Your Road Map to Internet Anywhere

There are many books today which tell you about the Internet. However, the book you're holding now goes one step further: it provides you with software that lets you connect with the Internet for *electronic mail* and *Usenet news*. The software is a version of the MKS Internet Anywhere package, and much of the book is devoted to helping you learn how to use the package.

What You Need to Get Started

In order to use the software, you need:

- An MS-DOS system running Microsoft Windows (Version 3.1 of Windows or a later release)

- A Hayes-compatible modem (almost all modems sold today are Hayes-compatible)

- At least 7 megabytes of disk space to store the package

 If you intend to use MKS Internet Anywhere to read Usenet news, you need additional disk space to store incoming news articles. The amount of space you need depends on the news topics that you wish to follow—the more topics you wish to read, the more disk space you need for holding the articles. If you read a lot of topics, you may need many megabytes of disk space to hold the news.

Access Providers

To begin using the Internet, you need to set up a connection...think of it as an "on-ramp" to the information highway. Two companies have kindly agreed to provide Internet connections for anyone who buys this book: the Rabbit Network and Portal Information Network.

> **Thanks to Rabbit and Portal, you can start using the Internet immediately, without having to negotiate terms with other companies.**

The Rabbit Network

The Rabbit Network will provide Internet access to anyone purchasing this book. The access is free for the first 30 days; after that, you'll be charged at Rabbit's normal rates. You connect with Rabbit through an 800 phone number, so you don't have to pay long distance charges.

For the details of Rabbit's free trial offer, see the description at the end of this book.

Portal Information Network

Portal Information Network will also provide readers with a free month of Usenet and electronic mail usage, including free signup and five free hours of connection time. Since Portal has local phone lines in 700 U.S. cities and more than 100 countries worldwide, there's almost certainly a local connection near you.

For the details of Portal's free trial offer, see the description at the end of this book.

During Installation

When you install the software, it will offer you the choice of setting up an Internet connection through Rabbit. If you accept the offer, the installation routine automatically tries to set an appropriate connection.

If the lines to Rabbit happen to be busy three times in a row, or if Rabbit fails to answer, the installation program asks for permission to connect with Portal instead. If you agree, the installation program sets up your Internet connection with Portal instead of Rabbit.

> **The prearranged connections with Rabbit and Portal only work inside the U.S. and Canada.** If you live in another country, you will have to make your own arrangements with an access provider; see Chapters 20 and 21 for more information.

If you prefer to deal with some company other than Rabbit or Portal, you'll have to enter all the relevant information yourself (the company's name, its phone number, and so on). Chapter 20 of this book discusses the information you'll need when you are talking to access providers, and Chapter 21 provides a directory of access providers all around the world.

How to Begin

The book is divided into several sections:

- *Getting Started* (Chapters 1–6)
- *Usenet News* (Chapters 7–10)
- *Electronic Mail* (Chapters 11–17)
- *Other MKS Internet Anywhere Software* (Chapters 18–19)

- *Information on Access Providers* (Chapters 20–21)

- *The Appendices and Glossary*

> **Step 1:** If you aren't familiar with the Internet at all, read Chapter 1 before anything else. This offers some brief background about the Internet, and answers the question, "What *is* the Internet anyway?"

Once you know a bit about the Internet, you're ready to install the software by working through the *Getting Started* section. The section tells you how to install the software on your hard disk and personalize it for your needs.

> **Step 2:** Work through Chapters 2–6 to install the software on your machine and personalize it for your use. *Note:* If you do not intend to use the prearranged connections with Rabbit or Portal, you must arrange your own Internet connection before you install the software. See Chapters 20–21 for information about arranging Internet connections.

Chapters 7–19 explain how you can use the software to work with the Internet. They also provide background information about the services supplied by MKS Internet Anywhere: electronic mail and Usenet news.

> **Step 3:** Work through Chapters 7–19 to learn how to work with Usenet news and electronic mail.

A Word About the Software

The software that accompanies this book is an *evaluation version* of the full MKS Internet Anywhere package. It will help you explore electronic mail and Usenet news on the Internet; however, it's not intended to be a substitute for MKS Internet Anywhere itself. The evaluation software has the following limitations:

1. **The evaluation software will only work for 30 days after you install it.** If you want to keep using it beyond that time, you must upgrade the software (as described in the next section).

2. With the evaluation software, the maximum allowable modem speed is 9600 bits per second. (The full MKS Internet Anywhere allows any speed.)

3. The full MKS Internet Anywhere can automatically connect with the Internet according to any schedule you choose. The evaluation version has no automatic connection abilities; in effect, you must tell the software, "I want to connect now."

4. The full package accepts up to four different users. The demonstation version only allows for one user.

5. The evaluation version only lets you subscribe to a maximum of 30 Usenet newsgroups. The full version lets you subscribe to any number.

6. The evaluation version automatically assigns a name to your computer (a *site name*). The full version lets you choose your own name.

7. The evaluation version automatically adds "MKS Internet Anywhere Evaluation Copy" on the end of every mail message or news article you send out. The full version doesn't do this.

Upgrading to the Full MKS Internet Anywhere

If you wish to continue using the software after the initial one-month period, you must upgrade to the full package before the month expires. For a complete description of how to upgrade your software, press the *Register* button in the *Prentice Hall Control Center program*. Chapter 4 of this book tells how to do this.

> You can upgrade to the full MKS Internet Anywhere package at any time by calling MKS. In the U.S. and Canada, you can phone MKS at 1-800-463-8269. In other countries, you should use the phone number given in the Register screen of the Prentice Hall Control Center program.

When you upgrade your software, MKS will ask for a Visa credit card number so that they can charge you for the upgrade.

> **The cost of upgrading to the full MKS Internet Anywhere package is**
>
> > **$49.50 (U.S.)**
> >
> > **$59.50 (Canada)**
>
> **Since the MKS Internet Anywhere package normally retails for $149.00 (U.S.), readers of this book are getting a real bargain: you're saving about $60.00.**

MKS will tell you how to upgrade your evaluation software immediately to get a full MKS Internet Anywhere package. You don't have wait to receive new disks, or go through any complicated procedure. Basically, you just give your evaluation software a password that tells it to start behaving like the full MKS Internet Anywhere package. The upgraded version does not have the limitations listed earlier.

Good Luck and Have Fun!

We hope you'll enjoy your time with the Internet. At times it may make you angry or swamp you with trivialities; but it will also prove to be an invaluable way to share information with friends and colleagues in every country on Earth. You're about to become a citizen of a huge electronic world...welcome to the Internet!

Table of Contents

1 *Introducing the Internet*

This chapter provides background about the Internet. It discusses:

- What the Internet is

- What it isn't

- What Internet facilities are available through MKS Internet Anywhere

The purpose of this chapter is to provide enough basic information so that you can talk intelligently with access providers. For more detailed information, see Appendix A, *The Insides of the Internet*.

Describing the Internet

It's difficult to define what the Internet is, but there are two approaches we could take:

1. The *internal* approach. If we wanted to describe the internal workings of Internet, we'd look at the communication signals that computers on the Internet use when they're exchanging information with each other.

2. The *external* approach. This approach describes the Internet by looking at the services it provides.

Many Internet purists would say that the internal approach is the only correct one; they define the Internet as the set of all computers that can communicate with each other in a certain way.[1] However, we suspect that most people reading this don't care much about the underlying technical details. You're more interested in what the Internet can do for you. With that goal in mind, we'll take the external approach to describing what the Internet is.

So What Is the Internet?

The Internet is a worldwide computer network, linking more than two million computers. Furthermore, the Internet is estimated to grow by more than 100,000 additional computers every month.

Unlike other well-known networks like CompuServe and GEnie, the Internet as a whole isn't owned or controlled by anyone. Some parts of it are owned by commercial companies, some are controlled by government agencies, and some belong to private individuals, with no central authority dictating how everything works.

The Internet is frequently called an *information highway*, but it's more like an interlocking system of highways and roads. For example, a car can drive from a city street to a county road, to a major superhighway, and even across a national border. Different roads are regulated and maintained by different jurisdictions, but these jurisdictions coordinate their activities so that traffic can flow from one place to another.

In the same way, the Internet consists of thousands of smaller computer networks, each of which operates independently. These member networks

---

1. Specifically, using a set of communication signals called the *TCP/IP protocols*. For further information on protocols, see Appendix A.

are all free to make their own rules—some exert strong restrictions on what their users can do, while others are wide open. However, no one governs the Internet as a whole. It only works by the cooperation and goodwill of everyone in the Internet community.

Internet Services

The Internet offers many services to its users: access to hundreds of databases, the ability to transfer files from one computer to another, various programs that search for information, and much, much more. However, the two most widely used services are those provided by MKS Internet Anywhere: electronic mail and Usenet news.

Electronic Mail

Electronic mail (or more simply, *E-mail*) is a good example of the cooperative nature of the Internet. Suppose you're in North America and you have a friend in England who has also installed MKS Internet Anywhere. You can type a message on your computer and ask for that message to be delivered to your friend. Then:

- The software in the MKS Internet Anywhere package automatically uses your modem to transfer your message to a computer on the Internet.

- That computer may transfer the message to another computer that is closer to the final destination.

- The next computer transfers the message to another computer, which transfers it to another, and so on. The Internet has facilities which let computers figure out a *route* that moves your message in a series of short *hops* from one computer to another. Often, each hop is just a local phone call from one computer to another so that nobody has to pay long distance charges.

- Eventually, the message is transmitted across the Atlantic…but almost certainly it is shipped over a high-speed transmission line at the same time as a lot of other messages, so the cost of sending your particular message is minimal.

- Computers on the other side of the Atlantic continue to transfer the message in short hops until it is finally placed directly on your friend's computer. The MKS Internet Anywhere package tells your friend that mail has arrived, so your friend can read the message whenever convenient.

As this process shows, the computers in the Internet cooperate with each other to help send your message to its destination.

You may think this process of messages hopping from one machine to another would be slow. In practice, however, it is usually quite fast. For example, an E-mail message sent out by a computer anywhere in North America can travel to almost any other computer on the continent in under a minute. Even messages to the far side of the globe seldom take more than 12 hours to reach the final destination (and the delay is usually caused by sites along the way that only connect with each other every few hours).

> Chapters 11–17 explain how to use the E-mail facilities of MKS Internet Anywhere.

Usenet News

Usenet news is another good example of the cooperative nature of the Internet. Usenet news provides a forum where Internet users can share information and opinions about every topic imaginable.

As a simple example, suppose you've just bought a new microwave oven and you're having trouble getting it to work. With Usenet news, you could *post* a *news article* saying:

```
I just bought a Brand X microwave oven
and I can't find the switch to turn it
on.  My whole family is waiting for
supper, so I need help desperately.
```

This news article can be sent to Internet sites all around the world, where it may be read by thousands of people. With so many readers, your article is almost sure to catch the attention of someone who knows the answer to your question. That person may use E-mail to send you a personal answer. Alternatively, he or she may choose to post the answer in another public news article, in case other readers have the same problem.

> Chapters 7-10 explain how to use the Usenet news facilities of MKS Internet Anywhere.

Other Internet Services

As you read Usenet news, you'll probably see references to other Internet services. For example, you might read an article that talks about obtaining information "via FTP." FTP is a way for Internet users to obtain files from other computers. Many Internet computers keep large collections of files that are free for the taking: files providing anything from financial statistics to hints about computer games. Using FTP, people can find out what files are available and get copies of any files that happen to be of interest.

Unfortunately, this version of MKS Internet Anywhere does not let you use FTP. However, many access providers offer a way around this. Basically, you send an E-mail message to your access provider, requesting that the provider use FTP to obtain a particular file. The provider does so, then sends the file to you by E-mail. You can't use FTP directly, but your access provider can supply you with an equivalent service.

The same goes for several other popular services. For example, *Archie* is an Internet program that searches for files on a large number of Internet computers; if you're looking for a particular file, Archie can tell you where that file is available via FTP. This version of MKS Internet Anywhere doesn't have the ability to find files using Archie, but again, many access providers can make Archie available indirectly through E-mail.

> For information about these and other Internet services, see Appendix A.

2

Installing the Software

This chapter tells you how to install the MKS Internet Anywhere package on your computer. It also explains a number of concepts you'll need to understand as you're installing the software.

Starting Out

To start the installation process, you run the `setup` program from the first diskette of the package. Follow these steps:

1. Start Microsoft Windows, if you do not have it running. Go to the Program Manager window. (One way to go to the Program Manager is to hold down the ALT key and keep pressing TAB until you see the words *Program Manager*. When you let go of the ALT key, you end up in the Program Manager.)

2. Put the first diskette of the MKS Internet Anywhere package into an appropriate drive. For most people, this is drive A:, but it could also be drive B:.

3. Pull down the *File* menu of the Program Manager window and choose the *Run* item. This prompts you to enter a command line. If you inserted the diskette in drive A:, type

```
a:setup
```

If you inserted the diskette in drive B:, type

```
b:setup
```

Press ENTER when you've entered this setup command.

Once you press ENTER, the installation process will begin.

Installation Location

The setup program takes a few moments to get started, then displays the following box:

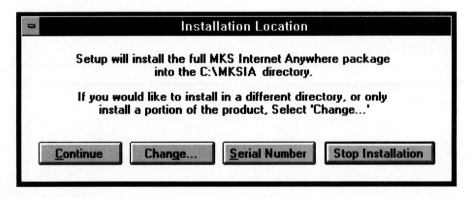

This says that the setup program normally sets up the software in the MKSIA directory on your C: disk drive. For many people, this is a good choice. However, if you have several hard disk drives, it's best to install MKS Internet Anywhere on the drive that has the most free space. (The software itself only takes about seven megabytes of space, but the daily news articles from Internet may take up much more space, especially if you choose to follow a lot of topics.)

If you want to install the software on some disk drive other than C:, use the left button of the mouse to click on the *Change* button. As the box says, you should also click on *Change* if you only want to install part of the software package. For example, some people may only install the electronic mail software, instead of both electronic mail and Usenet news.

If you want to install the full package and you have enough space on your C: drive to hold the software, use the left button of the mouse to click on *Continue*. This continues the normal installation process.

> **Note:** When you are using MKS Internet Anywhere, you always click using the left button of the mouse.

Installation Directory and Partial Installation

If you clicked on *Change* to change the installation location, you'll see a box something like this:

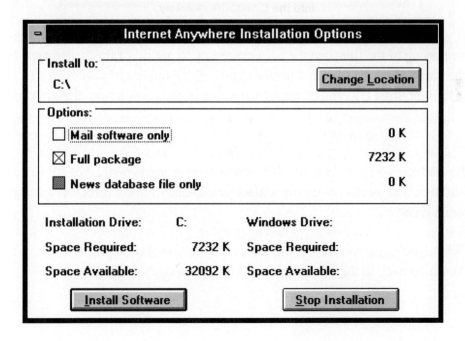

If you only want to install electronic mail (instead of both electronic mail and Usenet news), click on the box beside *Mail software only*.

If you want to install the software on a different drive, click *Change Location*. This displays a box where you can enter the name of your preferred directory:

If you want to install the software to a different drive, click on the C: at the beginning of the line, use the backspace key to get rid of the C, and type in the name of the drive you'd prefer to use. For example, if you want to install on drive D:, you'd change the name of the installation directory to

```
D:\MKSIA
```

If you like, you can choose a different directory name instead of MKSIA, but there's no reason to do this unless you already have a directory of the same name.

When you've entered the new name, click on *Continue with this Path*. You'll go back to the previous box. Then click on *Install software*.

Once again, you'll go back to a previous box. Click on *Continue* to proceed with the rest of the installation.

Copying the Files

After you've finished answering all these questions, the installation pro-gram begins to copy the software from the diskettes. It asks you to insert each diskette in turn and to press ENTER when the correct diskette is in place.

Rebuilding the Program Manager Group

If you have installed MKS Internet Anywhere before, the installation pro-gram displays:

This asks if you want to remake the existing MKS Internet Anywhere application group so that it refers to the new software. (An application group is basically a window in the Microsoft Windows Program Manager, with icons for the various program in the MKS Internet Anywhere pack-age.) We recommend that you answer *Yes* to the above question.

The Share Program

The share program makes it possible for several DOS or Windows programs to share a file simultaneously. This program has to be running in order for MKS Internet Anywhere to work properly. More specifically, share has to be running with a particular option (written as /1:500).

Many software packages need to use share, so it's quite possible that your system is already set up to have share running with the appropriate option. If so, the MKS Internet Anywhere installation program simply checks that share is running properly, then skips ahead to the next step of installation.

However, if share is not running with the correct option, MKS Internet Anywhere has to adjust the way your system is set up. Therefore, the installation program displays the following box:

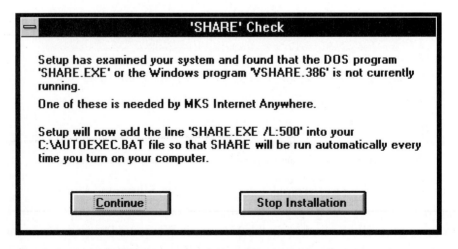

The autoexec.bat file mentioned in the above box is a file of instructions that are executed every time you boot (start up) your computer. The box says that the setup program is going to add an appropriate share command to these start-up instructions so that share will start running every time you boot your system. Click on *Continue* to keep going with the installation. The `setup` program changes your `autoexec.bat` file, then displays:

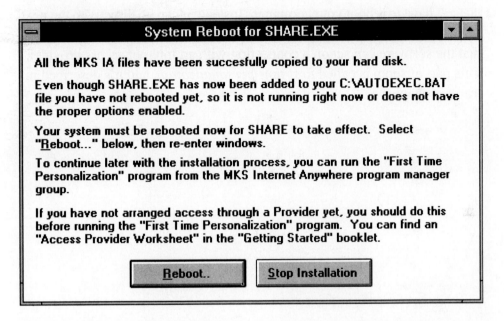

This new box says that MKS Internet Anywhere has changed your computer's start-up instructions so that `share` will begin running whenever you boot your computer. However, `share` still isn't running at the moment; it will only start running the next time you boot your computer. Therefore, it's time to reboot your computer.

If you'd like to go ahead with the process, click on *Reboot*. This reboots your computer. Once your computer has rebooted, start Windows again (if it doesn't start automatically) so you can go on to the next phase of setup.

If You're Already Running Share...

If you're already running the `share` program, MKS Internet Anywhere doesn't have to reboot your computer. Instead, it can go directly to the next stage of setup: finding out information about you and your computer so that the software can set up a connection with an Internet access provider. This part of setup is called *first-time personalization*, and it's described in the next chapter.

3 *First-Time Personalization*

This chapter explains the *First-Time Personalization* process. The process lets you provide the software with information that MKS Internet Anywhere needs, such as:

- Who you are and how you wish to be known to the world; for example, should your electronic mail messages show your real name or some nickname?

- How you want your computer to be known to the world; all Internet computers must have their own names.

- What type of modem you have and how it is attached to your computer.

- How to connect with your Internet access provider.

> Note: You should make sure your modem is connected to your computer and plugged into an appropriate phone jack before you start this phase of setup.

Starting the Personalization Program

The previous chapter described the first phase of the installation process: setting up your computer to run the MKS Internet Anywhere software. There were several ways the process might have ended.

1. If your computer was already running the `share` program, the installation process goes directly into first-time personalization. If so, go now to the *Beginning Personalization* section on the next page.

2. If you had to reboot your system because the `share` program wasn't running, start up Windows again and go to the MKS Internet Anywhere application group in the Program Manager.

The MKS Internet Anywhere application group looks like this:

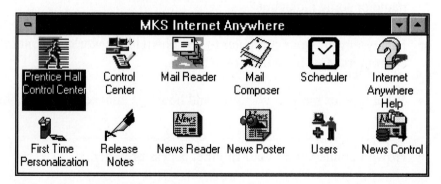

It shows all the major programs of the MKS Internet Anywhere package. You can run the Personalization program any time by double-clicking on the *First Time Personalization* icon.

Beginning Personalization

Whether you start the personalization process directly from the installation process or start it later by double-clicking on the *First Time Personalization* icon, the Personalization program starts by displaying:

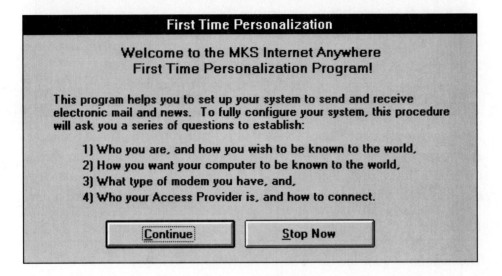

Click on *Continue* to start the personalization process.

Personal Information and Organization

The personalization process begins by displaying a box that asks for your full name, your street address, and other personal information. Fill in the blanks of this box with the requested data. If you make a typing mistake, you can backspace to correct it. To move from one blank to the next, press TAB. Press *Continue* when you've entered your name to your satisfaction.

Next, the personalization program displays:

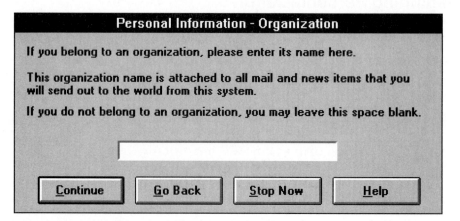

This lets you enter the name of your company, if you're using MKS Internet Anywhere in a business setting. If you enter an organization name, the name is included in all mail messages and news articles you send out. You can also leave this blank if you prefer. Press *Continue* when you're done.

User ID

The next box you'll see is:

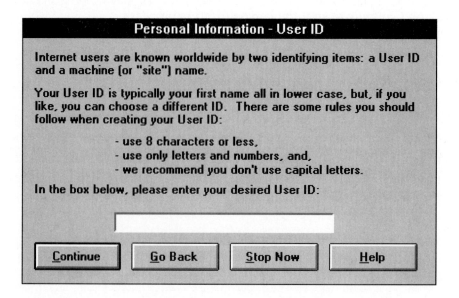

As the box explains, Internet users are identified by a short name, called a *User ID* (or *userid*). This name is also called a *username*. For example, the user Romeo Montague might choose `romeo` to be his username.

As the box says, your username cannot be longer than eight characters, and it can only contain letters and digits; for example, it cannot contain blank characters. By long-standing tradition, Internet names almost never have upper-case letters; some Internet sites have old software that doesn't handle upper-case letters very suitably.

Choose a username and enter it in the blank provided. Press *Continue* when you're done.

> **Note:** We'll use `romeo` as our sample username in the rest of this book.

Naming Your Computer

The next box deals with your computer's *site name*. The box explains that many other people on Internet almost certainly have the same username as the one you have chosen. To identify yourself properly on the Internet, you also need to give your computer a name; that way, you can tell people that you are the person named X who uses the computer named Y.

Any computer using the Internet is called a *site*. Remember this—you'll see the word "site" a lot, in this book and on the Internet itself. **A site is simply a computer that can connect with the Internet.** Because computers are called sites, computer names are *site names*.

> **Important:** The evaluation software that comes with this book automatically chooses a site name for you. You can select a more personalized site name if you upgrade your software to the full MKS Internet Anywhere package.

Your computer's site name must follow these rules:

1. It should only contain letters and numbers, and it's best to avoid upper-case letters.

2. The name can have up to eight characters.

Those are the only hard-and-fast rules. Here are some additional tips for choosing a site name:

1. Don't start your site name with a number.

2. In a business setting, avoid naming a computer after its user. For example, don't call a computer `joesmith`; some day, Joe may leave the company. A site name is a name for a *computer*, not for someone using that computer.

Unfortunately, there are a lot of computers out there already, and most of the "good" names have already been taken. You won't be able to get away with simple names like `Jack` or `Marie`—there are almost certainly computers with those names already.

Many service providers help their customers choose a site name. Some may impose extra restrictions on the type of name you can choose, beyond the restrictions we've already given.

If you prefer a more personal site name, you may be able to combine words to get a good name. For example, if your name is Jean and you live on Park Street, you might choose `jeanpark`. This is easy to spell and remember, but probably hasn't been used for some other computer.

> **Note:** We'll use the sitename `montague` in many of the examples for this book.

Registering Your Site Name

Once you have decided on a name for your system, it's a good idea to *register* the name so that no one else uses it. Registering your name also lets other computers "find" your computer when people want to send you electronic mail.

Many access providers automatically register the site names of all their customers, or will register site names on request. If your access provider doesn't offer this service, Appendix B explains how to register your site name yourself.

Time Zone

The next box you'll see is:

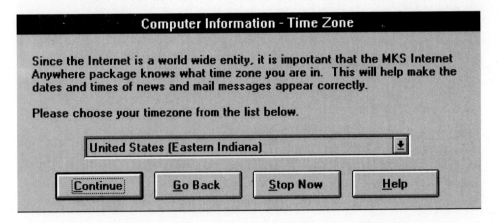

As the box explains, it's important for MKS Internet Anywhere to know your time zone so that it can relate the date and time on your computer to dates and times elsewhere in the Internet. Click on the arrow button and choose your time zone region from the set offered. Click on *Continue* when you've made your choice.

> **Note:** Many of the choices in the time zone list are accompanied by cryptic-looking codes like EST5EDT. You can ignore these codes; the computer uses them in references to your time zone.

Describing Your Modem

The next step in the personalization process is to tell the software what kind of modem you have. To help you do this, MKS Internet Anywhere displays the following box:

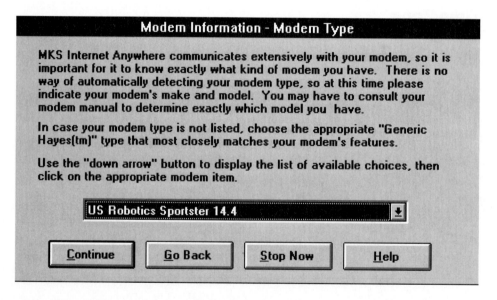

Using your mouse, click on the arrow button in the box. This displays a list of various brands of modems. If the list shows your type of modem, click on the modem name. You'll see that this name then appears in the box.

If you don't see your type of modem in the list, choose one of the entries that begin with the word *Generic* (for example, *Generic 1200 bps*). If you choose one of the generic modem types, the software assumes that your modem can be controlled by a basic set of instructions first developed by Hayes Microcomputer Products. Such modems are said to be *Hayes-compatible* because they are controlled by the basic Hayes instructions. Almost all modems built today are Hayes-compatible, so if MKS Internet Anywhere sends Hayes instructions to your modem, your modem will probably understand the instructions and work properly.

Once you have selected an appropriate modem type, click on *Continue*. The program then tries to identify the port where your modem is attached. You'll see a box like this:

Modem Search						
Scan finished, Modem Found!						
Modem Found on Port:						
COM1:	300	600	1200	2400	4800	9600	19200
COM2:	300	600	1200	2400	4800	9600	19200
COM3:	300	600	1200	2400	4800	9600	19200
COM4:	300	600	1200	2400	4800	9600	19200
COM5:	300	600	1200	2400	4800	9600	19200
COM6:	300	600	1200	2400	4800	9600	19200
COM7:	300	600	1200	2400	4800	9600	19200
COM8:	300	600	1200	2400	4800	9600	19200

Continue   Go Back   Stop Now   Help

One by one, the first-time personalization program tries all the COM ports on your system and checks to see if there is a modem connected to that port which responds at the given transmission speed (300 bits per second, 600, 1200, and so on). The program tries all the ports at all the speeds. When it has finished checking, click on *Continue*.

Once you have pressed *Continue*, the program displays a box like this:

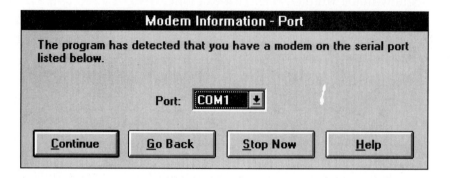

Of course, the port chosen on your computer may be different from the example shown. However, the box will tell you if MKS Internet Anywhere found a modem attached to your computer.

If you only have one modem attached to your computer and MKS Internet Anywhere found that modem, simply click on *Continue*. You don't have to change the port shown in the box unless you have several modems and want MKS Internet Anywhere to use a different modem than the one shown, or if you want to limit the interface speed between your computer and the modem.

If you want to switch to a different modem or change the speed, click on the arrow beside the chosen port. You'll see a list of all the ports where the setup program found modems. Click on the port you want, and the result will be filled into the appropriate blank. When you're finished, click on *Continue*.

> **Note:** The maximum speed accepted by the evaluation version of MKS Internet Anywhere is 9600 bits per second. If you upgrade to the full package, this limitation is removed.

Access Provider Information

From this point onward, the personalization program takes over to connect with an access provider. As explained in *Your Road Map to Internet Anywhere* at the beginning of this book, MKS Internet Anywhere first tries to establish a connection with the Rabbit Network. If this fails, it tries the Portal Information Network.

> **Note:** The setup program will test your hardware and software configuration by dialing in to your access provider. As soon as your provider's computer answers, the setup program hangs up, *without making a real connection*. In this way, the setup program tests that the connection is ready to work, but doesn't actually pick up Usenet news or e-mail. In order for this test to work, make sure that your modem is connected to your computer and plugged into your phone jack.

During this phase of the setup process, you'll be asked to provide several types of information:

Dialing prefix:
> Some phones may need to dial a special code before getting a normal phone line. For example, with many office telephone systems you have to "dial 9" to get an outside line. If the phone you'll be using requires this kind of prefix before dialing a normal phone number, MKS Internet Anywhere asks you to enter the prefix.

Phone type:
> The setup program will ask you if you have a rotary dial phone or a Touch-tone. Note that some phones have pushbuttons but still aren't Touch-tone phones. If you hear a series of clicks when you push a button on your phone, you have a dial (pulse) phone; if you have a single beep for each number, you have a Touch-tone.

Connecting with Rabbit:
> The automatic connection with the Rabbit Network uses an 800 number, so there is no charge to check the connection.

Connecting with Portal:
> The automatic connection with Portal is designed to use the Portal connection line that is closest to you. You will be asked to enter your state or province, and choose the closest available city to you.

The Personalization Is Complete

When the first-time personalization program is finished, it will display a box saying that you're ready to go. Just click on *OK* and you're finished.

> **Important:** Remember that the evaluation software will only work for 30 days after you've installed the package. If you are interested in continuing to use electronic mail and Usenet news, you must upgrade the package before the 30 days are up. *Your Road Map to Internet Anywhere* at the beginning of this book explains how to upgrade the package.

See Chapter 4 for an explanation of how to connect with your access provider and start using the Internet.

4 *A First Look at the Software*

This chapter gives a brief overview of the software in the MKS Internet Anywhere Package.

The MKS Internet Anywhere Application Group

The installation process sets up a window that you can use to start any of the major programs in the MKS Internet Anywhere package. The window looks like this:

On your computer, the little pictures (called *icons*) may be shown in a different order, but that doesn't matter. Each of the icons corresponds to one of the major programs in the MKS Internet Anywhere package. You can start any of the programs by double-clicking on the appropriate icon.

Note: the *Scheduler* and *Users* icons shown in the preceding picture will not appear until you have upgraded your evaluation software to the full MKS Internet Anywhere package.

The Look and Feel of a Program

As an introduction, we'll show you one of the programs in the MKS Internet Anywhere package: the Mail Reader. This program lets you read electronic mail messages that other users send you. We won't go into much detail about using the program—see Chapter 14 or the on-line help for information—but we'll show you how to start the program and what you'll see when you do.

The Mail Reader Program

To start the Mail Reader, double-click on the Mail Reader icon in the MKS Internet Anywhere application group. This displays the Mail Reader window:

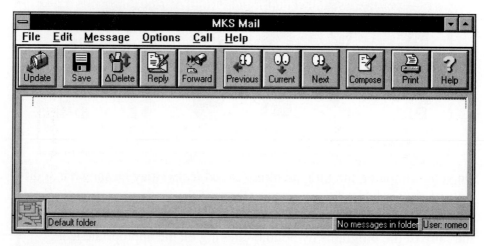

As you can see, this window is divided into several parts:

The Menu Bar
> This is at the top, where you see the menu headings `File`, `Edit`, `Message`, `Options`, `Call`, and `Help`.

The Toolbar
> This comes under the Menu Bar, and contains various icon buttons that you can push with the mouse. For example, the *Save* button lets you save any mail messages you receive, while the *Delete* button lets you get rid of mail messages you no longer want to keep.

The Message Area
> This is the white space under the toolbar. The Mail Reader uses this area to show you a list of mail messages waiting to be read, or to display the text of a single mail message.

The Status Bars
> These appear at the bottom, showing information about your mail.

Quitting the Mail Reader

There are two ways to quit the Mail Reader (and any other MKS Internet Anywhere program):

- Choosing *Exit* from the *File* menu

- Pressing ALT-F4.

Some programs also offer toolbar icons as a shortcut for quitting.

Other Programs in the Package

You've just had a short look at the Mail Reader. The other major programs of the package are:

The Mail Composer
> This lets you type in mail messages and send them to other users.

The News Reader
> This lets you read Usenet news articles.

The News Poster
> This lets you type in news articles and send them to the Internet.

When you're using MKS Internet Anywhere, you'll spend 99% of your time with the four major programs: the Mail Reader, the Mail Composer, the News Reader, and the News Poster. In addition to these major programs, there are several others that you might need once in a while:

Prentice-Hall Control Center:
> This is discussed later in this chapter.

Control Center
> This lets you set up and change the information describing how to connect with other sites.

Scheduler
> This lets you set up schedules for automatically running various activities. (In the evaluation version of MKS Internet Anywhere, the Scheduler is disabled.)

News Control
> This controls how news articles are stored on your computer.

Users
> When several people read news and send mail from your computer, the *Users* program lets those people identify themselves. For example, *Users* lets each person send out mail under his or her own name. (In the evaluation version of MKS Internet Anywhere, the Users program is disabled.)

These programs are described later in this book and in the on-line help facilities.

The Nightly Program

Finally, there's one other program you should know about: a program called *Nightly*. *Nightly* takes care of a number of chores that should be done regularly. These chores include:

- Getting rid of old news articles that you've already read, so there will be room for new articles

- Connecting with your Internet access provider to obtain any incoming electronic mail and news articles

- Shipping out any of your own news articles and electronic mail messages that are waiting to be sent to the Internet

> **Important Note:** In the evaluation software that comes with this book, the *Nightly* program does not automatically connect with your access provider to send or receive material. Later in the chapter, we'll discuss what to do about this.

It's important for the *Nightly* program to run on a regular basis. Otherwise, old news articles never get cleaned away; old news keeps filling up more and more disk space until you run out of room for new articles.

The full MKS Internet Anywhere automatically runs *Nightly* for you every night. You don't have to do anything except leave your computer turned on overnight! (With the evaluation software, you'll have to run *Nightly* by hand, as explained later in this chapter.)

Once you upgrade your software, *Nightly* can run automatically every night. In order for this to work properly, you must do the following:

1. Leave your computer running overnight.

2. Make sure that your computer's modem is plugged into a phone line.

3. Since *Nightly* is a Windows program, you must leave Windows running on your computer.

4. Finally, you should make sure that the News Reader and News Poster programs are **not** running overnight, since *Nightly* won't work properly if those other News programs are running.

If there's some reason you can't leave your computer running overnight, you must use the *Scheduler* program to set things up so that *Nightly* runs sometime during the day. We warn you that *Nightly*'s clean-up work can take quite a bit of time, especially if you follow a lot of news topics. Therefore, you should schedule *Nightly* for some time when you don't expect to be using your computer or the phone line.

Whenever *Nightly* runs, you should make sure that the four conditions listed above are true (your computer is on, your modem is plugged in, Windows is running, and the News programs are not).

The Prentice Hall Control Center

The evaluation software that comes with this book has a special program not found in the normal MKS Internet Anywhere package: the *Prentice Hall Control Center* (or PH Control Center for short).

The purpose of the PH Control Center is to make it easy for you to perform certain tasks that are performed automatically by the full version of MKS Internet Anywhere. To see what we mean, double click on the PH Control Center icon in the MKS Internet Anywhere application group. This displays the *PH Control Center Window*:

The main feature of this window is the set of icons in the toolbar. These perform the following tasks:

Exit:
Pressing this button quits the program.

Call:
Pressing this button immediately attempts to connect with your access provider. Once the connection is established, you will receive any incoming Usenet news and electronic mail that is waiting to be shipped to your computer. Your computer will also ship out any news articles that you've posted and electronic mail messages you've sent to users elsewhere on the Internet.

> **Note:** When your computer attempts to connect with your access provider, it may not succeed. For example, your access provider's phone may be busy. In this case, simply wait and try again later on.

Mail Call:

> Pressing this button also connects with your access provider. However, it only sends and receives electronic mail messages; it does not attempt to obtain your Usenet news or ship out any news articles you may have posted. *Mail Call* is helpful when you only have a few minutes, but want to check for any incoming mail. It's much faster than the normal *Call*, since shipping Usenet news almost always takes a lot longer than just obtaining e-mail.

Nightly:

> Pressing this button starts the *Nightly* program. As we mentioned earlier in this chapter, you should run *Nightly* on a regular basis—ideally every day. Running *Nightly* may take quite some time, since it often has a lot of work to do. Therefore, you should pick a time when you don't intend to use the computer again for a while.

Register:

> Pressing this button will explain how to upgrade your evaluation software into a full version of MKS Internet Anywhere. It will show you phone numbers that you can use to call MKS; it will also display the registration number for your software. Finally, the program will ask you for an upgrade code number.

> Call MKS at the given phone number and tell them the registration number; they will give you the appropriate upgrade code number. Type in the code number, and the PH Control Center will do all the work required to upgrade the evaluation software to the full MKS Internet Anywhere. (For price information, see *Upgrading to the Full MKS Internet Anywhere* in the section titled *Your Road Map to Internet Anywhere* at the beginning of this book.)

Important: With the evaluation software that comes with this book, you must use *Call* or *Mail Call* to connect with your access provider. If you do not, you'll never get any news or e-mail. Furthermore, any news and e-mail that you might want to send out will never get delivered to the Internet, because your computer never connects with your access provider.

You should also make a habit of running *Nightly* on a regular basis to perform required clean-up operations.

5

Connecting and Scheduling

This chapter tells how to connect with the Internet, and how to schedule regular connections.

Connecting Directly

With the evaluation software that comes with this book, you must always tell your computer when you want to connect with the Internet. To do this, you must use the Control Center program.

Click on the *Control Center* icon in the MKS Internet Anywhere application group. This calls up the Control Center window:

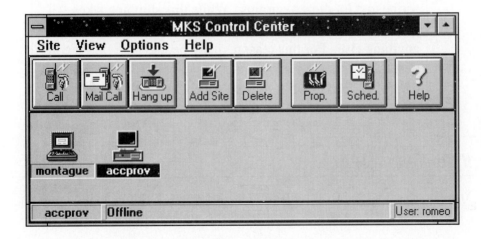

Notice that the window has little pictures of computers in the middle area.
Most people will have at least two of these:

- One labeled with your own computer's site name; in our example,
  this is `montague`. This picture stands for your own computer.

- One labeled with the name of your access provider. This stands for
  your connection to the Internet.

If you have configured connections to other computers, you'll see more
pictures in the Control Center window.

Now click on the picture of the computer representing your access provider
so that the picture is highlighted. Finally, click on the *Call* icon in the toolbar. This says that you want to call the chosen computer.

MKS Internet Anywhere will immediately try to connect with the access
provider. If the connection succeeds, the software will proceed to pick up
any mail messages and news articles waiting for you, and will send out any
messages or articles waiting to be delivered to other sites on the Internet.

> **Warning:** It may take quite some time to ship all the incom-
> ing news articles to your computer, especially if you sub-
> scribe to a lot of newsgroups. While this shipping takes
> place, you probably won't be able to use your computer for
> anything else. For this reason, many people may find it con-
> venient to connect just before going to bed so that the news
> can be shipped in while you're asleep.

If You're in a Hurry...

You'll notice that the Control Center window has a button labeled *Mail
Call*. If you click on *Mail Call* instead of *Call*, MKS Internet Anywhere

will call your access provider to obtain your electronic mail; however, it will not try to pick up any Usenet news articles. This is useful if you only have a few minutes to spend at the computer—you can check up on your mail without having to wait for your news to arrive.

The *Mail Call* button doesn't just fetch your mail from the Internet; it also sends out any mail messages that may be waiting to go to other computers. Therefore, *Mail Call* is also useful if you've just composed a message and want to send it to its destination fast. Create the message first, then start the Control Center program and use *Mail Call* to send the message out.

> **Note:** The *Call* and *Mail Call* buttons of the Control Center work exactly like the corresponding buttons of the PH Control Center.

Setting Up a Schedule

If you have the full version of MKS Internet Anywhere, you can set up a schedule so that your computer automatically connects with your access provider at preselected times. For example, you might set up the schedule so that your computer does all its work in the middle of the night.

> **Note:** With the evaluation software that comes with this book, you cannot set up this kind of schedule. Therefore, if you're using the evaluation software, you may as well skip the rest of this chapter. If, however, you upgrade your software to the full MKS Internet Anywhere, the rest of this chapter tells you how to set up a connection schedule that meets your needs.

To start setting up a schedule, start the Control Center program by double-clicking on the *Control Center* icon in the MKS Internet Anywhere

application group. This calls up the Control Center window you've
seen before:

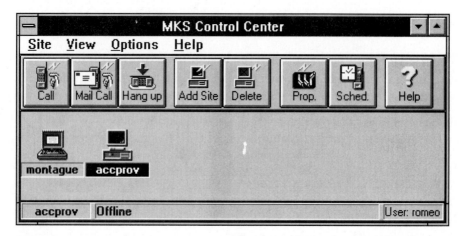

Click on the computer labeled with the name of your access provider, then
click on the *Sched.* icon to start the scheduling process.

You'll see the *Schedule dialog box* appear. It looks something like this:

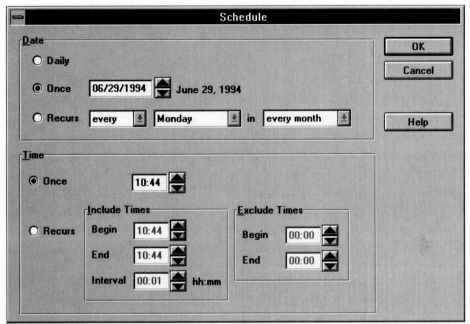

The Scheduling dialog box lets you set a schedule for connecting with the chosen site. The Date selection area offers these items:

Daily   Connects with the remote site every day, at all the times given in the Time selection area.

Once   Only connects once with the other computer. This is used for situations where you connect one time with a site but never expect to do so again. The Time selection area only applies to that one day.

Recurs   Lets you set up a regular connection schedule. For example, you can set up for a connection on every weekday in the month, for the first weekend in the month, or for the first of January every year. By clicking on the arrows in the Recurs line, you can get an idea of what possibilities are available.

Below the Date selection area is the Time selection area. This lets you specify the times of day when a connection can be made. Again, you have a choice of schedules:

Once   Only tries to make the connection at the specified time of day. Times are given using a 24-hour clock, with 0:00 standing for the beginning of the day and 24:00 for the end of the day.

Recurs   Connects at regular intervals throughout the day. You can set the interval between connections, the included times (when the software can try to connect), and the excluded times (when the software should not try to connect).

As an example of a recurring time, suppose you want to connect every two hours on weekday nights, between 11:00 p.m. and 8:00 a.m. (Why would you try to connect several times a night? If you only try once, the phone might be busy and you won't get through.) You can set up the schedule with the following Scheduling dialog box:

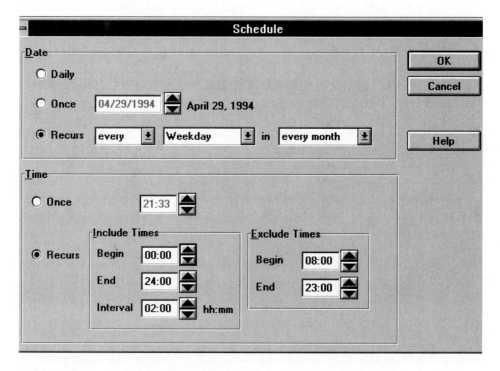

Notice that we set the *Include* time to all day (0:00 to 24:00), then set the *Exclude* time to the hours we don't want to make connections (8:00 to

23:00). This ensures that the software only tries to make connections between the desired hours. Since the *Interval* is set for two hours, the package tries to connect every two hours (for example, midnight, 2:00 a.m., 4:00 a.m., and so on).

Once you've set the schedule, click on *OK*. You'll go back to the original Control Center window, where you can quit the Control Center program.

Other Scheduling

The MKS Internet Anywhere application group has a separate icon for a program called the *Scheduler*. This lets you set or change the schedule for running any program in the software package. For example, you can use the *Scheduler* program to change the time for running the important *Nightly* program.

The *Scheduler* is available in your MKS Internet Anywhere application group (in the Program Manager) and in the Startup group. For further information about the Scheduler, go to the appropriate group, then double-click on the *Scheduler* icon. From there, you can use the on-line help facilities for more information.

> **Note:** Since the *Scheduler* is in your Startup group, it will start every time you start Windows.

6

Getting Help

While this book covers the basic principles of using the MKS Internet Any-where software, it doesn't tell you everything. Complete documentation for the software is available through the on-line help facilities. This chapter discusses those facilities and the various ways of obtaining help.

Starting the On-Line Help

In the MKS Internet Anywhere application group, there is an icon labeled *Internet Anywhere Help*. You can start the on-line help by double-clicking on the icon.

Alternatively, you can also start the on-line help within any program: simply pull down the *Help* menu and choose a topic from the menu. The on-line help facility then explains what types of help are available.

Finally, many of the windows that you see while working with MKS Internet Anywhere have *Help* icons in their toolbars. Clicking on the *Help* icon calls the on-line help facilities.

For help on a particular topic, use the *Help Search* facility in the *Help* menu to find that topic in the full list of available help.

Help in Context

As you are working with MKS Internet Anywhere, you can get help on any aspect of the software by pressing the F1 function key. For example, suppose you are working with the Mail Reader program. If you press F1, the on-line help facilities will tell you about the Mail Reader.

7 *Introducing Usenet News*

This background chapter introduces the basics of Usenet news, also called Netnews. We'll cover the following:

- What Usenet news is

- How news articles are organized

- What a news article looks like

> If you're already familiar with Usenet news, you can skip this chapter and go to Chapter 8, where we show how to start reading news.

Usenet News

Usenet news is something like a bulletin board where people can post information and opinions for other people to read. More precisely, Usenet news is made up of hundreds of such bulletin boards, each devoted to its own topics.

There's one big difference between Usenet news and other computer bulletin boards you may have used. Most computer bulletin boards are stored on a single computer; to read the bulletin board, people must connect with that particular computer. Usenet, on the other hand, is spread over hundreds of thousands of computers, with each computer keeping copies of the posted news articles. When someone submits a new article, copies of the article are automatically sent to all those thousands of computers. Thus, when you want to read an article, you don't have to connect with another computer—the latest batch of articles have automatically been shipped to your computer already.

Newsgroups

The bulletin boards that make up Usenet news are called *newsgroups*. Each newsgroup has a name suggesting the kind of topics covered by that group. For example:

news.announce.newusers
> A newsgroup that provides information about the Internet for people who have just started using the network.

news.newusers.questions
> A group where new Internet users can ask questions.

rec.humor
> A place where anyone can post jokes.

rec.humor.funny
> Like *rec.humor*, but moderated by an editor who is more selective about what gets posted.

As these examples show, the names of newsgroups are broken into components. For example,

```
news.announce.newusers
```

has three components:

```
news
announce
newusers
```

The components are separated from each other by dots. When people talk about newsgroups, they often pronounce the dots; for example, *rec.humor.funny* is referred to (affectionately) as "humor dot funny" (in this case, the *rec* is silent). On the other hand, people may ignore the dots; for example, *rec.humor* is usually pronounced as "wreck humor" (which may be appropriate). There's no rhyme or reason to this, and different people choose different pronunciations—just be aware that sometimes people pronounce the dots and sometimes they don't.

News Hierarchies

Newsgroups are arranged in *hierarchies*, based on the components of the newsgroup name. To explain what this means, let's look at the newsgroup *news.announce.newusers*. We'll examine this name component by component:

news
> Any newsgroup whose name starts with *news* deals with information about Usenet news itself. For example, the group *news.lists* provides statistics about Usenet news (such as which newsgroup received the most articles in the past week), and the group *news.answers* provides basic information on many other newsgroups.

news.announce
> Any newsgroup whose name starts with *news.announce* contains announcements of interest to the Usenet community. For example, *news.announce.conferences* contains announcements for conferences related to Internet, while *news.announce.newgroups* informs you when new newsgroups are formed.

news.announce.newusers
> This is the name of the group itself. Conceivably, there could be subgroups under this name, in the same way that *rec.humor.funny* is related to *rec.humor*. (In fact, all newsgroups are separate bulletin boards; *rec.humor.funny* isn't a subset of *rec.humor*, it's a completely separate group.)

Newsgroups can be split into major divisions, according to the first part of their names. For example, *news* indicates groups that discuss Usenet itself, while *rec* groups deal with various types of recreation. People use the term *hierarchy* for groups whose names all have the same first component. For example, people speak of "the *news* hierarchy", "the *rec* hierarchy" and so on.

Here's a list of some other popular hierarchies:

biz   Topics related to business, or newsgroups run by commercial enterprises.

comp   Groups dealing with computers and computing.

misc   Miscellaneous topics.

rec   Recreational pursuits.

sci   Science, engineering, and math.

soc   Groups for socializing and discussing current social issues.

alt   "Alternative" subjects. This is a catch-all hierarchy, which tends toward the bizarre and even the childish. On the other hand, the *alt* hierarchy also contains important newsgroups dealing with subject matter considered too contentious to fit in other hierarchies.

In many hierarchies, new groups undergo an approval process before they can be created; readers vote whether a proposed group is necessary or if existing groups already cover the topic adequately. In the *alt* hierarchy, however, no approval process is used. This means that people who want to create absurd groups can do so in the *alt* hierarchy without needing anyone else's agreement. On the positive side, the lack of approval process means that *alt* groups can be created very quickly to deal with sudden events like earthquakes or other fast-breaking news stories.

Local News Hierarchies

In addition to the news hierarchies just mentioned, Usenet allows for *local news hierarchies*. These contain groups of local interest.

For example, a company may create its own news hierarchy, containing newsgroups relevant to that company. If the company's name is ABC Manufacturing, the news hierarchy might start with the letters abc, and have newsgroups like:

abc.notices
    For notices of general interest to employees

abc.vacations
    To let other people know when you're going on vacation

abc.questions
    For questions about company policy, who borrowed the stapler
    from the photocopier room, and so on

In short, people at the company can create whatever newsgroups they wish. The abc on the newsgroups names establishes that these are in-house groups that normally shouldn't be distributed to outsiders.

News Articles

Below, we show a typical news article as displayed by MKS Internet Anywhere. The article has two parts:

- *Header lines*, which provide information about the article itself—
  for example, who posted it, when it was posted, what the article is
  about, and so on

- The *body* of the article, which provides the actual contents of the
  article

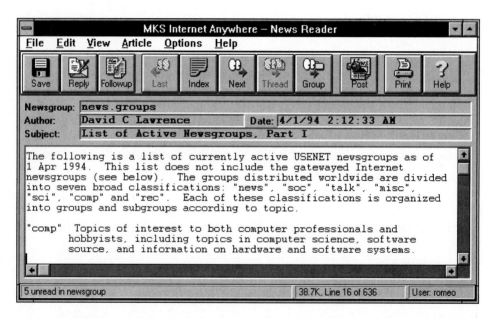

As you can see, the screen shows the following header lines:

Newsgroup
    The name of one or more newsgroups where this article has been
    posted. In this case, the newsgroup is *news.groups*.

Author, Date
    The person who posted the article and the date it was posted.

`Subject:`
A brief description of what the article is about, like the headline of a real newspaper article. You can help other users by creating clear and meaningful *Subject* lines for your articles.

These header lines are the only ones you'll normally see, since they're the only ones that MKS Internet Anywhere usually displays. However, news articles may have many additional header lines that aren't displayed. These additional header lines don't usually supply useful information, so the software doesn't bother showing them.

Newsgroups of Interest

To end this chapter, we'll list some newsgroups of particular interest to people who are just getting started with Usenet. No access provider carries all the newsgroups in the world, but the groups listed below have such widespread popularity that you can get them from almost every access provider.

news.announce.newusers
news.newusers.questions
These were described earlier in the chapter.

news.answers
This provides information about other groups. In many newsgroups, the readers of the group draw up a document answering questions that are asked again and again in the group. Such a document is called an FAQ, short for Frequently Asked Questions. A group's FAQ provides an excellent introduction to the newsgroup and usually answers all of a new reader's questions. The *news.answers* group collects the FAQs from all the other groups. If you want a lot of information very quickly, you can't beat *news.answers*.

comp.sys.ibm.pc.hardware

comp.sys.ibm.pc.digest

comp.sys.ibm.pc.misc

comp.sys.ibm.pc.net

comp.sys.ibm.pc.programmer

These newsgroups are devoted to various aspects of using IBM PC computers and PC clones.

> **Usenet vs. Internet:** *Usenet* is the set of all computers that receive Usenet news. Some Internet sites don't receive news, while other sites aren't connected to the Internet but do get news. Technically speaking, therefore, Usenet and Internet are two separate things. However, Usenet news is closely linked with the Internet, and in the minds of most people who read news, Usenet is the "voice" of Internet.

8 *Reading News Articles*

This chapter explains how to read Usenet news articles with MKS Internet Anywhere.

> **Note:** The evaluation software that comes with this book starts out with a few news articles so that you can get a feel for reading news. However, you won't get any new articles until you connect to your access provider (as described in Chapter 5), and your provider ships some news to your computer.

The News Reader Program

To make it easier for you to start reading news, MKS Internet Anywhere automatically subscribes you to a few sample groups. Chapter 9 tells how to unsubscribe to these groups if you don't like them, and how to subscribe to other groups you want to read.

To start reading news, double-click on the *News Reader* icon in the MKS Internet Anywhere application group. After some setup, the program displays the *News Reader Window*, which looks something like this:

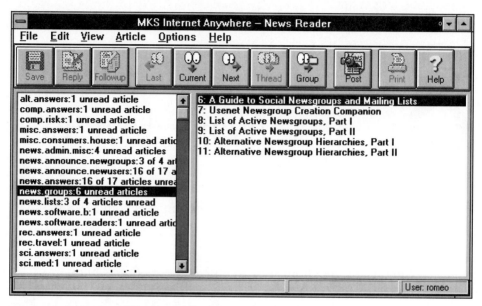

The main part of this window is called the *index area*. The index is divided into two parts: the *Newsgroup list* and the *Article list*.

- The Newsgroup list occupies the left side of the index. It shows newsgroups to which you subscribe. For each group, the list shows the number of articles in the group and how many of these articles are unread.

- The Article list occupies the right side of the index. It summarizes articles from the newsgroup highlighted in the Newsgroup list. For each article, the Article list shows the name of the person who posted the article and the article's *Subject* line.

Listing the Contents of a Newsgroup

To list the contents of a newsgroup, point to the group in the Newsgroup list and double-click on it. The Article list changes to reflect the contents of your selected group.

You can use the standard scroll bars beside the Article list to look through all the articles currently in the newsgroup. The *Subject* lines help you decide which articles you want to read.

> **Good Advice:** A meaningful *Subject* line helps readers decide whether they want to read a news article. Therefore, when you start posting your own articles to Usenet, you should put some effort into choosing good *Subject* lines. For example, a *Subject* like
>
> ```
> I need help
> ```
>
> isn't very informative. It's better to use something like
>
> ```
> I need help installing my Brand X printer.
> ```
>
> Then other readers can instantly tell whether to read the article.

Reading a News Article

You can read any article in the Article list by double-clicking on the corresponding list entry. When you do, the News Reader window changes to display the article:

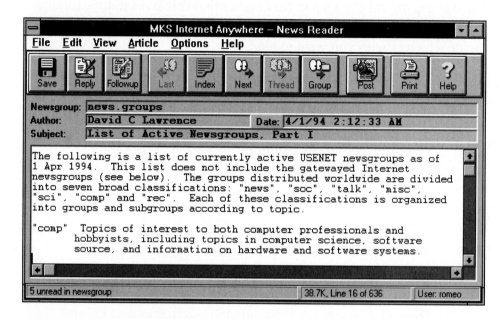

The middle of the screen shows header information about the article. The text of the article appears below the header lines. You can use the scroll bars beside the article to read the article.

Reading More Articles

The toolbar contains a number of icon buttons that help you move from one article to another:

Next   Goes to the next unread article in this newsgroup. If you have reached the last article in the current group, Next goes to the first unread article in the next group.

Last   Goes to the article that you read just before this one.

Group   Goes to the first article of the next group in the Newsgroup list.

Thread   Goes to the next article in the current newsgroup, with the
          same Subject line as the current article.

The *Thread* icon is useful for following the "thread" of a conversation.
Many times, someone posts an article, someone else posts a response,
someone replies to the response, and so on. However, this thread of conversation is mixed in with many other articles on different subjects. *Thread*
makes it easy for you to skip through the newsgroup, reading a sequence of
related articles.

Threads often have *Subject* lines starting with the letters Re: (short for
"regarding"). For example, if the first article in a thread has the *Subject*

```
Let's go to the zoo!
```

later articles in the thread often have the *Subject*

```
Re: Let's go to the zoo!
```

If you like, you can set an option so that your Article List arranges articles
by thread instead of sorting them by reference number. We'll tell you how
to do this later in this chapter.

> You can read all your news if you just keep clicking on *Next*.
> This reads everything in the current group, then moves on to
> the next group.

Once you've read an article, the News Reader tries not to show you that
article again. For example, the *Next* button generally skips over articles
you've already read.

When You've Read All You Want to Read

Newsgroups often contain a lot of articles, and you may not be interested in reading them all. Many times, you'll look at the *Subject* lines of all the articles in the group, read the articles that appeal to you, and decide to skip the rest.

In this case, pull down the *Article* menu and choose the item *Mark Newsgroup as Read*. This marks all the remaining articles in the newsgroup as if you had read them. Under normal circumstances, the *Nightly* program will then discard those articles in the usual clean-up process, making room for new incoming articles.

Saving Articles

If you want to save an article, click on the *Save* icon. A standard *Save* box comes up, to let you specify the name of the file where you want to save the article.

A file may hold any number of articles. Whenever you save an article in a file, the article is normally appended to the end of the file, after any other articles that the file may contain.

Returning to the Index

Clicking on the *Index* icon returns to the original form of the News Reader window showing the Newsgroup list and Article list. This time, however, the articles that you've read have been crossed out to indicate that you've seen them. However, you can still reread them by double-clicking on the appropriate lines.

If you start reading another newsgroup, then go back to the previous group, you'll see that the Article list no longer shows the articles that were crossed out. To save space, the Article list only shows the articles you haven't read yet. (If you really want to see the articles you've already read, the next section tells you how.)

> **A Curious Thing:** As you read through threads, you may see the response to an article before the article itself. This just means that the original article and the response took different routes through the Internet, and the response happened to take a faster route than the original.

News Views

Pull down the *View* menu of the News Reader window, and you'll see a variety of options for displaying newsgroups:

Subscribed Newsgroups Only:
> If this option is on, the News Reader window only shows the groups to which you currently subscribe. This is the default. If you turn this option off, the News Reader shows you all available newsgroups.

Unread Articles Only:
> If this is on, the News Reader window ignores articles that you've already read. This is the default. If you turn this option off, the News Reader shows all available articles, even if you've already read them.

By Thread:
> If this is on, news articles are grouped according to thread. Otherwise, news articles are sorted by reference number. By default, this option is off.

Empty Newsgroups:
> If this is off, the News Reader window only shows groups that con-
> tain articles for you to read. Usually, this means it only shows
> groups that contain at least one unread article; however, if you have
> also turned off the *Unread Articles Only* option, it shows all groups
> that contain articles, whether or not the articles are unread. By
> default, the *Empty Newsgroups* option is off.

> If the *Empty Newsgroups* option is on, the window shows all
> groups, whether or not they contain articles for you to read.

Newsgroups Matching Pattern:
> This lets you select newsgroups whose names contain a certain
> string of characters. If you click on this item, the program displays:

> You can then type in a string of characters that you want to find. If,
> for example, you type in `arts`, the News Reader window lists all
> the newsgroups whose names contain that character string.

Sort by Newsgroup Name:
> If this is on, the News Reader window sorts all the displayed news-
> groups in alphabetical order by name. Otherwise, it displays the

groups in the order given by your subscription list. See Chapter 9 for more on subscription lists.

Quit the News Reader at Night

By default, the MKS Internet Anywhere package performs numerous clean-up operations overnight, such as getting rid of news articles that are no longer needed. In order for this clean-up to work properly, you should quit the News Reader program when you're finished. **Don't leave the News Reader active overnight.** (For more information about automatic clean-up, see Chapter 4.)

9

Subscribing to Newsgroups

This chapter discusses the process of subscribing and unsubscribing to newsgroups.

The Subscription Dialog Box

The first time you start the News Reader, it automatically subscribes to some sample newsgroups. However, many of these groups won't interest you, so you'll want to unsubscribe.

To do this, start the News Reader by double-clicking on the *News Reader* icon in the MKS Internet Anywhere application group. As explained in the last chapter, this displays the News Reader window.

In the menu bar for this window, pull down the *Options* menu and choose the *Subscription List* entry. This displays the *Newsgroup Subscription List dialog box*:

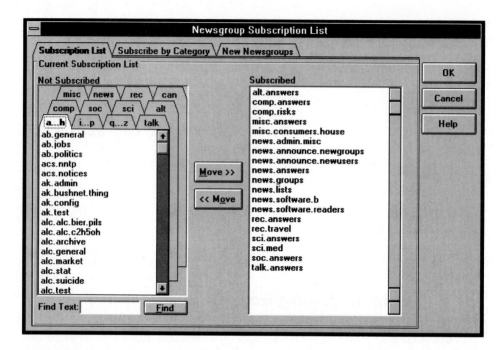

This box has two major regions: a *Subscribed* list and a *Not Subscribed* list. If you want to "unsubscribe" to a group, you just move it from the *Subscribe* half to the *Do Not Subscribe* half.

To make the move, click on the name of the newsgroup, then click on the appropriate *Move* button. One button moves groups to the *Not Subscribed* list, and the other button moves them in the opposite direction.

Subscribing by Category

You can also subscribe to groups by category. At the top of the Newsgroup Subscription List dialog box, click on the *Subscribe by Category* tab. The box changes to:

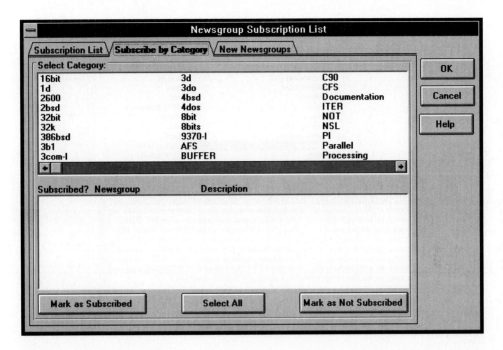

The list at the top of this box shows every component part of every news-group name. By double-clicking on an item, you can find out all the news-groups which contain that component. For example, double-clicking on msdos produces the following:

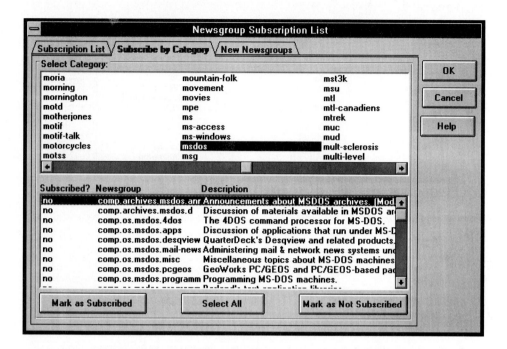

The area at the bottom lists all newsgroups that have `msdos` in their names. At the beginning of each line, you'll see `yes` or `no`, indicating whether or not you've subscribed to the group. After each newsgroup name is a brief description of that group.

If you want to subscribe or unsubscribe to any of the groups shown in the bottom part of the screen, click on the group; then click on *Mark as Subscribed* if you want to subscribe to the group, or *Mark as Not Subscribed* if you want to unsubscribe.

You can select all the groups shown in the bottom part of the screen by clicking on *Select All*. Once you have selected the groups, you can subscribe or unsubscribe by clicking on the appropriate *Mark* button.

When you have subscribed to any newsgroups that catch your interest, click on *OK* to go back to the News Reader program. If you click on *Can-*

cel, you can go back to the News Reader without changing your subscription list.

> **Note:** With the evaluation software that accompanies this book, you can only subscribe to a maximum of 30 newsgroups. If you upgrade to the full MKS Internet Anywhere, this limit is removed.

New Newsgroups

From time to time, other Usenet users create new newsgroups. In fact, you may see new groups almost every day.

If new groups have been created since the last time you read news, the News program displays the following box as it is starting up:

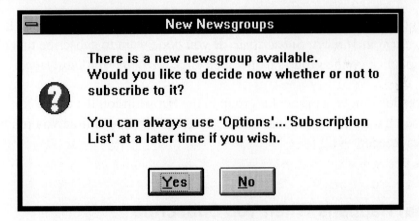

You can see what the new group is by answering *Yes*. If you do this, you'll see a new form of the Newsgroup Subscription List dialog box:

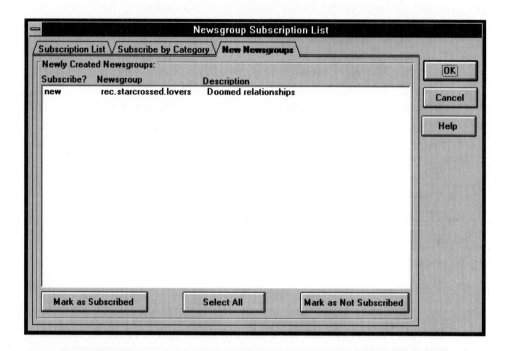

To subscribe to one of the new groups listed, click on its name in the list, then click on *Mark as Subscribed*. If you don't want to subscribe to a new group, click on the group's name, then click *Mark as Not Subscribed*.

If you don't move a particular group to the Subscription list or the Not Subscribed list, you'll be told about the group again the next time you run the News Reader.

What Happens When You Subscribe

If you subscribe to a particular newsgroup, you probably won't see articles from that group appear immediately. The reason is simple: even though you've told your own computer that you want to read that newsgroup, you also have to tell your access provider to start shipping that newsgroup to you. If your access provider doesn't send you the news, you simply won't have anything to read.

Different access providers have different procedures for finding out what you want to read:

- With some providers, you have to contact them personally: you must phone or fax, giving the names of the groups to which you want to subscribe.

- With other providers, you can just send an E-mail message, telling what groups you want to receive.

- Still others use an automatic process where software lets your computer automatically tell your access provider that you want to subscribe to one or more specified newsgroups. One of the most common pieces of software for handling subscription requests in this way is called Gensys.

MKS Internet Anywhere can send Gensys subscription requests automatically, if your access provider accepts such requests. The package can also send E-mail messages, if that's what your provider wants. If your provider wants direct contact (phone or fax), you'll have to remember to do this yourself.

> **Note:** The software that comes with this book is already configured so that your subscription requests are automatically relayed to Rabbit or Portal. Thus if you are using Rabbit or Portal as your access provider, you can ignore the next section.

Setting Up Subscription Requests

If your access provider accepts E-mail or Gensys requests, you can set up MKS Internet Anywhere to create such requests automatically. To do this, you must use the *Control Center* program. This is the same program you use when you want to start a connection with your access provider.

Start the Control Center program and click on the little computer icon that stands for your access provider. Then click on the *Prop* (Properties) icon in the toolbar. This displays the following window:

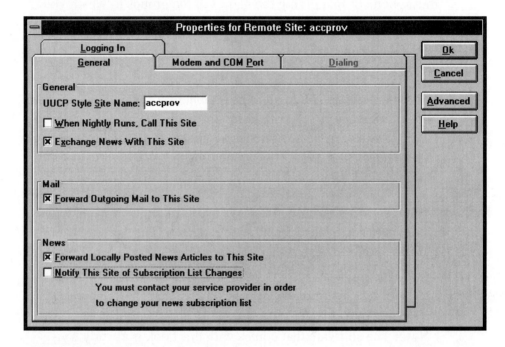

This window specifies various kinds of information for connecting with your access provider.

Near the bottom of the box, you'll see a line that reads *Notify This Site of Subscription List Changes*. If the little box beside this line is blank, it means that you must contact your access provider by phone or fax when you wish to subscribe or unsubscribe to a newsgroup.

If your access provider accepts automatic subscription changes, click on the box beside *Notify This Site of Subscription List Change*. You'll see that the dialog box changes to:

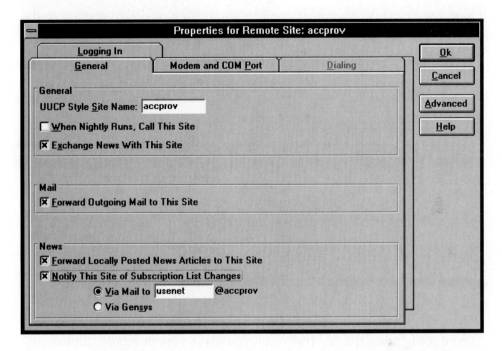

This now lets you tell the software how to pass on subscription requests to your access provider.

1. Clicking on *Via Mail to* says that you want MKS Internet Anywhere to send an electronic mail message to someone when you subscribe or unsubscribe to newsgroups. The software sends the mail message automatically, whenever you change your subscription information.

   Note that you must fill in the electronic mailing address of the person you want to notify about subscription changes. For more information about electronic mail addresses, see Chapter 11.

2. Clicking on *Via Gensys* says that you want MKS Internet Anywhere to notify your access provider using the Gensys automatic subscrip-

tion software. In order for this to work, your access provider must accept Gensys requests. Talk to your access provider for more information.

Once you've set the appropriate information, click on *OK* to go back to the Control Center window. To quit the Control Center program, press ALT-F4 or pull down the *Site* menu and choose *Exit*.

Disk Space Considerations

You may be tempted to subscribe to a lot of newsgroups when you first start reading Usenet news. However, you should be aware that some newsgroups receive several megabytes of articles a day, and that's a lot of data. It takes a long time for your access provider to ship that much news to you every day; if you pay by the minute, the costs can really add up.

Even worse, you'll need sufficient disk space to store all those news articles. The disk space can *really* add up—by default, MKS Internet Anywhere starts up in the middle of the night to clean away all the articles you've read during the day (provided you leave your computer turned on). But what happens if you don't have time to read your news for a few days? If you subscribe to a lot of newsgroups and you go away for the weekend, you may find that you have 30 or 40 megabytes of news waiting for you when you get back. That can eat up all your available disk space very quickly.

Unless you have huge amounts of available disk space, you should only subscribe to a small number of newsgroups. This is especially true for newsgroups that receive a lot of articles every day. Usenet news is the biggest conversation in all of human history; unless you're careful you'll get in trouble, like trying to sip a drink from a firehose. To avoid problems, you should only subscribe to a few groups at first, then expand the number if you have the time and the disk space to handle it.

Long-Term Absences

What happens if you go on vacation for a few weeks? If you turn off your computer, you don't have to worry about news filling up your disk while you're gone—you can't receive news if your computer's off. However, if your access provider can't send you news, the news simply piles up on your provider's computer, waiting for the day when you finally turn on your computer again. Then, that great backlog of news gets dumped onto your computer, taking up enormous quantities of disk space and requiring who knows how many hours to ship to you.

To avoid this kind of problem, talk to your provider before you go on vacation and discuss how to prevent a flood of news when you get home. It may make sense to unsubscribe to almost all your newsgroups a few days before you leave, so that a significant backlog doesn't pile up. Your access provider may have other suggestions for handling the situation. The key is to work things out ahead of time, *before* you start getting swamped by the flood; fixing things afterward is sure to be more complicated.

> **Warning:** Don't just unsubscribe to all your newsgroups, then turn off your computer as you walk out the door. Even if you've set up your computer so that it automatically tells your access provider when you subscribe or unsubscribe to groups, it takes time for your computer to send the notification to your provider. Allow at least two days for your computer to prepare a notification and deliver it.

> **Note:** Due to space limitations, some *alt* newsgroups have been left off the subscription list. The on-line release notes explain how to add these to your subscription list.

10 *Posting News Articles*

This chapter explains how to post a news article to one or more news-groups.

> **Important Note:** If you are unfamiliar with Usenet, you should read Appendix D before posting a news article. The appendix explains the etiquette of posting, and suggests ways to avoid snubs from your fellow users.

The News Poster Program

You post news articles using the *News Poster*. To start this program, double-click on the *News Poster* icon of the MKS Internet Anywhere application group. You can also call the News Poster by pushing the *Post* or *Followup* buttons in the News Reader. Either way, you'll see the *News Poster* window:

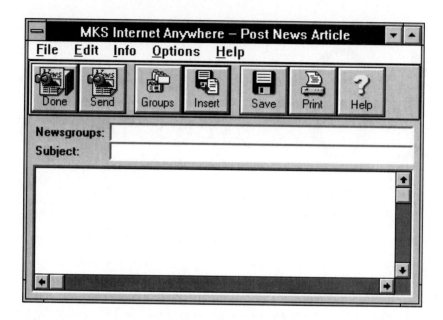

Sending a Simple Article

Posting an article is just a matter of filling in the blanks:

- One or more newsgroups where you want to post the article.

- A suitable *Subject* line for the article.

- The body of the article itself.

Selecting Newsgroups

To send a simple article, you should first choose one or more newsgroups where you want to post the article. To choose newsgroups, double-click on the *Newsgroups* line. This calls up the *Newsgroup Selection dialog box*:

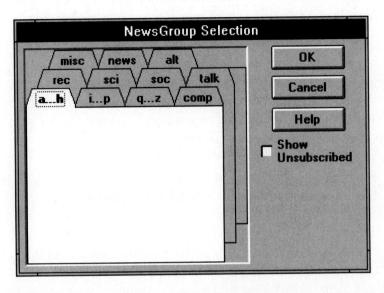

This box shows all the groups to which you currently subscribe. If you click on the *Show Unsubscribed* box, it will also show groups to which you don't subscribe. You can choose a newsgroup simply by clicking on its name. When you choose a newsgroup, the name of the group is highlighted. If you decide not to post to that newsgroup after all, you can just click on the name again, and the highlighting goes away.

If you highlight more than one name in the list, your article will be sent to all the selected newsgroups. Sending an article to more than one group is called *cross-posting*.

 Think twice about cross-posting articles. Some people get in the habit of posting their articles to every group that is even vaguely related to the subject of the articles. This can annoy other readers and earn you some nasty mail messages. Don't post to more than one group unless your article is directly related to all the groups you choose.

After you have chosen one or more newsgroups, click on *OK*. You'll return to the News Poster window, where you can continue preparing your article.

Finishing an Article

Once you have chosen the newsgroups where you want to post your article, you can keep going to finish the article:

1. First, fill in a suitable *Subject* line. To do this, just click on the *Subject* line and enter a brief "headline" for your article.

2. You can then enter the body of your article in the blank area at the bottom of the window. To get to the article area from the *Subject* line, press TAB or simply click on the article area.

3. When you're ready to send the article, click on *Send* or *Done* to post the article. *Send* sends the article, then clears the screen so you can start another article. *Done* sends the article, then quits the News Poster.

> **A Word About Line Length:** Many people read news articles on monitor screens that are only 80 characters wide. It's therefore a good idea to keep the lines in your articles shorter than 80 characters. Don't bother counting characters—just keep your lines reasonably short. At the end of each line, press ENTER to start a new line.

When you have finished posting an article, the News Poster displays a box of the form:

Other Icons

The News Poster window has a number of other icons on the toolbar:

Groups Has the same effect as clicking on the Newsgroups line. It displays the Newsgroups Selection dialog box so you can choose groups where you want to send your article.

Insert Lets you insert the contents of a text file into your article. If you click on this icon, a standard file search dialog box appears to let you find the file. **Note:** You can only insert text files; for example, you cannot insert databases, spreadsheets, and other special types of files. Since most word processors produce non-text files, you can't insert word processor files either.

Save Saves the current article in a file. A standard file search dialog box appears so that you can choose a file.

Print Prints the article you have just been working on.

All icons are also available through menu items.

Sending Replies to Other Articles

You can reply to articles as you're reading news. Remember that the News Reader window looks like this:

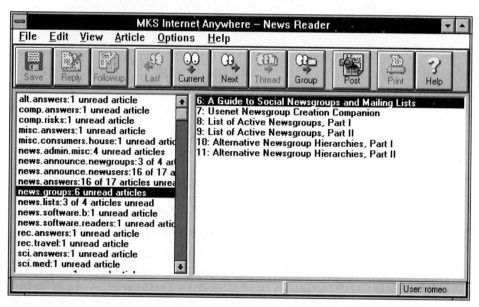

There are two icons on the toolbar that let you reply to the article:

Reply   sends an electronic mail message to the person who posted the original article. If you click on this icon, the News Reader calls the Mail Composer program to let you write and send the message. Chapter 13 discusses the Mail Composer.

Followup   posts a news article to the newsgroup(s) where the original article appeared. If you click on this icon, the News Reader calls the News Poster to let you write and post the article.

You may be asking which is better—a mail message or a news article. In many cases, it's better to send a mail message, especially when your message is mostly of interest to the person who submitted the original article. The reason is simple:

- A mail message is simply transmitted from your computer to the recipient's computer.

- A news article, on the other hand, is sent to every computer in the world that carries this particular newsgroup. Your article will take up disk space in tens of thousands of computers, it will cost money for all those computers to transmit, and it will take up a few moments of time from everyone who reads that newsgroup.

If you use a news article instead of a mail message, it costs hundreds or even thousands of dollars to send that article around the Internet, not to mention the valuable time that you waste for all those readers.

Only use *Followup* to reply with a news article if what you have to say is truly of value to a significant portion of the Usenet community. Otherwise, use *Reply* and send a personal mail message.

The Text from a Previous Article

If you use *Followup* to post an article in response to a previous article, the News Reader calls the News Poster, and you'll see something like this:

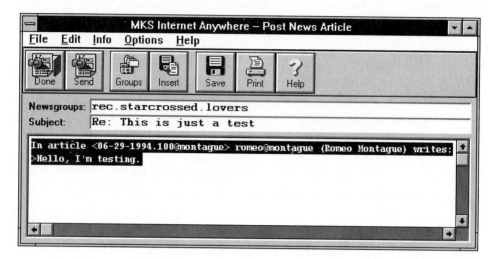

The News Poster automatically fills in the *Subject* and *Newsgroups* fields for you. Because you're responding to a previous article, the News Poster can figure out the necessary information from that article.

The News Poster also fills in a copy of the text of the original article to start your reply. The text starts with a line of the form:

In article <ref-string> user@sitename (Real Name) writes:

This identifies the original article by its reference string and tells who submitted the article. After this line, the News Poster puts the text of the original article, with > characters at the beginning of each line so that the text stands out.

If you don't want to include the text of the original article, simply press the DEL key when the News Poster window appears. This deletes everything that's highlighted, which happens to be the text of the original article.

If you don't press DEL to delete all of the original article, you should still trim irrelevant passages from the original text. It costs time and money to ship articles around the Internet. Reducing articles to the shortest practical length means savings for everybody.

> You can delete text from the window by clicking your mouse on the beginning of the text you want to delete, then dragging the pointer to the end of the text. This highlights the relevant text. Then, just press the DEL key to delete the text.

Quit the News Poster at Night

By default, the MKS Internet Anywhere package performs clean-up operations overnight. In order for this to work properly, you should quit the News Poster program when you're finished. **Don't leave the News Poster active overnight.** (For more information about automatic clean-up, see Chapter 4.)

11

Introducing E-Mail

This chapter explains the basic principles of electronic mail (E-mail) in MKS Internet Anywhere. In particular, we look at:

- How electronic mail works

- What an Internet mail address looks like

- Internet mailing lists: a way for Internet users to hold discussions by E-mail

How Electronic Mail Works

Perhaps the easiest way to understand electronic mail is to follow the trail of a mail message from one user to another.

Suppose Juliet wants to send Romeo an invitation to an upcoming masquerade ball. Let's also suppose that the site name of Juliet's computer is `capulet`, and the site name of Romeo's computer is `montague`.

Juliet starts the process by typing a *mail message* on her computer. The message is mostly just lines of text, as in:

```
Dear Romeo:
    How about some dinner and dancing
Friday night around eight?

P.S. The balcony is open.
```

The message also has *header lines* (like the header lines of a news article) providing information such as the time the message was sent. You can think of these header lines as the "envelope" of the mail message: they provide information about sending and receiving the message. Most header lines are automatically created when the message is entered; the only ones Juliet has to fill in by hand are Romeo's address and the *Subject* line.

Once Juliet finishes composing her message, MKS Internet Anywhere *stores* the message. The software may send out the stored message immediately, or hold onto it until the next scheduled time for Juliet's computer to connect with Romeo's—it depends whether Juliet has set up a schedule or uses the *Call on Demand* feature. Either way, the delivery happens automatically; the software decides when to make the connection and sends off the message at the next scheduled time.

> **Note:** With the evaluation software that comes with this book, messages are not sent out until you use the Control Center program to connect with your access provider. If you upgrade to the full MKS Internet Anywhere package, messages will be sent out according to a schedule whenever your computer connects with your access provider.

Let's say that Juliet has set up her computer to connect with Romeo's in the middle of the night. (Somehow that seems appropriate.) When the time comes, Juliet's computer automatically dials up Romeo's computer and ships over the stored message.

> **Important:** Remember that automatic connection is only available once you upgrade to the full MKS Internet Anyhere package. Until then, you must explicitly use the Prentice Hall Control Center to connect with your access provider (as explained in Chapter 4).
>
> When you have the full package, your modem has to be attached to the computer and to a phone jack, so your computer can call out automatically. **For best results, MKS Internet Anywhere users should leave their computers turned on overnight and their modems plugged in.**

When Romeo's computer receives the message, it stores the message in a special file, waiting for Romeo to read it. This file is called a mail *folder*. A folder can hold any number of mail messages.

The next time Romeo checks his mail, he'll see that he has received a new message. He can use the Mail Reader to read the message. After that, he can save the message in case he wants to read it again, or he can just delete the message from the folder. He can also reply to the message with a message of his own. Romeo's reply will be stored, then transmitted to Juliet's computer the next time Juliet's computer connects with Romeo's.

Mail Through the Internet

In the example just discussed, Juliet's computer connected directly to Romeo's. Mail can also be sent indirectly.

For example, suppose Juliet's computer can connect to an Internet access provider. Juliet can then send a mail message to anyone anywhere on the Internet. First, the message passes to the provider's computer; then the provider's computer forwards the message through one or more other Internet computers until it reaches its final destination.

Internet Addresses

When you send an E-mail message to someone, you have to put an *address* on the message so it goes where it's supposed to. An address needs two pieces of information:

- The username of the person who will receive the letter

- The site name of the computer that person uses

An E-mail address consists of a person's username and site name in a special format. The next section discusses this format.

Address Formats

The standard format of an Internet address is

        username@sitename

where `username` is a person's username, and `sitename` is the site name of the computer the person uses. For example, Romeo's address is

        romeo@montague

and Juliet's address is

        juliet@capulet

The @ character is pronounced "at" so you would pronounce Juliet's address as "Juliet at Capulet".

Domains

With millions of computers on the Internet, it's difficult to come up with a unique site name for each computer. Therefore, Internet site names often have special codes attached to them, called *domains*.

A domain works much like a telephone area code. Just as an area code distinguishes a Toronto phone number from a New York one, a domain can distinguish similar site names from each other. For example,

```
site.ca
site.uk
```

are two similar site names, with domain names attached on the end. The domain name .ca indicates a computer in Canada; the domain name .uk indicates a computer in the United Kingdom. The "." character is pronounced "dot" so the above names would be pronounced "site dot see ay" and "site dot ewe kay".

Not all domains are geographical. Some domains are based on the nature of the computer site. For example, here are some domains you might see while using the Internet:

.com	Commercial companies
.edu	Educational institutions
.gov	Government agencies
.mil	U.S. military
.org	Non-profit organizations

For example, the site name for the U.S. White House is

```
whitehouse.gov
```

indicating that it is associated with the U.S. government.

Subdomains

Some mailing addresses have subdomain codes as well as domain codes. For example, system.on.ca has a domain of .ca (Canada) and a subdomain of .on (Ontario, a province within Canada). Notice that the domain (.ca) is on the far right and you read backward on the line to find the subdomain (.on) and then the computer itself.

An address may have a domain, a subdomain, a sub-subdomain, and so on; however, you don't have to worry about such things. The point is simply that subdomains make it easier for Internet software to figure out the location of a particular computer.

Other Address Formats

The Internet is a network of networks, and some of the member networks use different formats for mailing address. Thus, you may see mailing addresses that are complicated snarls of @, !, and % characters. Don't worry about it. If you ever have to send mail to such an address, just copy out the address exactly as you see it—the MKS Internet Anywhere software can handle many different address formats.

> **Your E-Mail Address:** The form of your E-mail address depends on how your access provider sets up your connection. For more information, ask your access provider what address you should give to others (or print on your business card).

Internet Mailing Lists

A mailing list is a simple way for people with some common interest to share information and opinions. There are literally hundreds of mailing lists, covering every topic imaginable, from tax advice to women's issues to Harley-Davidson motorcycles.

Mailing lists work very simply:

1. People who belong to the mailing list can use E-mail to send relevant messages to some central address.

2. A person or special software at that central address collects the incoming messages and sends them back to *all* the people who belong to the list.

The central receiver may send out messages as soon as they arrive, or the messages may be stored temporarily, then sent out on some regular schedule (for example, once a day).

Some lists are *moderated*, which means that the central receiver selects which incoming messages are actually sent out to the mailing list members. Other lists are *unmoderated*, which means that all incoming messages are sent out, without editing. Both types of lists have good and bad points. Many people like the "uncensored" nature of unmoderated lists; on the other hand, a good moderator can save everyone a lot of time by eliminating junk and only sending out messages of real interest.

Finding Out About Mailing Lists

The Usenet newsgroups *news.announce.newusers* and *news.lists* list hundreds of mailing lists open to anyone who'd like to join. The list tells the topic covered by each mailing list, and explains how to subscribe to the list.

If you want to join a list, it's important that you follow the instructions exactly. The subscription process is often supervised by computer programs, and the programs can only handle subscription requests that have the right format.

Mailing Lists vs. Newsgroups: Mailing lists serve much the same purpose as newsgroups, but they work differently. With mailing lists, messages are mailed personally to the members of the list. With newsgroups, articles are posted publicly for anyone who wants to read them.

12 *Getting Started with E-mail*

Now that you've learned the basics of E-mail, you're ready to use the mail facilities of MKS Internet Anywhere. This chapter tells you how to start the Mail Reader and what you'll see when you do.

Starting the Mail Reader

To start the Mail Reader program, double-click on the *Mail Reader* icon of the MKS Internet Anywhere application group.

As the Mail Reader starts up, it displays the MKS Internet Anywhere logo. You may also see a box that says the program is updating information about incoming mail; however, if you do not have any incoming mail, the *Updating* box appears and disappears very quickly.

The Mail Reader Window

When the Mail Reader is ready to go, it displays the following:

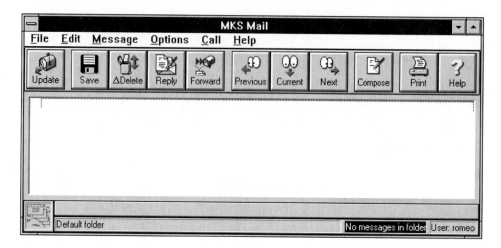

This is the *Mail Reader window,* and it lets you read incoming E-mail. The white empty area is called the *Message List* or *Index,* and that's where you can see if you have any incoming mail messages.

Folders

The information lines of the screen give the name of a *folder.* You'll recall from Chapter 11 that a folder is just a file that can contain mail messages.

To begin with, the Mail Reader window shows the name *Default Folder.* When mail messages come in, you'll read them from your default folder. Chapter 15 explains how you can move messages to other folders if you want to save the messages.

Quitting the Mail Reader

Chapter 14 explains how to read messages with the Mail Reader. However, you probably don't have any messages at this point, so you can quit the Mail reader by:

- Choosing *Exit* from the *File* menu, or

- Pressing ALT-F4

When you quit, the Mail Reader may display the following box:

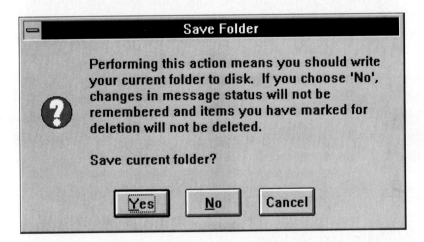

What does this mean? Remember that a folder is a file containing mail messages. The folder also contains information about messages; for example, the folder contains information telling which messages you've read and which you haven't.

While you work with the Mail Reader, the program keeps its own records of what you do with the messages in the folder—the program remembers which messages you read, which you delete, which you save, and so on. When you quit the Mail Reader, the program displays the above box to see if you want to store all these records in the original folder.

- If you choose *Yes*, the Mail Reader adjusts the contents of the folder to reflect what you've done during your mail session. For example, if you've deleted a message during the session, the Mail Reader deletes the same message from the folder.

- If you choose *No*, the Mail Reader doesn't change the folder. For example, even if you've deleted a message, the Mail Reader leaves the message in the folder. In other words, the folder stays the same as it was when you started using the Mail Reader, with no record of any changes you might have made while using the program.

- If you choose *Cancel*, the Mail Reader doesn't quit after all. Instead, you go back to using the program.

In most cases, you should choose *Yes*, so that your folder is updated. However, if you think you've made mistakes during the session, you can always choose *No*; that way, the Mail Reader doesn't change your folder, so you can quit and start again.

> **Note:** If you haven't done anything that would change the contents of your folder, the Mail Reader doesn't ask if you want to save the folder.

13 *Sending Messages*

This chapter explains how to send a mail message—to yourself, to other people using your computer, and to anyone in the Internet.

Starting the Mail Composer

To send a mail message, you use the *Mail Composer*. There are two ways to start the Mail Composer:

1. If you are in the main MKS Internet Anywhere application group, double-click on the *Mail Composer* icon.

2. If you are in the Mail Reader window, click on the *Compose* icon.

Whichever way you choose, the Mail Composer displays the following window once it starts up:

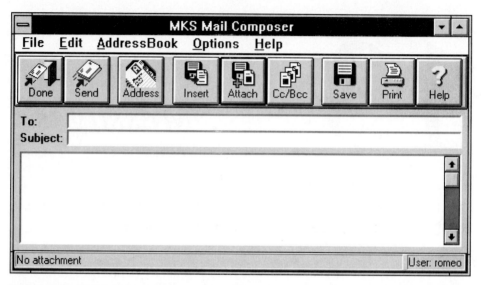

This is the *Mail Composer window.* Below the toolbar are lines that contain *header information* for your message. These lines serve the same purpose as the header information lines in news articles.

Using settings from the *Options* menu, you can control which header information lines are displayed. By default, the Mail Composer displays:

To:

> You fill in the blank with the Internet addresses of one or more people who should receive this message. For example,

> > To: romeo@montague

sends a message to the user romeo at the computer whose site name is montague.

> You must fill in at least one address on the To header line. Chapter 16 describes the *Address Book*, which can give you a lot of help when you have to supply an Internet address.

Subject:

> The *Subject* line explains what your message is about, just as in news articles. You should make an effort to enter a meaningful *Subject* line so people can identify the message from a one-line summary.

Entering Your Message

To fill in a header information line, click on the line and enter the required information. Press TAB when you've finished typing, and the cursor moves down to the next header line. You can keep pressing TAB to move through all the header information lines.

To show how this works, we'll show you how to send a message, just for practice. Follow these steps:

1. In the `To:` line, enter your own username.

2. Press TAB to move to the `Subject:` line. Then enter

   ```
   Just an experiment
   ```

3. Press TAB again to move into the big blank space at the bottom of the Mail Composer window. Type the message

   ```
   This is just an experimental message.
   ```

Sending a Message

When you're finished entering the message, there are two icons you can click on to send the message:

Send   sends the message, then clears the Mail Composer window so you can start writing a new message.

Done   sends the message and quits the Mail Composer.

Try sending yourself a message with *Send*, then send yourself another message and quit with *Done*.

 Messages sent to people using other computers will not be delivered immediately. Your computer won't send messages to other sites until you connect with your access provider. With the evaluation software that accompanies this book, you must directly tell your computer to connect with your access provider, as explained in Chapter 5. If you upgrade to the full MKS Internet Anywhere package, you can set up a regular schedule when your computer connects with your access provider automatically.

Message Lengths

MKS Internet Anywhere lets you send messages of any length. However, your message may be passed from one computer to another before it is finally delivered, and some of those computers may not be able to handle extremely long messages. (Some systems still run outdated software that limits the size of messages.)

Usually, you're safe if your messages are less than 10,000 characters in length. This works out to about 120 lines of text.

Sending Copies of a Message

You'll notice that the Mail Composer toolbar has an icon labeled *Cc/ Bcc*. This icon lets you send copies of your message to people not mentioned in the *To* list.

Click on the *Cc/Bcc* icon and you'll see the Mail Composer window change:

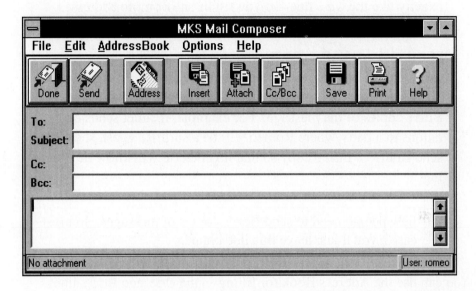

It now displays two more header lines above the message area:

Cc:

"Cc:" stands for *Carbon Copies*. If you enter one or more addresses on this line, the message is sent to those addresses as well as the people named on the To: header line.

There's not much difference between Cc: recipients and To: recipients, since they all get copies of the message; however, the distinction is occasionally useful. For example, suppose Romeo wants to ask Mercutio to be the best man at his wedding. Romeo might send an E-mail message To: Mercutio, then add a Cc: to Juliet—the message is mainly for Mercutio, but the Cc: is a nice way to let Juliet know what's going on.

You can leave the Cc: line blank if you don't need to send Cc: copies to anyone.

Bcc:

"Bcc:" stands for *Blind Carbon Copies*. The Bcc: line is almost exactly like the Cc: line—if you fill in one or more addresses, those people all receive a copy of the message.

The difference is that people who receive a message are automatically told the names of people who receive Cc: copies of the message. However, they are not told about any people who receive Bcc: copies of the message. For example, if Juliet sends out invitations to a party where Romeo will be a surprise guest, she could send Romeo a Bcc: copy so that no one else will know he is coming.

> Few people need to send Bcc: copies of messages. In most cases, you'll just leave this line blank.

You can use the Address Book for filling in the Cc: and Bcc: lines. See Chapter 16 for more details.

14

Reading
Messages

This chapter explains how to read mail messages using the Mail Reader.

> **Note:** In the last chapter, we suggested that you send yourself a couple of mail messages as practice for sending messages to other people. If you haven't done that already, do so now so that you'll have some messages to read in this chapter.

Checking Your Mail

Start the Mail Reader by double-clicking on the *Mail Reader* icon in the MKS Internet Anywhere application group. You'll see something like this:

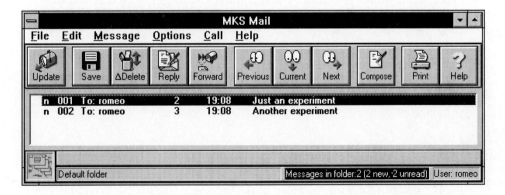

The message list area shows the messages that you sent to yourself as an experiment. (If it does not, push the *Update* button on the toolbar. *Update* tells the software to go out and see if there are any messages waiting.)

Message List Items

The first line in our sample list reads:

n 001 Romeo Montague 2 19:08 Just an experiment

This line provides several pieces of information about the message, mostly taken from the message's header lines:

n
> The "n" beginning the line tells you this is a new message.

001
> This is just a reference number. Messages in the message list are numbered sequentially.

Romeo Montague
> The next item on the line is the name of the person who sent you the message. Since you sent yourself these messages, you'll see your own name here.

2
> After the name of the sender comes a count of the number of lines in the message.

19:08
> This tells when the message was sent, using a 24-hour clock (so that 19:08 means 7:08 p.m.) If the message was sent today, all you'll see is the time; otherwise, you'll see the date the message was sent.

`Just an experiment`
The line ends with the `Subject` you specified when you sent the
message. If there isn't enough room to show the full subject line,
you'll see as much as can fit into the available space.

Reading a Message

Now, let's read the first message. You can see that the line describing the
message is already highlighted in the message list. Just double-click on the
message line, and the program displays the following:

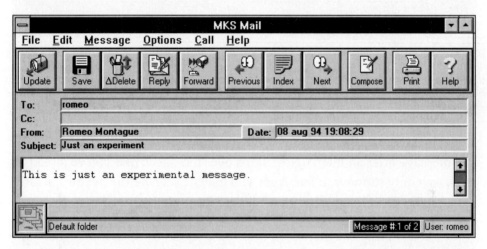

In the white area at the bottom of the window, you can see the body of the
message. Above that, you can see various pieces of information about the
message, including the name of the person who sent the message, the subject, and the date it was sent.

If the message is too long to fit in the white area of the window, use the
scroll bars or arrow keys to move through the message.

Moving Through a List of Messages

Once you've read the message, you're ready to read the next message.
Click on the *Next* icon in the toolbar, and the Mail Reader shows you the
next unread message.

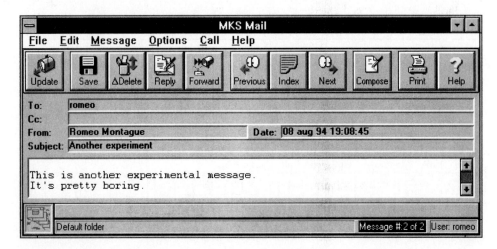

If you had more messages, you could continue to use *Next* to read through
one message after another. (*Next* skips over messages that you've already
read, so it only shows you messages you haven't seen before.) You can also
click on the *Previous* icon to go backward through the list of messages.

Replying to a Message

As you read through your list of messages, you can reply to any of the messages in the list. Simply click on the *Reply* icon. This calls up the Mail
Composer to let you enter your reply.

> **Note:** When you reply to a message, the Mail Composer automatically fills in the `To:` line with the name of the person who sent you the original message; that way your reply goes to that person. The Mail Composer also fills in the *Subject* line with `Re:` followed by the original subject.

Once you have finished composing your reply, choose *Done* to send the reply. When you quit the Mail Composer, you'll return to the Mail Reader window so you can read more mail.

Returning to the Index

When you have finished reading through the list of messages, click on *Next* or *List* to return to the original message list. When you return, you'll see one difference:

- When you first saw this list, each message line was marked with the letter **n** to indicate the message was new.

- Now the lines no longer start with the letter **n**. You've read the messages, so they're no longer new.

If You Quit...

If you quit now, the Mail Reader asks if you want to save your current folder. As explained in Chapter 12, the program keeps its own records of which messages you've read. If you save to the current folder, the program's records are stored in the folder. If you don't save, the folder is not changed.

What's the difference? In this case, not much. If you save, the information in the folder is updated to show which messages you have and haven't read.

- Messages that you haven't read yet are marked **o** for **old**.

- Messages that you have read aren't marked at all.

If you don't save, the next time you start the Mail Reader, you'll see the same messages and once again they'll be marked **n** for **new**. You told the program not to save its records, so the Mail Reader doesn't know that you've read these messages before.

15

Saving Messages

This chapter looks at the process of saving messages in files and deleting messages that you don't want to save.

Saving a Message

Last chapter, you read several messages using the Mail Reader window. After reading the messages, you should have seen something like this:

Let's save the message that's highlighted in the window. To do this, click on the *Save* icon in the toolbar. This calls up a *Save Message dialog box*:

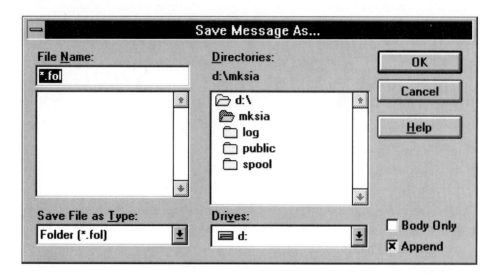

This box lets you save the message in a file. The default is to create a file whose name ends in the extension `.fol` (standing for "folder"). However, you can use a different style of file name if you wish.

If you want to save the message in a new file, just enter the file's name in the blank *File Name* area. You can also save the message in an existing file: either type in the name of the file, or use a standard file search procedure to move from one directory to another until you find the file.

For the sake of experiment, type in the name `sample.fol` in the *File Name* area and press ENTER. This saves the highlighted message in a (new) file named `sample.fol` under the indicated directory.

Now, try the same thing again. Highlight another message in the message list (by using the mouse or arrow keys) and click on the *Save* icon again. The *Save File* dialog box appears again, but now it has `sample.fol` in the *File Name* area. Just press ENTER, and the message you just highlighted is added to the other message in the file.

You'll notice that the Save Message dialog box has a check box labeled *Append*. When this box is check-marked, new messages are added (appended) at the end of any other messages in the folder. If the *Append* box is blank, new messages **replace** the current contents of the folder—when you save a message, the old contents of the folder are thrown away, so the folder only contains the new message. Most of the time, you'll want to leave *Append* turned on so that you don't lose the current contents of the folder.

Changing Folders

You've just saved two messages in a folder called `sample.fol`. Suppose you want to look at those messages some time in the future—how do you look into the folder?

To look at the messages in `sample.fol`, follow these steps:

1. In the Mail Reader window, click on the word *File* in the menu bar. This calls up the *File Menu*.

2. From the *File Menu*, choose the *Open Folder* item by clicking on it. This pops up a dialog box of the following form:

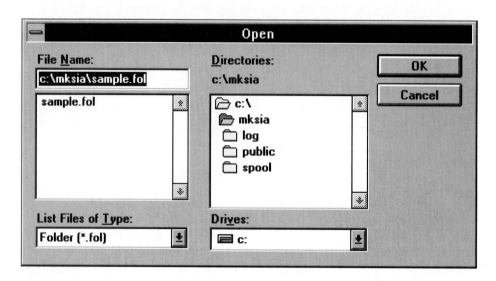

This box lets you open an existing mail folder. You'll notice that `sample.fol` is shown in the list of existing folders. Click on the name, then press ENTER.

You'll see that the Mail Reader displays the following dialog box:

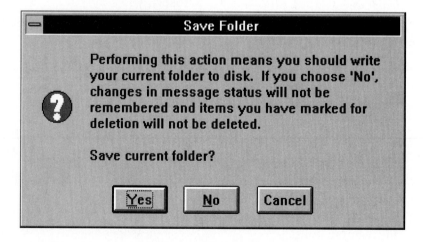

You've probably seen this box before. Before you switch to the new folder, the Mail Reader wants to know if you want to save updated information about the previous folder. If you choose *Yes*, the Mail Reader saves the information; if you choose *No*, it doesn't. In our situation, it doesn't really matter, so choose *Yes*.

Once you click on *Yes*, the Mail Reader shows you the contents of the new folder:

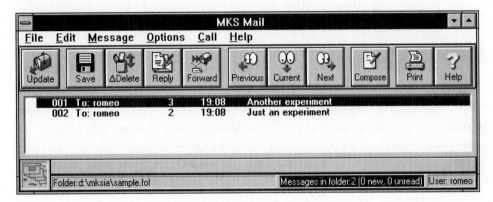

These are the same messages you saved, listed in the order they were saved. (If you followed our instructions closely, you saved the second message first, then went back to the first message, so the two messages are in reverse order.)

Effective Use of Folders

You may be wondering what the point of this operation is: you started with two messages in a folder, and you saved the same two messages in another folder. Why bother?

The point is that multiple folders can help you organize your incoming mail. For example, Romeo might save all his messages from Juliet in a file named `juliet.fol`, and save messages from other people in other files.

This makes it easier to find a particular message if you search for it later. If Romeo wants to find some specific message from Juliet, he can just open up `juliet.fol` and scan the messages for the one he wants. This is easier than keeping all your messages in one big folder, and searching through everything each time you want to find a particular message.

> You can organize your mail by creating separate folders for each person whose messages you want to keep. However, there are other possible ways to get organized. For example, you might create separate folders for mail on different topics or projects. You can decide what works best for you.

Deleting a Message

So far, we've talked about saving the messages you receive. However, you'll find that most of your messages aren't worth saving for long. To save disk space, and to make it easier to find the messages that are really worth keeping, you should delete most messages when you no longer need them.

To show you how to delete messages, let's go back to the Mail Reader window where the contents of `sample.fol` are displayed. Highlight the first message in the list (using the mouse or the arrow keys), then click on the *Delete* icon in the toolbar. You'll see the following:

There's now a "d" beside the highlighted message. This means that the message is scheduled for deletion. It isn't deleted yet, and you can still read it if you want. You can even "undelete" the message. Just click on the *Delete* icon again, and you'll see that the "d" disappears—the message won't be deleted after all.

Updating Your Folder

We still have to show you how to delete a message, so click the *Delete* icon once more to mark the highlighted message for deletion. Now, click on the *Update* icon. *Update* tells the Mail Reader to go ahead and delete the message for real, and to update the folder file to make the message go away.

You'll see a box flash by briefly, showing that the Mail Reader is updating the folder. Then the window changes to:

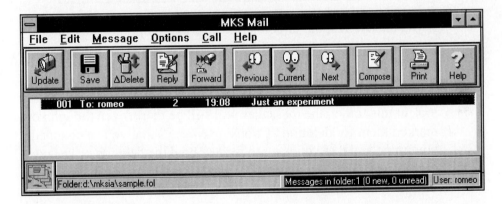

As you can see, the message you marked for deletion is gone. You can no longer retrieve it.

Updates When You Quit

Messages marked for deletion go away when you do an *Update*. If you quit the Mail Reader without doing an *Update*, you'll see a dialog box you've seen before:

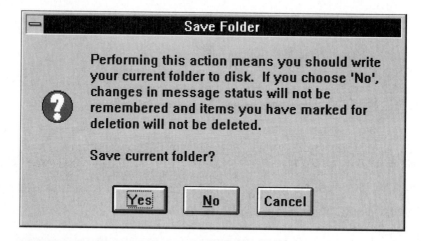

- If you choose *Yes*, the effect is like an *Update* option—any messages marked for deletion will disappear. The next time you look at this folder, the messages will be gone.

- If you choose *No*, the messages are not deleted. The next time you look at this folder, the messages will still be there, even though you marked them for deletion. Choosing *No* says that you've changed your mind and that you want to forget about the deletions. The next time you read mail, the messages won't even be marked for deletion.

> We recommend that you delete messages as soon as you don't need them anymore. This saves disk space and makes it easier to manage the messages you really do need.

Saving a Message Body

Normally, when you save a mail message, the Mail Reader saves all the header information associated with the message as well as the message itself. This header information is saved as a sequence of text lines at the beginning of each message. These text lines start with words like To, Subject, and so on, much like the information lines you see when you are reading a mail message with the Mail Reader.

If you want, you can save a mail message without all those header lines. Highlight a message, and click on the *Save* button. Once again, you'll see the dialog box:

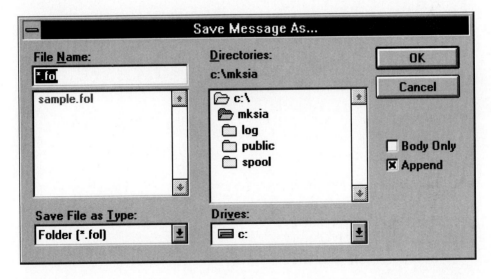

If you click on the *Body only* box before you save the message, the Mail Reader saves only the main part of the message, not the header information. This is useful if someone sends you a lot of information and you want to save that information in a file all on its own.

Warning: There's one drawback when you only save the body of a message. Since you've explicitly asked the program to get rid of all the header information, the saved text is no longer recognizable as a mail message. This means that you can no longer read the text using the Mail Reader. You must use other software, like the *Notepad* accessory of Windows or the DOS `type` command to look at the file.

16 *The Address Book*

This chapter discusses the *Address Book* facilities available through the Mail Composer. The Address Book makes it easy to keep track of complicated Internet mailing addresses and reference them quickly when you send a mail message.

The Address Book

The Address Book is managed by the Mail Composer. Double-click on the *Mail Composer* icon in the MKS Internet Anywhere application group to get the Mail Composer window. Then click on the *Address* icon in the Mail Composer toolbar.

This calls up a window containing the *Address Book*. The Address Book is a way to record the names and postal addresses of people, along with their Internet addresses. It can really help when you're trying to send mail to people, because Internet addresses can get very long and hard to remember.

When you click on the *Address* icon, you'll first see a window that looks like this:

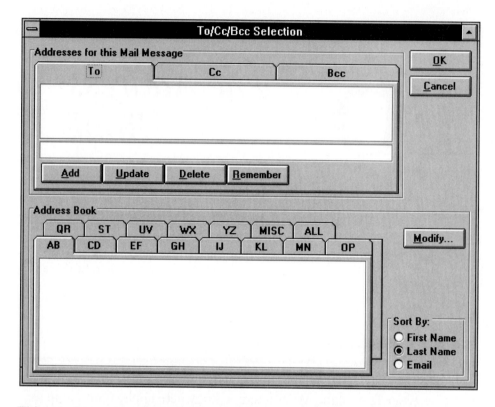

This window makes it easier to enter Internet addresses in the To:, Cc:, and Bcc: lines of mail messages. Basically, you can find Internet addresses in the Address Book area of the window, then copy those addresses to the upper part of the window. The addresses in the upper part of the window will be added to the mail message you're composing.

We'll get back to that in a minute. First, however, we have to put some names into the Address Book. To do this, click on the *Modify* button. The Mail Composer responds by displaying a window that says:

Welcome to the MKS Internet Anywhere Address Book!
There are no records in your Address Book.
Use the 'Add' button to add an address.

This window also has an *Add* button. Press *Add* and you'll see the *Address Book dialog box*:

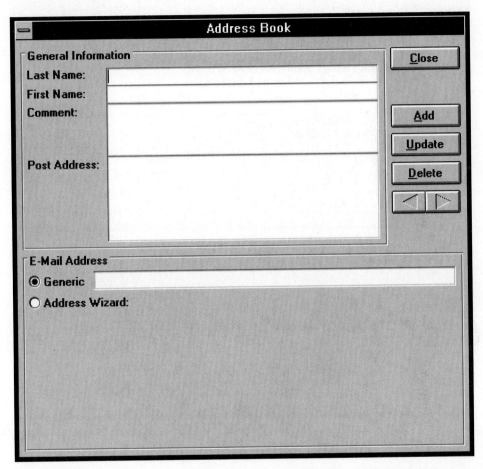

This lets you create an *Address Book entry*, containing information on people with whom you exchange messages. For example, Romeo might fill in information about Juliet, entering her last name, first name, and so on.

For practice, fill in general information for someone you know. To move from one field to the next (e.g., from *Comments* to *Post Address*), just press TAB. Once you've filled in all the information, you might have something like this:

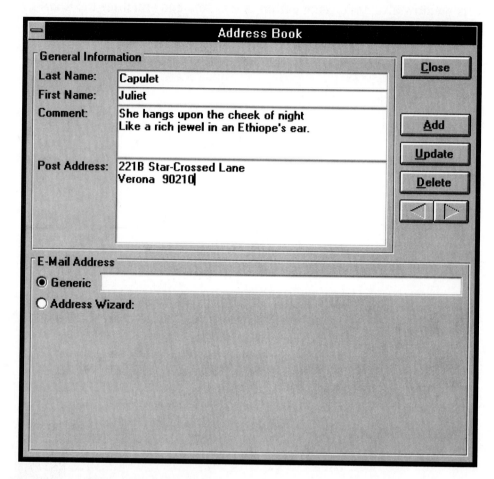

Filling in E-Mail Addresses

After you've filled in the *General Information* area, it's time to fill in the
E-mail address. There are two ways to do this:

1. If you know the complete E-mail address, you can just click on the
   blank beside *Generic*, then type in the address. For example,
   Romeo might type in

   ```
   juliet@capulet
   ```

2. Otherwise, you can use the *Address Wizard* to figure out the best address to use for someone.

The Address Wizard

To see how the Address Wizard works, click on the *Address Wizard* button. The bottom part of the window changes to:

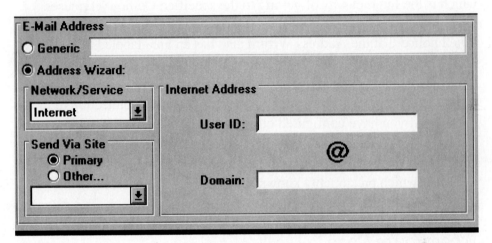

This lets you create an Internet address by filling in the *User ID* field with the person's username and the *Domain* field with `sitename.domain` or whatever is appropriate.

The Address Wizard recognizes many other forms of address as well. Click on the arrow under *Network/Service* and you'll see that the Wizard can create addresses for America Online, CompuServe, MCI Mail, and many others.

To create an address, just choose the appropriate address type from the *Network/Service* list. The Address Wizard changes the *Address* part of the screen to ask for the information that MKS Internet Anywhere needs in order to create an appropriate Internet address for this person.

For example, if you choose CompuServe from the *Network/Service* list, the Address Wizard asks for the person's CompuServe User ID. Once you fill in the User ID, the Address Wizard can create an appropriate (Internet style) address you can use to send mail to that CompuServe user. If you fill in the User ID 73260,1043 (which is MKS's CompuServe User ID), the Address Wizard creates the Internet address,

73260,1043@CompuServe.com

which is the Internet way of getting to the specified CompuServe user.

You'll notice that the Address Wizard also has an area labeled *Send Via Site*. This area provides more information that the Address Wizard can use to create an appropriate E-mail address. If you click on *Primary*, your E-mail to this person will be sent out via your primary connection to the Internet. If you have configured other connections to other machines, you can fill in the *Other...* blank with the name of a different machine; when you do this, mail to this person is sent from your computer to the specified machine (which presumably knows how to direct the message to the intended recipient).

When You're Done

When you've finished filling in the *General Information* in the Address Book dialog box, and when you've filled in an E-mail address (in the *Generic* blank or using the Address Wizard), you're ready to add all this information to your Address Book.

To add this entry to the Address Book, click on the *Add* button. This adds all the information to your Address Book, then clears the dialog box so that you can add another person to your Address Book. When you're finished adding to the Address Book, click on *Close*.

When you return to the previous window, you'll see that the Address Book contains the information you entered, as shown on the next page. You'll notice that the example shows Juliet's last name first, as in

Capulet, Juliet juliet@capulet She hangs upon the cheek...

By clicking the buttons in the bottom right hand corner of the dialog box, you can arrange Address Book entries by first name or by E-mail address, if you don't like arranging entries by last name.

You'll also notice that the window has alphabetic tabs at the bottom, to help you flip through your Address Book quickly. For example, if you have a lot of addresses, clicking on the ST tab moves directly to names beginning with S and T. However, if you only have a few addresses in your book, the Address Book shows all of your addresses, no matter which alphabetic tabs you click.

Here is a typical screen showing an Address Book entry:

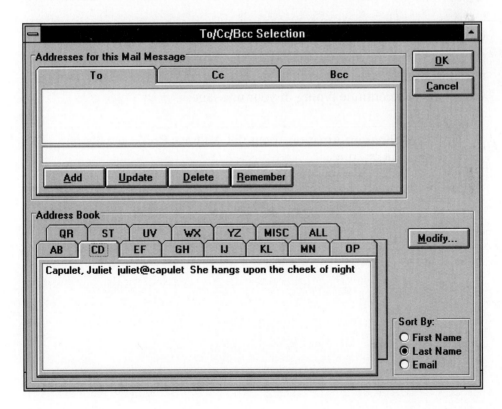

Using the Address Book

Now suppose Romeo wants to send a message to Juliet. First, he clicks on the *To* tab in the top half of the window, because he wants to send the message to Juliet. (For Cc: lines, he would click on the *Cc* tab and for Bcc: lines he would click on the *Bcc* tab.)

Next, Romeo clicks on Juliet's name in the Address Book, then drags the name up to the blank area at the top of the window. This adds Juliet's Internet address to the To: line of the message being composed. If Romeo wants to send the message to several other people too, he can also drag their names from the Address Book to the area labeled *Addresses for this Mail Message*.

Using the Address Book in this way, you can set up the addresses of all the people who'll receive a copy of the message. When you're finished getting the addresses, choose *OK*. You'll go back to the Mail Composer window, where you can continue typing in your message.

> For further information about the Address Book, see the on-line help facilities.

17

Attachments and Inserts

This chapter explains how to send existing files to other users, by inserting them into the body of messages or by "attaching" them indirectly to messages.

Attaching Files to Messages

Using the Mail Composer, you can attach a file to any mail message you send out. To do this, simply click on the *Attach* icon in the Mail Composer window's toolbar. The Mail Composer displays the *Attach dialog box*:

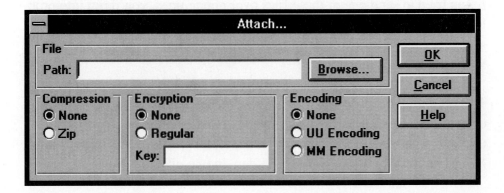

If you know the name of the file you want to attach, fill the file name into the blank area after *Path:* (standing for "pathname"). If you don't know the name, you can click on *Browse* and use standard file search procedures to locate the file you want.

You'll notice that the Attach box has several areas, each of which contain various options for *Compression*, *Encryption*, and *Encoding*. The sections that follow describe each of these in detail.

Encoding

In the process of exchanging data over phone lines, computers send each other many special signals. These signals are often sent using *control characters*: special characters that can't be confused with normal text characters like letters and digits.

Unfortunately, the same control characters are used for lots of different purposes by different programs. For example, word processing programs use control characters to indicate things like changes in fonts or other formatting commands; and control characters are often found in spreadsheet files, databases, and files containing executable programs.

If you tried to send one of these files over phone lines, you'd run into problems: the software wouldn't be able to tell when a control character was a special signal related to transmitting data, or when the control character was part of the data itself.

To get around this problem, you have to *encode* data files to get rid of the control characters. Basically, this means translating the data into normal characters like letters and numbers: characters that are "safe" to transmit. MKS Internet Anywhere can encode data in two different ways:

UU encoding:
> This is a type of encoding that originated on UNIX computing systems (hence the letter "U").

MM encoding:
> This is a form of encoding based on the MIME standard for data exchange on the Internet.

In general, *UU encoding* is more widely accepted.

> If you are sending a non-text file as an attachment to a mail message, you should use *UU encoding* unless you have a good reason for using *MM encoding*. You **must** encode the file; encoding is the only way to make sure that non-text files are correctly transmitted.

Compression

Compressing an attached file makes it smaller. This can speed up the rate of transmission from one computer to another (and save you money). While there are a variety of different ways of compressing data, the *Zip* compression technique is very popular in the Internet world. To compress an attached file, click on the *Zip* button in the Attach box.

You'll notice that when you click on *Compress*, it automatically marks *UU encoding* too. A compressed file always contains non-text characters, so it must go through the *UU encoding* process before it can be shipped to another computer.

Encryption

Encryption disguises data to make it difficult for other people to read. Remember that mail messages can pass through many computers before they are finally delivered to their intended recipients, so it is theoretically possible for the people who own those computers to intercept and read mail messages as they pass through. This isn't something you should normally worry about—most people have better things to do than hijacking electronic mail—but if you are sending confidential information, you'll certainly be more secure if you encrypt it first.

To encrypt the message, simply click on the *Regular* button in the *Encryption* area. You'll notice that the cursor moves to the blank area after the word *key*. The process of encrypting a file uses a formula that is based on a string of characters, called the *encryption key*. In order for anyone to decrypt the file contents, they have to know the key string that you used in the encryption. Thus, the encryption key is something like a "password" that lets you into the file. You can choose any string of characters for your encryption key.

People who receive an encrypted file must know the encryption key you used when you sent the message; otherwise, they won't be able to decrypt what you send. And don't send a message along the lines of

```
Here's a file I encrypted
with the key ABCDEFG.
```

The only reason to encrypt a file is if you're worried about people reading it. If someone really does read your mail, they'll be able to use the key to decrypt the attached file, thereby defeating your attempts at security. Tell people your encryption keys some other way (for example, by phoning the intended recipient).

> **Warning:** Be sure you remember what encryption key you use. If you forget the key, there's no hope of decrypting the attached file.

When you attach a file to a mail message, the bottom of the Mail Composer window changes to show there is an attachment, as in:

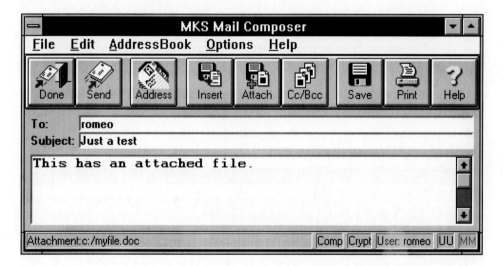

The file name is shown after the word *Attachment*. The same line also shows if you've used any special attachment options. In this case, we've used all three: UUencode, Compression, and Encryption. The window also shows MM, but this is greyed out because we have not used MM encoding.

Receiving Messages with Attached Files

If you receive a message that has an attached file, you will see the message marked with a file folder in your message list, as in:

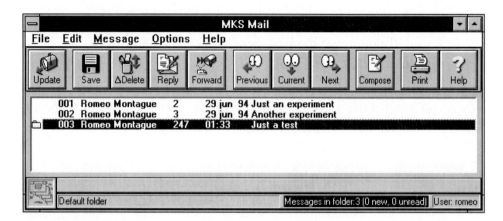

In this example, the last message in the list has an attached file, as indicated by the little picture on the left side of the line. If you double-click on this line to read the message, you'll see something like:

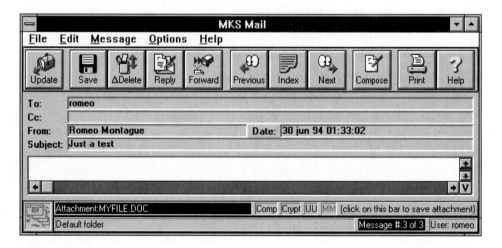

The line under the message area says *Click this bar to save the attachment.* This gives you the chance to save the attached file to a file on your own computer. If you click the bar, the Mail Reader displays a box of the form:

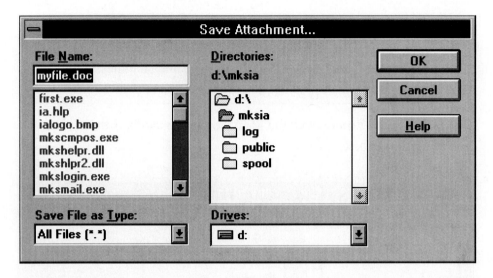

This box lets you specify where you want to save the attached file. When you save the file, the Mail Reader automatically reverses any encoding and compression that occurred when the file was attached.

If the file was encrypted, the Mail Reader displays a box asking you to enter the password (encryption key) for the file. You must enter the encryption key that was used when the message was sent; otherwise, the result is gobbledygook.

Inserting Files

The Mail Composer window has an *Insert* icon on the toolbar. This lets you insert the contents of a text file into the body of a message.

> **Note:** When you *insert* a file, its contents become part of the message itself. When you *attach* a file, you don't see the file as part of the message; the file accompanies the message separately.

If you click on the *Insert* icon, the Mail Composer displays the *Insert File* dialog box:

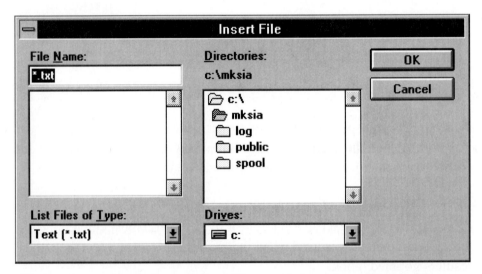

This lets you go through a standard file search in order to find the file you want to insert. If you already know the name of the file you want to insert, you can type it in directly in the *File Name* area.

 Note: You can only insert *text* files; you cannot insert files that contain non-text (control) characters. Since most word processors use non-text characters to represent formatting instructions, you usually can't insert word processing files. If you want to send someone a word processing file, a spreadsheet, a database, an executable program, or some other kind of non-text file, you must attach the file rather than insert it.

18

The User Program

This chapter discusses the *User* program. This program lets you identify all the people who will be using MKS Internet Anywhere on your computer.

> **Note:** The evaluation software that comes with this book does not allow for several different people to read news or send mail; therefore, the features described in this chapter are unavailable. However, if you upgrade to the full MKS Internet Anywhere package, you will be able to use all these features.

Starting the User Program

To start the program, click on the *Users* icon in the MKS Internet Anywhere application group. This displays the *User window*:

Adding New Users

When you first call the User program, you'll only see one user: the person
who installed the software. To add another user, follow these steps:

1. Click on the *Login* field and enter a username for the new user.
   Remember that a username should be from one to eight characters
   long, consisting only of letters and digits, and the first character
   can't be a digit. For example, if the new user is Juliet, enter
   `juliet`. **Don't** press ENTER when you've typed in the name.

2. Press TAB to go to the *Full Name* field, then type in the full name of
   the new user. There are no special rules on the full name; use whatever format the person prefers. For example, you might type

       Juliet Capulet

3. When both the *Login* and *Full Name* fields have been filled in, pull down the *User* menu and choose the *Add* item. You'll see the new name appear in the list of users.

The list can contain a maximum of four different users.

Switching Users

Suppose Romeo and Juliet share the same computer. Obviously, when Romeo uses the Mail Reader, he wants to see his mail; and when Juliet uses the Mail Reader, she wants to see *her* mail. For this to happen, they have to tell the software who they are—the computer equivalent of saying "Hello, I'm Romeo" or "Hi, I'm Juliet."

It's even more important to identify yourself when you're reading news. First of all, Romeo and Juliet may subscribe to different newsgroups— Romeo likes to read *rec.sport.fencing*, but Juliet doesn't. The software can keep a personalized subscription list for each person, but the News Reader has to know who's reading before it can use the correct subscription list.

Even worse, suppose that Romeo and Juliet both subscribe to some group (like *alt.feuds.verona*). If Juliet reads all the articles in the group and then Romeo starts reading his news, Romeo would certainly like a chance to read the articles too. The software can keep track of things like "Juliet has read this article already but Romeo hasn't," and can give each person a chance to read all the appropriate articles…but only if people identify themselves first.

Identifying Yourself

To identify yourself to the software, follow these steps:

1. Make sure that the four main programs of MKS Internet Anywhere are not running. These programs are the News Reader, the News Poster, the Mail Reader, and the Mail Poster. If you are currently running one or more of these programs, you must quit before you change users.

2. Once you have quit any other MKS Internet Anywhere programs, double-click on the *Users* icon in the MKS Internet Anywhere application group. This calls up the User window.

3. Click on your name in the list of users in the *Set Current User* part of the window. You'll see that this highlights your name.

4. Quit the program.

That's all you have to do. Once you've told the software who you are, you can use all the other programs to read your own mail and news, and to send out messages and articles under your own name.

> **Important:** When several people use the same computer for news and E-mail, they should all get into the habit of identifying themselves through the *User* program before they do anything else.

Variations Between Users

Some facilities are shared by users; for example, the information for connecting to other computers is shared by all users. On the other hand, some features can be set individually for each user; for example, each user has a separate newsgroup subscription list, so that each user can choose which groups he or she wants to read.

The following features can change from user to user:

- Username (used when sending out mail messages and news articles)

- Mail folders; each user has a different default folder

- Address book

- Newsgroup subscription lists

- Option settings in the four major programs (Mail Reader and Composer, News Reader and Poster); for example, one user can set options to have the News Reader show empty newsgroups, while another user can set options so that the News Reader only shows newsgroups that contain unread messages

The following features are the same for all users:

- Information for connecting to other systems

- Schedules for connecting to other systems and for operations like the nightly clean-up

- The set of newsgroups your access provider ships to your computer

19

Advanced Concepts

This chapter briefly introduces a number of other features of MKS Internet Anywhere. We won't describe these features in detail; we merely want to mention that these features are available, then direct you to the on-line documentation where you can find complete explanations.

The Control Center

Chapters 2–5 described the most basic features of the Control Center. However, it skipped a few advanced features. Procedures for using these features can be found in the Control Center section of on-line help, under the *Procedures/How To* topic. The advanced features include:

Login sequence
> The login sequence dictates the procedure that your machine follows when it connects with another computer. For further details, see the *Creating a Login Sequence* entry in the on-line help, or Appendix C in this book.

The News Reader

Several features of the News Reader have not yet been mentioned in this guide. Descriptions of these advanced features can be found in the *Usenet*

News section of on-line help, under the *Commands* topic. The advanced features include:

The Article Menu

The News Reader's *Article* menu lets you perform various actions on articles. For example, the *Mark Article As Unread* item can be applied to an article that you've already read, so that the article doesn't disappear in the next clean-up. This is useful if you start to read an article, then quit but want to come back to it another time.

The *Cancel Posted Article* item of the *Article* menu lets you cancel an article that you posted yourself. For example, if you've just posted an article, then notice it has a significant typing mistake, you may want to cancel it and have another try.

For further information on these features and others, see *News Reader: Article Menu Commands* in the on-line help.

The Options Menu

The News Reader's *Options* menu controls various aspects of reading news. For example, the entries *Primary font* and *Alternate font* give you the choice of two different type fonts for displaying news articles.

The *Disguise (Rot13)* menu item comes from a long-standing tradition in Usenet news. When an article contains vulgar language or other objectionable material, the person posting the article may "scramble" the article using a technique called *Rot13* encoding. As a result, you may see gobbledygook instead of a comprehensible article. By clicking on the *Disguise* menu item, you can "unscramble" and read the original article. (Of course, if you may be offended by such material, you might prefer to skip the scrambled article.)

For further information on these features and others, see *News Reader: Options Menu Commands* in the on-line help.

The News Poster Program

The following features of the News Poster have not yet been mentioned in this guide:

The Info Menu
> The News Poster's *Info* menu lets you add extra information to a news article's header lines. For more information, see *News Poster: Info Menu Commands* in the on-line help.

The Options Menu
> The *Options* menu controls various aspects of the News Poster. For example, it lets you change the font of articles and the header lines.
>
> The *Signature* item of the *Options* menu lets you create a signature that is automatically added to every article you post. As you read Usenet, you'll see many people who have standard signatures, giving information about themselves and their companies, possibly including a quotation or motto. You can use the *Signature* item to create a similar signature for yourself. However, don't go overboard—a signature more than a few lines long just adds to the clutter of Usenet.
>
> For further information on these features and others, see *News Poster: Options Menu Commands* in the on-line help.

The News Control Program

The News Control program controls the way that Usenet news works on your system. In particular, it manages the *news database*, the file that contains all the news articles on your system. For example, News Control lets you control the way that old articles are cleaned out of the database, in order to make room for incoming articles.

MKS has chosen automatic settings to suit the needs of users who are unfamiliar with the internal workings of Usenet. We strongly recommend that you do not change the settings unless you have a solid understanding of Usenet and have special needs which the default settings do not satisfy.

> **Note:** In the evaluation software that comes with this book, the features that let you feed Usenet news to other sites are disabled.

The Settings Menu

News Control's *Settings* menu controls the way the database receives and holds news. This includes the following:

System Distribution
> The System Distribution Table is used if you feed newsgroups to other sites; the table controls which kinds of newsgroups you'll send out. For example, you could say that you'll send anything in the *comp* hierarchy but nothing from the *alt* hierarchy. For further information, see *System Distribution Table* in the on-line help.

Active Newsgroup
> The Active Newsgroup Table lets you change the characteristics of the newsgroups you receive from your access provider. For further information, see *Active Newsgroup Table* in the on-line help.

Expiration List

This list controls how long news articles are retained on your system before they are cleaned out to make room for new articles. For further information, see *Expiration List* in the on-line help.

Incoming Batch Processing

This controls the way the software handles incoming batches of news articles. For further information, see *Incoming Batch Processing* in the on-line help.

The Database Menu

News Control's *Database* menu offers more features related to the news database.

Expire

The *Expire* item lets you immediately clean out unwanted news articles from the database. This overrides the normal automatic expiration process (which usually takes place overnight). For further information, see *Expire* in the on-line help.

Process Incoming Batch

From time to time, your Internet access provider sends you a file containing a batch of news articles. The articles must be moved from this file into the news database before you can read them. Normally, the software does this automatically according to a set schedule. For further information, see *Process Incoming Batch* in the on-line help.

Create Outgoing Batch

Just as your access provider feeds news to you, you can feed news to other computers. This is called *downstream feeding*, based on the idea that news comes to you from an "upstream" site and gets sent off to "downstream" sites. For more information, see *Create Outgoing Batch* in the on-line help.

Newsgroup Statistics

This item tells how much space is used to hold your news articles, how many newsgroups are known to your system, and how many articles they contain.

Compact Database

This attempts to shrink the amount of disk space occupied by the news database, by getting rid of the unused space in the file. This unused space is a result of articles being deleted or expiring, leaving "gaps" in the database file. The compaction process shifts the remaining articles to fill in the gaps, then gets rid of any excess space. For further information, see *Compact Database* in the on-line help.

Repair Database

This attempts to correct any problems in the database file. For example, if you have a power failure while your computer is working with the database, it's possible that the contents of the file may get mixed up. *Repair Database* tries to straighten things out. For more information, see *Repair Database* in the on-line help.

Advanced

This lets you examine and modify various tables used in controlling newsgroups and news articles on your system. Few users will ever have to worry about these tables—the software handles them automatically. However, if you have very specialized needs, you may have to adjust one or more of these tables by hand. For further information, see *Advanced* in the on-line help.

The Mail Reader

Earlier chapters have already discussed most of the features of the Mail Reader. The following list looks at some that haven't been mentioned yet.

System Folders
>Chapter 11 explained that a folder is a file that can hold mail messages. When mail messages arrive from other computers, the software puts them into a *system folder*, a special file that is exclusively used to hold incoming mail.
>
>When you have mail messages waiting in your system folder, the software lets you know that the messages are there by displaying the Notify box. When you click on the Mail Reader's *Update* icon, the new messages are moved from the system folder into your *working folder,* where you can then read the messages. After you have read the messages, you can save them from your working folder to other folders if you so choose.
>
>For further information, see the *Folders... Command* topic in the Electronic Mail section of the on-line help.

Mail Notification
>The *Notify* item in the Mail Reader's *Options* menu lets you change how the software shows that there's a mail message waiting for you. For further information, see the *Notify... Command* topic in the Electronic Mail section of the on-line help.

Headers
>The *Headers* item in the Mail Reader's *Options* menu lets you specify what header lines are displayed when you read a message, and what information is displayed in the one-line summaries of messages in the message list area. For further information, see *Headers Command* topic in the electronic mail section of the on-line help.

The Mail Composer

Previous chapters have discussed almost every feature of the Mail Composer. The only significant feature not discussed is the ability to cut and paste text from the Windows clipboard. Thus, you might use your favorite word processor to prepare a message ahead of time, then paste it from the clipboard.

Note that you can only paste **text**; you cannot paste pictures, spreadsheets, or other kinds of information.

The Scheduler

The Scheduler program lets you set or change the schedule that the package uses for running various programs automatically. For example, we've mentioned that the package normally runs an *expiration* program every night to remove old articles from your news database. This kind of clean-up operation can take quite a bit of time if you subscribe to a lot of newsgroups, so it's best to do the work when you aren't trying to use the computer for other things.

However, if you're a night owl who works from midnight to sunrise, you might prefer to schedule the clean-up work during the day. The Scheduler lets you set times to run every program in the MKS Internet Anywhere package, if you so wish. For further information, see *Scheduling Network Activity* in the Control Center section of the on-line help.

> **Note:** The Scheduler program has been disabled in the evaluation software that comes with this book. You won't be able to use the Scheduler unless you upgrade to the full MKS Internet Anywhere.

20 *Access Providers*

This chapter gives you some background on Internet access providers, and what you need to know about Internet connections before you arrange a connection for yourself.

> Remember, Chapter 1 of this book provides basic information about the Internet. You should read it before you talk to any access provider.

Internet Access Providers

An access provider is a company or organization that can provide you with an electronic connection to the Internet. If you think of the Internet as an information highway, access providers serve as on-ramps.

An access provider *feeds* you information from the Internet, and relays your information to the Internet. MKS Internet Anywhere works with your access provider to transmit this information.

> A *feed* is a collection of Usenet news articles and electronic mail messages, gathered by your access provider and sent to you in one big batch.

There are different types of Internet connections and feeds. MKS Internet Anywhere requires a specific kind of connection from the access provider: a *UUCP connection*.

UUCP Connections

UUCP is an acronym for UNIX to UNIX Copy Program. It is a well-established set of signals and procedures that computers can use to exchange data. MKS Internet Anywhere talks to other computers using the UUCP set of signals. This is called a *UUCP connection*.

 When you contact an access provider about connecting to the Internet, make sure you ask for a UUCP connection. There's more than one way to connect to the Internet, and MKS Internet Anywhere won't work if you get some other kind of connection. Some suppliers can't give you the right kind of connection, so you have to make it clear that your software needs UUCP. See the following sections for more details on how to choose and connect to an access provider.

Choosing an Access Provider

In order for an access provider to set up a connection for you, you'll have to give the access provider information about your system. This helps the access provider to understand your needs and to set things up appropriately.

This chapter tells exactly what you need to know about setting up connections for the MKS Internet Anywhere software. However, an access provider will also need information about your hardware, and you'll have to gather that information for yourself. On the next page, you'll find a sheet listing all the questions that an access provider may ask. Fill in the blanks with the appropriate answers about your computer.

MKS Internet Anywhere: Software Requirements	
What type of Internet Connection is needed?	UUCP
What do you need as a *feed*?	Usenet News & Electronic Mail
How do you notify the access provider when you want to subscribe to new newsgroups?	Send e-mail to a specified address, or issue GENSYS requests

Your System: Hardware Requirements	
What kind of modem do you have?	
What speed is your modem?	
What is the phone number to reach your modem?	
What is your voice phone number?	
How much free hard disk space do you have on your PC?	

Your Preferences: Personal Requirements	
What is the name you prefer to give your computer on the Internet? (site name)	
Do you want the access provider to help you register the name for your computer?	
What is your preferred user name for your computer to log in?	
What is your preferred password for your computer to log in?	
Which newsgroups (topics) do you want to receive? (Subscribing to many newsgroups takes more space on your computer and more time and money to receive, so limit your requests accordingly.)	
When, and how often, do you want to call the access provider during the day to pick up your *feed* of news and mail?	
What is your desired price range? (per minute/month/year, etc.)	

(Permission granted to photocopy this page for personal use)

The Access Provider's System and Requirements

As you contact providers, they may talk about things that are unfamiliar to you. You must ask the right questions to get the information you need. When you find answers to the following questions, ensure that they match the requirements you listed for your system.

Questions to Ask a Potential Access Provider

> Do you supply UUCP connections?
> Do you supply Usenet News?
> Do you carry every newsgroup, or just selected groups?
> Will you register my computer's site name for me?
> Do you support the speed of my modem?
> Are there restrictions on the number of times I can call you?
> Are there certain hours when I cannot call?
> If I have problems getting started, how can I get help?
> What are your current prices?
> How do you charge for services? Are there discount times?
> Do you have a local or toll-free number I can call for my feed?

When You Have Found an Access Provider

Once you have decided on a particular access provider, you need information about connecting with the Internet through the provider. Below, we list some questions that you should ask; on the next page, we've provided a worksheet where you can write down the answers, since you'll need this information when you start personalizing MKS Internet Anywhere (as described in Chapter 3).

Information to Get From Your Provider

> What is your Internet site name?
> What are your phone numbers? (both modem and support lines)
> What will my computer's Internet mailing address be?

What username and password will I use to login at your computer?

Does my computer need to use a detailed login sequence? If so, what is the sequence?

(See Appendix C for a discussion of login sequences.)

What are your possible baud rates?

(Baud rate is one way to measure the speed with which a modem transmits information.)

What are your parity and stop bits?

(Parity bits are used to detect transmissions errors, and stop bits are used to stop transmission temporarily after a bit of information is sent.)

Things to Find Out from Your Access Provider

Access Provider's site name: _____

Access Provider's phone number: _____

What will your mailing address be: _____

Login name you'll use when you call: _____

Password you'll use to login: _____

Possible baud rates: _____

Parity and stop bits: _____

Login:

Your Computer Sends: *Access Provider Responds:*

_____   _____

_____   _____

_____   _____

_____   _____

The questions given here serve as a guideline for dealing with Internet access providers. There may be other issues to discuss, so make sure you have plenty of time to straighten out any questions you or your access provider might have.

 Some access providers may try to talk you into another kind of connection, such as TCP/IP, SLIP, or PPP; they may also offer you "login access" to get mail and news directly on their system. However, none of these possibilities will work with MKS Internet Anywhere. Insist that you really do want a UUCP connection and a Usenet feed. If they can't help you, thank them for their time and try another access provider. Note that all providers listed in Chapter 21 have assured us they provide UUCP connections.

Connecting to Your Access Provider

Once you have all the information from your chosen Internet access provider, you're ready to install and personalize the MKS Internet Anywhere package that comes with this book.

During the personalization process, you'll be asked to enter a site name for the access provider, as well as other information such as the phone number, login sequence, and other details.

> **Note:** If you change access providers, you'll have to use the *Control Center* program to set up a connection to the new access provider. For further information, see *Adding a Remote Site* in the on-line help facility.

21 *Access Provider Directory*

This is a comprehensive directory of organizations that provide UUCP connections to the Internet. Whether you are looking for a connection for yourself or a connection for your business, this directory will help you select the most appropriate access provider to suit your needs.

The directory is sorted alphabetically by geographic area, broken down into five regions of the world:

North America: United States, Canada

Europe: All of Europe, Austria, Belgium, Croatia, Czech Republic, Denmark, France, Germany, Hungary, Iceland, Ireland, Luxemburg, The Netherlands, Portugal, Slovak Republic, Slovenia, Spain, Sweden, Switzerland, United Kingdom

Eurasia: Lithuania, Russia, Ukraine

Africa: Egypt, South Africa, Tunisia

Pacific Rim: Australia, Hong Kong, Japan, Malaysia, Taiwan

About the Listings

Each entry displays the following information:

Name of the Organization or Service

Mailing Address
Telephone and Fax Numbers
E-mail Address for General Inquiries
Internet Domain

Service Area:	At what locations does the provider offer service? *City, State/Province,* and/or *Country*
1-800 Service:	Can the customer access the service using an 800 number? *Yes* or *No*
UUCP Service:	What UUCP services are offered? *Usenet News* and/or *Electronic Mail*
Domain Registration:	Does the access provider offer to register your computer name in the Internet domain (i.e., help customers with the registration paperwork and submit the registration form on the customer's behalf)? *Yes* or *No* Check with the access provider to see if they charge for this service.
Consulting Services:	Are consulting services available? *Yes* or *No* (areas of specialization)
Commercial Traffic:	Does the access provider allow message traffic that is not in support of research or education? *Yes* or *No* If the access provider does not allow commercial traffic, you will not be permitted to conduct business correspondence unless it's related to research and education. Most providers in this book allow commercial traffic.
Sign Up Procedure:	How do you sign up with the access provider? *Instructions* (online or other)

Brief description of company and services.

Note that pricing information is not included in directory entries; contact the access provider for current rates.

Before you contact an access provider from this directory, you should make sure that you've read Chapter 20, and that you've gathered together all the information discussed in that chapter.

> **Warning:** All of the information in this chapter is subject to change. Contact the individual companies for more up-to-date details.

North America

The North American section of this directory lists access providers in the United States and Canada.

United States

The United States part of this directory lists information on the following:

National Access Providers
Arizona
California
Colorado
Connecticut
Delaware
District of Columbia
Florida
Georgia
Illinois
Louisiana
Maine
Maryland
Massachussetts
Michigan
Minnesota
Missouri
Nevada
New Hampshire
New Jersey
New Mexico
New York
Ohio

Oregon
Pennsylvania
Rhode Island
Texas
Utah
Vermont
Virginia
Washington
Wisconsin

National Access Providers

AlterNet

A service of UUNET Technologies, Inc.
3110 Fairview Park Dr.
Suite 570
Falls Church, VA 22042
Tel: (800) 488-6383 or (703) 204-8000
Internet Domain: We register individual domain names for our customers.

Service Area:	Worldwide UUCP service
1-800 Service:	Yes
UUCP Service:	Yes Usenet News and Electronic Mail
Domain Registration:	Yes
Consulting Services:	Yes
Commercial Traffic:	Yes
Sign Up Procedure:	Contact AlterNet Sales at (800) 4UUNET3

AlterNet operates a national TCP/IP network in the U.S., with direct connections to the Internet's component networks around the world. AlterNet provides UUCP, dialup PPP, dedicated SLIP/PPP, and dedicated 56 Kbps, T1, and 10 Mbps connections to its customers.

CNS (Community News Service), Inc.

1155 Kelly Johnson Boulevard
Suite 400
Colorado Springs, CO 80906
Tel: (719) 592-1240
Fax: (719) 592-1201
E-mail: info@cscns.com
Internet Domain: cscns.com

Service Area:	Nationwide via 800 Local Access in Denver, Colorado Springs. Pueblo and Alburq under construction.
1-800 Service:	Yes
UUCP Service:	Yes Usenet News and Electronic Mail
Domain Registration:	Yes
Consulting Services:	Yes
Commercial Traffic:	Yes
Sign Up Procedure:	By telephone: Call (800) 592-1240 By modem: Call (303) 758-2656 or (719) 520-5000 (userid: new pwd: newuser) For more information, send e-mail to info@cscns.com

CRL Network Services

P.O. Box 326
Larkspur, CA 94977
Tel: (415) 837-5300
Fax: (415) 392-9000
E-mail: support@crl.com
Internet domain: crl.com

Service Area:	National
1-800 Service:	No
UUCP Service:	Yes Usenet News and Electronic Mail
Domain Registration:	Yes
Consulting Services:	Yes
Commercial Traffic:	Yes
Sign Up Procedure:	Contact CRL at (415) 381-2800

CRL NETWORK DIRECT DIAL ACCESS: POINTS OF PRESENCE

ARIZONA: (602) 277-8045

CALIFORNIA: (415) 705-6060, (714) 517-6700, (213) 236-9944, (510) 603-2700, (415) 574-9001, (415) 225-0302, (415) 917-9995, (415) 389-8649, (707) 794-7150, (510) 232-7114, (415) 367-0706, (415) 461-1173, (707) 538-0251, (707) 746-0480

GEORGIA: (404) 577-3250

MASSACHUSETTS: (617) 577-9300

MISSOURI: (314) 241-7600

NEW YORK: (212) 695-7988

TEXAS: (214) 823-2000, (512) 472-2983, (210) 226-5151, (713) 236-9200

Information Access Technologies Inc. (HoloNet)

46 Shattuck Square
Suite 11
Berkeley, CA 94704-1152
Tel: (510) 704-0160
Fax: (510) 704-8019
E-mail: support@holonet.net
Internet Domain: iat.com and holonet.net

Service Area:	National
1-800 Service:	No
UUCP Service:	Yes Usenet News and Electronic Mail
Domain Registration:	Yes
Consulting Services:	No
Commercial Traffic:	Yes
Sign Up Procedure:	Modem to (510) 704-1058 8N1. Terminal emulation should be vt100 or vt102. Login as guest in lower-case letters. Or call (510) 704-0160 for more information.

IAT provides Internet access, including UUCP and custom domain name service for individuals, businesses and bbses nationwide.

Neosoft Inc.

3408 Mangun
Houston, TX 77092
Tel: (713) 684-5969
Fax: (713) 684-5922
E-mail: info@neosoft.com
Internet Domain: neosoft.com

Service Area:	Houston, New Orleans, St. Louis; provides service nationwide
1-800 Service:	Yes
UUCP Service:	Yes Usenet News and Electronic Mail
Domain Registration:	Yes
Consulting Services:	Yes For TCL/TK and systems administration
Commercial Traffic:	Yes
Sign Up Procedure:	Contact Neosoft at info@neosoft.com or call (713) 684-5969

NETCOM Online Communication Services

4000 Moorpark Avenue, Suite 209
San Jose, CA 95117
Tel: (408) 554-8649
Fax: (408) 241-9145
Internet Domain: netcom.com

Service Area:	National
1-800 Service:	No
UUCP Service:	Yes Usenet News and Electronic Mail
Domain Registration:	Yes
Consulting Services:	No
Commercial Traffic:	Yes
Sign Up Procedure:	Call for a business account representative at (800) 501-8649

NETCOM is the nation's leading commercial Internet Service Provider with local access points in major metropolitan areas throughout the United States. Full Internet Access is available for both the corporate or individual at 14.4, 56k, and T1 speeds.

NETCOM is entering its seventh year as a reliable provider of Internet products and services and maintains a 24/7 Network Operations Center. NETCOM's customers include defense contractors, semiconductor manufacturers, banks, and so on.

North Shore Access

A service of Eco Software, Inc.
145 Munroe Street, Suite 405
Lynn, MA 01901
Tel: (617) 593-3110
E-mail: info@northshore.ecosoft.com

Service Area:	Boston/Lynn/Salem area. U.S. and international access available
1-800 Service:	No

UUCP Service:	Yes Usenet News and Electronic Mail
Domain Registration:	Yes
Consulting Services:	Yes
Commercial Traffic:	Yes
Sign Up Procedure:	On-line sign-up, dial (617) 593-4557

Northwest Nexus

PO Box 40597
Bellevue, WA 98015-4597
Tel: (206) 455-3505 or (800) 539-3505
Fax: (206) 455-4672
E-mail: info@nwnexus.wa.com
Internet Domain: halcyon.com and wa.com

Service Area:	Primarily the Pacific Northwest, but we have customers from around the world.
1-800 Service:	No
UUCP Service:	Yes Usenet News and Electronic Mail
Domain Registration:	Yes
Consulting Services:	Yes
Commercial Traffic:	Yes
Sign Up Procedure:	Use a communications program emulating a VT100 (8,N,1) to dial 206.382.6245, and login as "new". Or call (800) 539-3505 for more information.

Northwest Nexus offers a wide range of low-cost options to give both private individuals and companies access to the vast resources of the Internet: millions of people interacting on thousands of subjects, and data available from countless sources, including the U.S. Government, universities, research labs, and private corporations.

Performance Systems International, Inc.

510 Huntmar Park Drive
Herndon, VA 22070
Tel: (703) 904-4100
E-mail: info@psi.com
Internet Domain: psi.com

Service Area:	Continental US
1-800 Service:	Yes Available with UUPSI
UUCP Service:	Yes Usenet News and Electronic Mail
Domain Registration:	Yes
Consulting Services:	Yes
Commercial Traffic:	Yes
Sign Up Procedure:	Contact 1.800.82psi.82 or send e-mail to "info@psi.com"

PSI, Inc. is a value-added network service provider that delivers a full spectrum of products for the user of electronic information with over 5,000 customers and hundreds of thousands of users. The PSI staff is a team of experienced networking professionals. They are proven leaders in offering the means for professional organizations and individuals to access and process information and communicate with other professionals in product development and support, news, financial services, government contracting, consulting, and academic pursuits.

Incorporated in 1989, PSI is headquartered in Herndon, VA, with its primary Network Operations Center (NOC) and Customer Support Group (CSG) near Albany, NY.

UUPSI - Mail/News: Electronic Mail and Bulletin Board services using the common UUCP protocol, a PC and a modem. It provides reliable electronic communications to the individual and corporate user at an inexpensive, fixed rate. UUPSI uses local numbers in over 80 cities throughout the continental U.S. or an 800-number incurring usage fees, and includes PSI's registering for a domain name on your behalf.

The Portal Information Network

20863 Stevens Creek Boulevard.
Suite 200
Cupertino, CA 95014
Tel: (408) 973-9111
Fax: (408) 725-1580
E-mail: info@portal.com
Internet Domain: portal.com

Service Area:	U.S. and International
1-800 Service:	No
UUCP Service:	Yes Usenet News and Electronic Mail
Domain Registration:	Yes
Consulting Services:	No
Commercial Traffic:	Yes
Sign Up Procedure:	Contact Portal via Voice: (408) 973-9111 Fax: (408) 725-1580 E-mail: cs@portal.com, info@portal.com

Portal provides a wide range of Internet connectivity solutions, including PPP, SLIP, UUCP, UNIX shell, and the menu-based Portal Online System. All these services are available nationwide through Sprint-Net, through our California modem pools, and through the Internet.

The Rabbit Network, Inc.

31511 Harper Avenue
St. Clair Shores, MI 48082
Tel: (800) 456-0094
Fax: (810) 790-0156
E-mail: info@rabbit.net
Internet Domain: rabbit.net

Service Area:	Entire USA via our 800 number and local access via our Cleveland, Ohio, terminal server and our Mt. Clemens, Michigan, terminal server
1-800 Service:	Yes
UUCP Service:	Yes Usenet News and Electronic Mail
Domain Registration:	Yes
Consulting Services:	Yes
Commercial Traffic:	Yes
Sign Up Procedure:	Contact us toll free at (800) 456-0094 or send e-mail to "info@rabbit.net"

We provide UUCP news and mail feeds, TCP/IP (SLIP/PPP) news and mail feeds, a telnet server for interactive sessions on the Internet, dial-up SLIP/PPP connections to the internet, domain name service and MX mail forwarding and (soon) an interactive internet BBS with GUI capabilities for Windows and MAC.

South Coast Computing Service Inc.

P.O. Box 270355
Houston, Texas
77277-0355
Tel: (713) 917-5000
E-mail: info@sccsi.com
Internet Domain: sccsi.com

Service Area:	Southern United States
1-800 Service:	No
UUCP Service:	Yes Usenet News and Electronic Mail
Domain Registration:	Yes
Consulting Services:	Yes
Commercial Traffic:	Yes
Sign Up Procedure:	Login to sccsi.com as newuser or send e-mail to info@sccsi.com or call (800) 221-6478

Arizona

CRL Network Services

See this complete listing under the state of California.

Data Basix

PO Box 18324
Tucson, AZ, 85731
Tel: (602) 721-1988
Fax: (602) 721-7240
E-mail: sales@data.basix.com or info@data.basix.com
Internet domain: data.basix.com

Service Area:	Arizona, Tuscon
1-800 Service:	No
UUCP Service:	Yes Usenet News and Electronic Mail
Domain Registration:	Yes
Consulting Services:	Yes
Commercial Traffic:	Yes
Sign Up Procedure:	E-mail sales@data.basix.com or call (602) 721-1988

Evergreen Internet Express

5333 North 7th Street
Suite B-220
Phoenix, Arizona   85014
Tel: (602) 230-9330
Internet Domain: libre.com

Service Area:	Arizona, Nevada, Utah, New Mexico
1-800 Service:	Selected, call for details
UUCP Service:	Yes Usenet News and Electronic Mail
Domain Registration:	Yes
Consulting Services:	Yes
Commercial Traffic:	Yes
Sign Up Procedure:	Call (602) 230-9330 in Arizona, or (702) 831-3353 in Nevada

California

a2i communications

1211 Park Avenue
#202
San Jose, California   95126-2924

Attn: Rahul Dhesi
Tel: (408) 293-8078
a2i network support account <support@rahul.net>
Internet Domain: rahul.net

Service Area:	San Francisco Bay Area
1-800 Service:	No
UUCP Service:	Yes Usenet News and Electronic Mail
Domain Registration:	Yes
Consulting Services:	Yes
Commercial Traffic:	Yes
Sign Up Procedure:	Voice (408) 293-8078 Modem (408) 293-9010, login 'guest'

Caprica Telecomputing Resources

2168 South Atlantic Blvd
#258
Monterey Park, CA
91754
Tel: (213) 266-0822
Internet Domain: caprica.com

Service Area:	Los Angeles
1-800 Service:	No
UUCP Service:	Yes Usenet News and Electronic Mail
Domain Registration:	Yes
Consulting Services:	Yes
Commercial Traffic:	Yes
Sign Up Procedure:	Login as "guest" at (213) 526-1195 for more information Voice (213) 266-0822

CRL Network Services

P.O. Box 326
Larkspur, CA 94977
Tel: (415) 837-5300
Fax: (415) 392-9000
E-mail: support@crl.com
Internet domain: crl.com

Service Area:	National
1-800 Service:	No
UUCP Service:	Yes Usenet News and Electronic Mail
Domain Registration:	Yes

Consulting Services:	Yes
Commercial Traffic:	Yes
Sign Up Procedure:	Contact CRL at (415) 381-2800

CRL NETWORK DIRECT DIAL ACCESS: POINTS OF PRESENCE

ARIZONA: (602) 277-8045
CALIFORNIA: (415) 705-6060, (714) 517-6700, (213) 236-9944, (510) 603-2700, (415) 574-9001, (415) 225-0302, (415) 917-9995, (415) 389-8649, (707) 794-7150, (510) 232-7114, (415) 367-0706, (415) 461-1173, (707) 538-0251, (707) 746-0480

GEORGIA: (404) 577-3250

MASSACHUSETTS: (617) 577-9300

MISSOURI: (314) 241-7600

NEW YORK: (212) 695-7988

TEXAS: (214) 823-2000, (512) 472-2983, (210) 226-5151, (713) 236-9200

Gordian

20361 Irvine Ave.
Santa Ana Heights, CA, 92707
Tel: (714) 850 0205 (Ask for uucp service)
Fax: (714) 850 0533
E-mail: uucp-request@gordian.com
Internet Domain: Users choose and use their own domain.

Service Area:	Southern California
1-800 Service:	No
UUCP Service:	Yes Usenet News and Electronic Mail
Domain Registration:	Yes
Consulting Services:	No

21: Access Provider Directory

Commercial Traffic:	Yes
Sign Up Procedure:	Please e-mail uucp-request@gordian.com or phone (714) 850-0205 for a signup form or more detailed information.

Gordian offers UUCP connectivity to the Internet for a small fee to sites in Southern California.

Information Access Technologies Inc. (HoloNet)

46 Shattuck Square
Suite 11
Berkeley, CA 94704-1152
Tel: (510) 704-0160
Fax: (510) 704-8019
E-mail: support@holonet.net
Internet Domain: iat.com and holonet.net

Service Area:	National
1-800 Service:	No
UUCP Service:	Yes Usenet News and Electronic Mail
Domain Registration:	Yes
Consulting Services:	No
Commercial Traffic:	Yes
Sign Up Procedure:	Modem to (510) 704-1058 8N1. Terminal emulation should be vt100 or vt102. Login as guest in lower-case letters. Or call (510) 704-0160 for more information.

IAT provides Internet access, including UUCP and custom domain name service for individuals, businesses, and bbses nationwide.

* See more details under the Nation wide section.

Kaiwan Corporation

12550 Brokhurst Street
Suite H
Garden Grove, CA   92640
Tel: (714) 638-2139
Fax: (714) 638-0455
E-mail: info@kaiwan.com
Internet Domain: kaiwan.com

Service Area:	Orange County, Los Angeles County, Riverside County, Ventura County, and San Diego County
1-800 Service:	No
UUCP Service:	Yes Usenet News and Electronic Mail
Domain Registration:	Yes
Consulting Services:	Yes
Commercial Traffic:	Yes

Sign Up Procedure:	1) Telnet kaiwan.com or
	2) Dial in to local POP
	    Garden Grove Station
	    Data Phone Lines# (714) 539-0829 (Multiple Lines), (714) 741-2920 (Multiple Lines)
	    Mission Viejo Station
	    Data Phone Lines# (714) 452-9166 (Multiple Lines)
	    Gardena Station
	    Data Phone Lines# (310) 527-4279 (Multiple Lines)
	    San Gabriel Valley Station
	    Data Phone Lines# (818) 579-6701 (Multiple Lines)
	    Van Nuys Station
	    Data Phone Lines# (818) 756-0180 (Multiple Lines)
	3) Type guest at the login prompt
	4) Register on-line
	5) Call us for more information

Maestro Technologies, Inc.

See this complete listing under the state of New York.

NETCOM Online Communication Services

4000 Moorpark Avenue, Suite 209
San Jose, CA 95117
Tel: (408) 554-8649
Fax: (408) 241-9145
Internet Domain: netcom.com

Service Area:	National
1-800 Service:	No
UUCP Service:	Yes Usenet News and Electronic Mail
Domain Registration:	Yes
Consulting Services:	No
Commercial Traffic:	Yes
Sign Up Procedure:	Call for a business account representative at (800) 501-8649

NETCOM is the nation's leading commercial Internet Service Provider with local access points in major metropolitan areas throughout the United States. Full Internet Access is available for both the corporate or individual at 14.4, 56k, and T1 speeds.

NETCOM is entering its seventh year as a reliable provider of Internet products and services and maintains a 24/7 Network Operations Center. NETCOM's customers include defense contractors, semiconductor manufacturers, banks, etc.

The Portal Information Network

20863 Stevens Creek Boulevard.
Suite 200
Cupertino, CA 95014
Tel: (408) 973-9111
Fax: (408) 725-1580
E-mail: info@portal.com
Internet Domain: portal.com

Service Area:	US and International
1-800 Service:	No
UUCP Service:	Yes Usenet News and Electronic Mail
Domain Registration:	Yes
Consulting Services:	No
Commercial Traffic:	Yes
Sign Up Procedure:	Contact Portal via Voice: (408) 973-9111 Fax: (408) 725-1580 E-mail: cs@portal.com, info@portal.com

Portal provides a wide range of Internet connectivity solutions, including PPP, SLIP, UUCP, UNIX shell, and the menu-based Portal Online System. All these services are available nationwide through Sprint-Net, through our California modem pools, and through the Internet.

Colorado

CNS (Community News Service), Inc.

1155 Kelly Johnson Boulevard
Suite 400
Colorado Springs, CO 80906
Tel: (719) 592-1240
Fax: (719) 592-1201
E-mail: info@cscns.com
Internet Domain: cscns.com

Service Area:	Nationwide via 800 Local Access in Denver, Colorado Springs. Pueblo and Alburq under construction.
1-800 Service:	Yes
UUCP Service:	Yes Usenet News and Electronic Mail

Domain Registration:	Yes
Consulting Services:	Yes
Commercial Traffic:	Yes
Sign Up Procedure:	By telephone: Call (800) 592-1240 By modem: Call (303) 758-2656 or (719) 520-5000 (userid: new pwd: newuser) For more information, send e-mail to info@cscns.com

Colorado SuperNet, Inc.

Colorado School of Mines
1500 Illinois
Golden, CO 80401
Tel: (303) 273-3471
Fax: (303) 273-3475
E-mail: info@csn.org
Internet domain: csn.org

Service Area:	There are currently 12 local calling areas served in Colorado: Alamosa, Fort Collins, Greeley, Boulder/Denver, Frisco, Gunnison, Colorado Springs, Glenwood Springs, Pueblo, Durango, Grand Junction. Telluride Access for the rest of the state (and from the U.S. for travelers) is provided via 800 service. (Frisco is pending.)
1-800 Service:	Yes
UUCP Service:	Yes Usenet News and Electronic Mail
Domain Registration:	Yes
Consulting Services:	Yes Call for information on contractor referral program.
Commercial Traffic:	Yes
Sign Up Procedure:	Call or send e-mail for information

Colorado SuperNet is a non-profit organization formed by the State of Colorado in 1986 with a mission of promoting use of the Internet for research, education, and economic growth. SuperNet offers both dedicated and dial-in connections; its dedicated network reaches most universities and large high-tech companies. We have numerous projects in K-12, state/city government, commercial, and library arenas.

Old Colorado City Communications

2502 West Colorado Avenue
Suite 203
Colorado Springs, CO 80904
Tel: (719) 632-4848
Internet Domain: oldcolo.com

Service Area:	Colorado Springs
1-800 Service:	No
UUCP Service:	Yes Usenet News and Electronic Mail
Domain Registration:	Yes
Consulting Services:	Yes From communications advice, training and education, to turnkey systems. They have formal education and training programs on-line.
Commercial Traffic:	Yes
Sign Up Procedure:	Call (719) 632-4111 or (719) 632-4848

Connecticut

Maestro Technologies, Inc.

See this complete listing under the state of New York.

Pioneer Neighborhood

See this complete listing under the state of Massachussetts.

Delaware

SSNet Inc.

1254 Lorewood Grove Road
Middletown, DE 19709
Tel: (302) 378-1386
Internet Domain: ssnet.com

Service Area:	Delaware, Philadelphia, South Jersey
1-800 Service:	No
UUCP Service:	Yes Usenet News and Electronic Mail
Domain Registration:	Yes
Consulting Services:	Yes
Commercial Traffic:	Yes
Sign Up Procedure:	Call (302) 378-1386

SSNet provides several levels of Internet services to both individuals and businesses.

District of Columbia

Clark Internet Services, Inc.

See this complete listing under the state of Maryland.

Florida

Cybergate, Inc.

662 So. Military Trail
Deerfield Beach, FL   33442
Tel: (305) 428-GATE(4283)
Fax: (305) 428-7977
E-mail: sales@gate.net
Internet Domain: gate.net

Service Area:	Florida southeast coast (Miami to West Palm Beach), Orlando, Tampa with other Florida cities to be added soon.
1-800 Service:	No
UUCP Service:	Yes Usenet News and Electronic Mail
Domain Registration:	Yes
Consulting Services:	Yes
Commercial Traffic:	Yes
Sign Up Procedure:	In Florida, call (305) 428-GATE or (800) NET-GATE

Gateway To The World Inc.

9200 South Dadeland Boulevard.
Suite 309
Miami, FL 33156
Tel: (305) 670-2930
Fax: (305) 670-2930
Modem: (305) 670-2929
E-mail: mjansen@gate.com
Internet Domain: gate.com

Service Area:	Dade and Broward County, Florida
1-800 Service:	No
UUCP Service:	Yes Usenet News and Electronic Mail
Domain Registration:	Yes
Consulting Services:	Yes
Commercial Traffic:	Yes
Sign Up Procedure:	On-line by Mastercard or Visa Off-line by business check or money order

Gateway To The World Inc., with offices in Dade and Broward County, offers dial up Internet access to businesses and personal users throughout South Florida. Using the powerful Galacticomm software and the revolutionary new Vircom software, accessing the Internet has never been easier.

For local businesses that want to advertise on our network, their product information can be delivered to those on the Internet that request literature through EMail callback (no form of direct advertising is allowed on the Internet).

Maestro Technologies, Inc.

See this complete listing under the state of New York.

Georgia

CRL Network Services

This access provider offers its services nationwide. See the complete listing under the National section.

Illinois

XNet Information Systems

P.O. Box 1511
Lisle, Il   60532
Tel: (708) 983-6064
Internet Domain: xnet.com

Service Area:	Points of presence: Naperville, Hoffman Estates
1-800 Service:	No
UUCP Service:	Yes Usenet News and Electronic Mail
Domain Registration:	Yes
Consulting Services:	Yes
Commercial Traffic:	Yes
Sign Up Procedure:	Please call (708)983-6064 or [telnet net.xnet.com]

Louisiana

Neosoft Inc.

See this complete listing under the state of Texas.

Maine

Pioneer Neighborhood

See this complete listing under the state of Massachussetts.

Maryland

Clark Internet Services, Inc.

10600 Route 108
Ellicott City, MD 21042 USA
Toll Free: (800) 735-2258
Tel: (410) 730-9764
Fax: (410) 730-9765
E-mail: info@clark.net
Internet domain: clark.net

Service Area:	Baltimore, Maryland Washington, D.C. Northern Virginia Clark Internet Services numbers Modem phone numbers to access to ClarkNet host computer: 1. Columbia area, covers half Balt. and half Metro DC. (410) 730-9786 2. Ellicott City area, covers full Balt. area. (410) 995-0271 3. Laurel area, covers Metro DC except VA. (301) 596-1626 4. Ashton area, covers full Montgomery County area. (301) 854-0446 5. Northern Virginia. (301) 621-5216
1-800 Service:	No
UUCP Service:	Yes Usenet News and Electronic Mail
Domain Registration:	Yes
Consulting Services:	Yes
Commercial Traffic:	Yes
Sign Up Procedure:	We offer you three ways to register the ClarkNet account: 1) If you plan to pay using credit card, you can enter "2) Instant Account Application (VISA or MC only)" in the main menu. You will need four things before you register online: a) Username of your choice, up to eight characters long. b) The full name that you want to be known by; it can be your real name or an anonymous name. c) Your credit card number, expiration date, and the name on the card. d) Be sure to read ClarkNet Connect Contract and Rules and Regulations. 2) You can download the Account Application by entering "3) Display Clark Net Connect Contract and Account Application" in the main menu. Be sure to enter "8) Toggle Text Display Mode" first so you can do ASCII capture. Print the ClarkNet Connect Contract and Account Application and then fill them out. If you plan to pay by check, include the first month's subscription fee. 3) You can enter "7) Give Us Your Postal Mail Address..." in the main menu, and we will mail you the packet which includes the brochure, ClarkNet Connect Contract, Account Application, and Rules and Regulations.

Basic Service provides Mail and News only (UNIX shell and easy-to-use menu). Internet Service provides Mail, News, FTP, Telnet, ARCHIE, and IRC (UNIX shell and easy-to-use menu). You have to be 18 years or older to join ClarkNet Services.

Massachussetts

Channel 1 Communications

P.O. Box 338
Cambridge, MA 02238-0338
Tel: (617) 354-3230
Fax: (617) 354-3100
Internet Domain: channel1.com

Service Area:	Massachussetts
1-800 Service:	No
UUCP Service:	Yes Usenet News and Electronic Mail
Domain Registration:	No
Consulting Services:	No
Commercial Traffic:	Yes
Sign Up Procedure:	Call direct via modem at (617) 354-3230 Call voice number: (617) 864-0100 or Fax: (617) 354-3100

Channel 1 Communications is more than an Internet access provider. Channel 1 is a large bulletin board service that offers UUCP and general Internet connectivity.

CRL Network Services

This access provider offers its services nationwide. See the complete listing under the National section.

DMConnection

Acorn Software, Inc.
267 Cox St.
Hudson, MA 01749
Tel: (508) 568-1618
Fax: (508) 562-1133
E-mail: postmaster@dmc.com or info@dmc.com
Internet Domain: dmc.com

Service Area:	New England and surrounding area
1-800 Service:	No
UUCP Service:	Yes Usenet News and Electronic Mail
Domain Registration:	Yes
Consulting Services:	Yes Full software development services for most platforms. Price dependent upon job.
Commercial Traffic:	Yes
Sign Up Procedure:	Send mail to info@dmc.com, fill out the form, and return it. Typical turnaround time is two working days. Or call for information.

Genesis Public Access Unix

453 Park Street West
North Reading, MA 01864
Data: (508) 664 0149
E-mail: steve1@genesis.nred.ma.us (Steve Belczyk)
Internet domain: genesis.nred.ma.us

Service Area:	North Reading and surrounding area
1-800 Service:	No
UUCP Service:	Yes Usenet News and Electronic Mail
Domain Registration:	Yes
Consulting Services:	Yes
Commercial Traffic:	No
Sign Up Procedure:	Call for information

North Shore Access

A service of Eco Software, Inc.
145 Munroe Street, Suite 405
Lynn, MA 01901
Tel: (617) 593-3110
E-mail: info@northshore.ecosoft.com

Service Area:	Boston/Lynn/Salem area. U.S. and international access available
1-800 Service:	No
UUCP Service:	Yes Usenet News and Electronic Mail
Domain Registration:	Yes

Consulting Services:	Yes
Commercial Traffic:	Yes
Sign Up Procedure:	On-line sign-up, dial (617) 593-4557

Pioneer Neighborhood

1770 Massachusetts Avenue
#273
Cambridge, MA 02140
Tel: (617) 646-4800
Fax: (617) 497-7162
E-mail: info@pn.com
Internet Domain: pn.com

Service Area:	New England
1-800 Service:	No
UUCP Service:	Yes Usenet News and Electronic Mail
Domain Registration:	Yes
Consulting Services:	Yes From installation of network software to holding seminars.
Commercial Traffic:	Yes
Sign Up Procedure:	Call. We accept MC and Visa. You'll have your connection in about one day.

Pioneer Neighborhood provides Internet access through regular phone lines. Established in 1993, the company's primary goal is to provide the easiest and most affordable access to the Internet for everyone.

Michigan

Maestro Technologies, Inc.

See this complete listing under the state of New York.

Msen Inc.

320 Miller Avenue
Ann Arbor, MI 48103
Phone: (313) 998-4562
Fax: (313) 998-4563
E-mail: info@mail.msen.com
Internet Domain: msen.com

Service Area:	Michigan
1-800 Service:	Yes Lower Michigan: $5/hour; outside Michigan: $8/hour
UUCP Service:	Yes Usenet News and Electronic Mail
Domain Registration:	Yes
Consulting Services:	Yes
Commercial Traffic:	Yes
Sign Up Procedure:	Call (313) 998-4562 or send e-mail to info@mail.msen.com

The Rabbit Network, Inc.

31511 Harper Avenue
St. Clair Shores, MI 48082
Tel: (800) 456-0094
Fax: (810) 790-0156
E-mail: info@rabbit.net
Internet Domain: rabbit.net

Service Area:	Entire USA via our 800 number and local access via our Cleveland, Ohio, terminal server and our Mt. Clemens, Michigan, terminal server
1-800 Service:	Yes
UUCP Service:	Yes Usenet News and Electronic Mail
Domain Registration:	Yes
Consulting Services:	Yes
Commercial Traffic:	Yes
Sign Up Procedure:	Contact us toll free at (800) 456-0094 or send e-mail to "info@rabbit.net"

We provide UUCP news and mail feeds, TCP/IP (SLIP/PPP) news and mail feeds, a telnet server for interactive sessions on the Internet, dial-up SLIP/PPP connections to the internet, domain name service and MX mail forwarding, and (soon) an interactive Internet BBS with GUI capabilities for Windows and MAC.

Minnesota

Minnesota Regional Network (MRNet)

511 11th Avenue South
Box 212
Minneapolis, MN 55415
Tel: (612) 342-2570
Email: info@MR.Net
Internet Domain: MR.Net

Service Area:	Minnesota
1-800 Service:	No
UUCP Service:	Yes Usenet News and Electronic Mail
Domain Registration:	Yes
Consulting Services:	No
Commercial Traffic:	Yes
Sign Up Procedure:	Call (612) 342-2570

Missouri

CRL Network Services

This access provider offers its services nationwide. See the complete listing under the National section.

Neosoft Inc.

See this complete listing under the state of Texas.

Nevada

Evergreen Internet Express

See this complete listing under the state of Arizona.

New Hampshire

Pioneer Neighborhood

See this complete listing under the state of Massachussetts.

New Jersey

Global Enterprise Services, Inc.

3 Independence Way
Princeton, NJ 08540
Tel: (800) 358-4437
E-mail: market@jvnc.net
Internet Domain: jvnc.net or ges.com

Service Area:	New Jersey
1-800 Service:	Yes
UUCP Service:	Yes Usenet News and Electronic Mail
Domain Registration:	Yes
Consulting Services:	Yes
Commercial Traffic:	Yes
Sign Up Procedure:	Sign up by contacting GES Sales Force at (800) 358-4437 or e-mail to market@jvnc.net

Maestro Technologies, Inc.

See this complete listing under the state of New York.

SSNet Inc.

See this complete listing under the state of Delaware.

New Mexico

Evergreen Internet Express

See this complete listing under the state of Arizona.

New York

American Network

60 East 56th St.
New York, NY 10022
Tel: (212) 758-3283
Fax: (212) 758-3453

Service Area:	Local
1-800 Service:	No
UUCP Service:	Yes Usenet News and Electronic Mail
Domain Registration:	No
Consulting Services:	No
Commercial Traffic:	Yes
Sign Up Procedure:	Call for information

CRL Network Services

This access provider offers its services nationwide. See the complete listing under the National section.

Maestro Technologies, Inc.

29 John Street
Suite 1601
New York, NY 10038
Tel: (212) 240-9600
E-mail: info@maestro.com or info-ps@maestro.com
Internet Domain: maestro.com

Service Area:	Mainly New York, but also Northeast U.S.
1-800 Service:	No
UUCP Service:	Yes Usenet News and Electronic Mail
Domain Registration:	Yes
Consulting Services:	Yes
Commercial Traffic:	Yes
Sign Up Procedure:	Call the modem number (212) 240-9700 and login as newuser; there is no password; go through the registration process. Or call (212) 240-9600.

PANIX Public Access Internet

15 West 18th Street
5th floor
New York City, NY
10011
Tel: (212) 787-6160, (212) 877-4854
E-mail: info@panix.com
Internet Domain: panix.com

Service Area:	(212), (516) area codes, and expanding to other area codes as of April 1994. We plan to offer X.25 access soon as well; check back for updated information.
1-800 Service:	No
UUCP Service:	Yes Usenet News and Electronic Mail
Domain Registration:	Yes
Consulting Services:	No
Commercial Traffic:	Yes
Sign Up Procedure:	(1) Telnet to panix.com and log on as "newuser" (no quotes); or (2) Dial (212) 787-3100 and log on as "newuser" (no quotes).

PANIX is a full-service Internet provider. Our services include dial-up Internet and UNIX accounts, Usenet news, e-mail, UUCP, SLIP, and more.

Ohio

APK Public Access UNI* Site

19709 Mohican Avenue
Cleveland, OH   44119
Tel: (216) 481-9428
Fax: (216) 481-9436 x33
E-mail: info@wariat.org
Internet Domain: wariat.org

Service Area:	216 area code
1-800 Service:	No
UUCP Service:	Yes Usenet News and Electronic Mail
Domain Registration:	Yes
Consulting Services:	Yes
Commercial Traffic:	Yes
Sign Up Procedure:	Dial (216) 481-9436, login as bbs, download user.new or e-mail info@war-iat.org. Or call us for information.

Maestro Technologies, Inc.

See this complete listing under the state of New York.

Oregon

Teleport

Suite 803
319 SW Washington
Portland, OR 97204
Tel: (503) 223-4245
Fax: (503) 223-4372
E-mail: jamesd@teleport.com   (James Deibele)
Internet Domain: teleport.com

Service Area:	Portland, OR
1-800 Service:	No

UUCP Service:	Yes Usenet News and Electronic Mail
Domain Registration:	Yes
Consulting Services:	Yes
Commercial Traffic:	Yes
Sign Up Procedure:	Call (503) 220-1016 and enter "new"

Pennsylvania

SSNet Inc.

See this complete listing under the state of Delaware.

Telerama Public Access Internet

Pittsburgh, PA
Tel: (412) 481-3505
E-mail: info@telerama.pgh.pa.us

Service Area:	Pittsburgh
1-800 Service:	No
UUCP Service:	Yes Usenet News and Electronic Mail
Domain Registration:	Yes
Consulting Services:	Yes
Commercial Traffic:	Yes
Sign Up Procedure:	Dial (412) 481-5302 or (412) 481-4644 and log in as "new".

Rhode Island

Pioneer Neighborhood

See this complete listing under the state of Massachussetts.

Texas

The Black Box

P.O. Box 591822
Houston, TX 77259-1822
Tel: (713) 480-2684
Internet Domain: blkbox.com

Service Area:	Houston
1-800 Service:	No
UUCP Service:	Yes Usenet News and Electronic Mail
Domain Registration:	Yes
Consulting Services:	No
Commercial Traffic:	Yes
Sign Up Procedure:	Send your name, phone, address and desired 3 to 8-character user name along with a check to: Marc Newman PO Box 591822 Houston, TX 77259-1822 Call in the evenings.

CRL Network Services

See this complete listing under the state of California.

Neosoft Inc.

3408 Mangun
Houston, TX 77092
Tel: (713) 684-5969
E-mail: info@neosoft.com
Internet Domain: neosoft.com

Service Area:	Houston, New Orleans, St. Louis; provides service nationwide
1-800 Service:	Yes
UUCP Service:	Yes Usenet News and Electronic Mail
Domain Registration:	Yes
Consulting Services:	Yes For TCL/TK and systems administration
Commercial Traffic:	Yes
Sign Up Procedure:	Contact Neosoft at info@neosoft.com or call (713) 684-5969

Real/Time Communications

6721 N. Lamar #103
Austin, TX 78752
Tel: (512) 451-0046
Data: (512) 459-4391, login as new
Internet domain.: bga.com

Service Area:	Austin, Texas
1-800 Service:	No
UUCP Service:	Yes Usenet News and Electronic Mail
Domain Registration:	Yes
Consulting Services:	Yes
Commercial Traffic:	Yes
Sign Up Procedure:	Anyone wanting a two-week trial regular (dial-up or telnet) account may request it as follows: 　　　* Call the Real/Time system at (512) 459-4391 and login as "new" 　　　* rlogin or telnet to bga.com and login as "new" 　　　* Mail a request via US Mail to the address below 　　　* Send email to hosts@bga.com 　　　* Call our voice number, (512) 451-0046 Requests for accounts should include a first and second choice of user name (a single word, four to eight alphanumeric characters), a full address, home and work phone numbers, and the type of your computer. You will receive a new user package via US Mail. New users, once validated, are given two weeks of free full access to evaluate our system and make a decision regarding a subscription for service.

Direct Internet access via FTP, telnet, IRC, rlogin, gopher and a variety of other standard Unix tools. Real/Time also provides UUCP e-mail, Usenet news and full access to the UNIX shell.

South Coast Computing Service Inc.

P.O. Box 270355
Houston, TX 77277-0355
Tel: (713) 917-5000
E-mail: info@sccsi.com
Internet Domain: sccsi.com

Service Area:	Southern United States
1-800 Service:	No
UUCP Service:	Yes Usenet News and Electronic Mail
Domain Registration:	Yes
Consulting Services:	Yes
Commercial Traffic:	Yes
Sign Up Procedure:	Login to sccsi.com as newuser or send e-mail to info@sccsi.com or call (800) 221-6478

Texas Metronet

860 Kinwest Parkway
Suite 179
Irving, TX   75063
Tel: (214) 705-2900
Fax: (214) 401-2802
Internet Domain: metronet.com

Service Area:	Area codes 214/817, North Texas
1-800 Service:	No
UUCP Service:	Yes Usenet News and Electronic Mail
Domain Registration:	Yes
Consulting Services:	Yes

Commercial Traffic:	Yes
Sign Up Procedure:	Call (214) 705 2901 or (817) 261 1127 and login as signup.

Utah

Evergreen Internet Express

See this complete listing under the state of Arizona.

Vermont

Pioneer Neighborhood

See this complete listing under the state of Massachussetts.

Virginia

AlterNet

A service of UUNET Technologies, Inc.
3110 Fairview Park Dr.
Suite 570
Falls Church, VA 22042
Tel: (800) 488-6383 or (703) 204-8000
Internet Domain: We register individual domain names for our customers

Service Area:	Worldwide UUCP service
1-800 Service:	Yes
UUCP Service:	Yes Usenet News and Electronic Mail

Domain Registration:	Yes
Consulting Services:	Yes
Commercial Traffic:	Yes
Sign Up Procedure:	Contact AlterNet Sales at (800) 4UUNET3

AlterNet operates a national TCP/IP network in the U.S., with direct connections to the Internet's component networks around the world. AlterNet provides UUCP, dialup PPP, dedicated SLIP/PPP, and dedicated 56 Kbps, T1, and 10 Mbps connections to its customers.

Clark Internet Services, Inc.

See this complete listing under the state of Maryland.

InfiNet, L.C.

801 Boush St.
Suite 203
Norfolk, Virginia 23510
Tel: (804) 622-4289
Fax: (804) 622-7158
E-mail: system@wyvern.com
Internet Domain: wyvern.com

Service Area:	VA: Norfolk, Virginia Beach, Portsmouth, Chesapeake, Newport News, Hampton, Williamsburg
1-800 Service:	No
UUCP Service:	Yes Usenet News and Electronic Mail
Domain Registration:	Yes

Consulting Services:	Yes
Commercial Traffic:	Yes
Sign Up Procedure:	Phone (804) 622-4289 or e-mail system@wyvern.com

Performance Systems International, Inc.

510 Huntmar Park Drive
Herndon, VA 22070
Tel: (703) 904-4100
E-mail: info@psi.com
Internet Domain: psi.com

Service Area:	Continental U.S.
1-800 Service:	Yes Available with UUPSI
UUCP Service:	Yes Usenet News and Electronic Mail
Domain Registration:	Yes
Consulting Services:	Yes
Commercial Traffic:	Yes
Sign Up Procedure:	Contact 1.800.82psi.82 or send e-mail to "info@psi.com"

PSI, Inc. is a value-added network service provider that delivers a full spectrum of products for the user of electronic information with over 5,000 customers and hundreds of thousands of users. The PSI staff is a team of experienced networking professionals. They are proven leaders in offering the means for professional organizations and individuals to access and process information and communicate with other professionals in product development and support, news, financial services, government contracting, consulting, and academic pursuits.

Incorporated in 1989, PSI is headquartered in Herndon, VA, with its primary Network Operations Center (NOC) and Customer Support Group (CSG) near Albany, NY.

UUPSI - Mail/News: Electronic Mail and Bulletin Board services using the common UUCP protocol, a PC, and a modem. It provides reliable electronic communications to the individual and corporate user at an inexpensive, fixed rate. UUPSI uses local numbers in over 80 cities throughout the continental

U.S. or an 800-number incurring usage fees, and includes PSI's registering for a domain name on your behalf.

Washington

Northwest Nexus

PO Box 40597
Bellevue, WA 98015-4597
Tel: (206) 455-3505 or (800) 539-3505
Fax: (206) 455-4672
E-mail: info@nwnexus.wa.com
Internet Domain: halcyon.com and wa.com

Service Area:	Primarily the Pacific Northwest, but we have customers from around the world.
1-800 Service:	No
UUCP Service:	Yes Usenet News and Electronic Mail
Domain Registration:	Yes
Consulting Services:	Yes
Commercial Traffic:	Yes
Sign Up Procedure:	Use a communications program emulating a VT100 (8,N,1) to dial 206.382.6245, and login as "new". Or call (800) 539-3505 for more information.

Northwest Nexus offers a wide range of low-cost options to give both private individuals and companies access to the vast resources of the Internet: millions of people interacting on thousands of subjects, and data available from countless sources, including the U.S. Government, universities, research labs, and private corporations.

Wisconsin

Freenet

4508 Wildwood Court
Eau Claire, WI 54701

Service Area:	Milwaukee, WI, metro area
1-800 Service:	No
UUCP Service:	Yes Usenet News and Electronic Mail
Domain Registration:	Yes
Consulting Services:	No
Commercial Traffic:	Yes
Sign Up Procedure:	Send postal mail for initial contact.

MIX Communications

Milwaukee, WI
P.O. Box 17166
Milwaukee, WI 53217
E-mail: info@mixcom.com for automated reply,
    sysop@mixcom.com for information
Internet Domain: mixcom.com

Service Area:	Milwaukee, WI, metro area
1-800 Service:	No
UUCP Service:	Yes Usenet News and Electronic Mail
Domain Registration:	Yes
Consulting Services:	No

Commercial Traffic:	Yes
Sign Up Procedure:	Mail application form, available by sending mail to info@mixcom.com or by calling BBS @ (414) 241-5469.

Canada

The Canada section of this directory lists information on the following:

National Access Providers
Alberta
British Columbia
Manitoba
Newfoundland
Ontario
Quebec
Saskatchewan

National Access Providers

UUnet Canada Inc.

1 Yonge Street
Suite 1400
Toronto, Ontario
M5E 1J9
Tel: (416) 368-6621
Fax: (416) 368-1350
E-mail: info@uunet.ca
Internet Domain: uunet.ca

Service Area:	National. Centered in greater Metro Toronto with points of presence in Montreal, Ottawa, Calgary, Vancouver, Kitchener, London, and Hamilton
1-800 Service:	No
UUCP Service:	Yes Usenet News and Electronic Mail
Domain Registration:	Yes
Consulting Services:	Yes
Commercial Traffic:	Yes
Sign Up Procedure:	Contact us by phone (416) 368-6621, fax (416) 368-1350, or e-mail info@uunet.ca

UUNET Canada Inc. provides network infrastructure and services to access the resources of the worldwide Internet/UUCP community. These resources include Usenet news, electronic mail, telnet, ftp, and numerous other services and file archives.

VRx Network Services Inc.

87 Seymour Ave
Toronto, Ontario
M4J 3T6
Tel: (416) 778-5955
Fax: (416) 962-0079
Internet Domain: vrx.net

Service Area:	Canada
1-800 Service:	Yes
UUCP Service:	Yes Usenet News and Electronic Mail
Domain Registration:	Yes
Consulting Services:	Yes
Commercial Traffic:	Yes
Sign Up Procedure:	Call (416) 778-5955

Alberta

Alberta SuperNet Inc.

#325 Pacific Plaza
10909 Jasper Avenue
Edmonton, Alberta
T5J 3L9
Tel: (403) 441-3663
Fax: (403) 424-0743
E-mail: info@tibalt.supernet.ab.ca
Internet Domain: supernet.ab.ca

Service Area:	Alberta
1-800 Service:	No
UUCP Service:	Yes Usenet News and Electronic Mail
Domain Registration:	Yes
Consulting Services:	Yes
Commercial Traffic:	Yes
Sign Up Procedure:	Call or send electronic mail for information

CCI Networks

A division of Corporate Computers Inc.
4130 - 95 Street
Edmonton, Alberta
T6E 6H5
Tel:(403) 450-6787
Fax:(403) 450-9143
E-mail: info@ccinet.ab.ca
Internet Domain: ccinet.ab.ca

Service Area:	Anywhere, but local calls only within the Edmonton calling area. Calgary local service available Summer '94.
1-800 Service:	No
UUCP Service:	Yes Usenet News and Electronic Mail
Domain Registration:	Yes
Consulting Services:	Yes
Commercial Traffic:	Yes
Sign Up Procedure:	Contact CCI Networks: Phone: (403) 450 6787, Fax: (403) 450 9143), Email: info@ccinet.ab.ca, or mail to the address above.

Internet service provider. Several levels of access are available: Terminal access to CCInet hosts (connected to Internet); UUCP; SLIP/PPP direct access to Internet, using either shared or dedicated dial-up; dedicated network connections (restrictions apply).

Telnet Canada Enterprises, Ltd.

419,1711 4th Street SW
Calgary, Alberta
T2S 1V8
Tel: (403) 245-1882
Internet Domain: tcel.com

Service Area:	Calgary, Local
1-800 Service:	No
UUCP Service:	Yes Usenet News and Electronic Mail
Domain Registration:	No
Consulting Services:	Yes
Commercial Traffic:	Yes
Sign Up Procedure:	Phone (403) 245-1882

AMT Solutions Group Inc. - Island Net

P.O. Box 6201, Depot 1
Victoria, British Columbia
V8P 5L5
Tel: (604) 479-7861
E-mail: mark@amtsgi.bc.ca (Mark Morley)
Internet Domain: amtsgi.bc.ca

Service Area:	Vancouver Island, Gulf Islands
1-800 Service:	Coming
UUCP Service:	Yes Usenet News and Electronic Mail
Domain Registration:	Yes
Consulting Services:	Yes
Commercial Traffic:	Yes
Sign Up Procedure:	Log into the service by dialing (604) 477-5163 or telnetting to amtsgi.bc.ca. Log in using the name "new" to fill out an application. Alternatively, you may call us at (604) 479-7861 (voice). A "guest" account is also available.

AMT offers a wide variety of computer and networking services, not the least of which is Island Net, a public access Internet service.

DataFlux Systems Limited

1281 Lonsdale Place
Victoria, British Columbia
V8P 5L3
Tel: (604) 744-4553
Fax: (604) 480-0899
E-mail: info@dataflux.bc.ca
Internet Domain: bc.ca

21: Access Provider Directory

Service Area:	Victoria and Vancouver Island
1-800 Service:	No
UUCP Service:	Yes Usenet News and Electronic Mail
Domain Registration:	Yes
Consulting Services:	Yes Communication solutions, implementation, and design. All services are on a custom basis.
Commercial Traffic:	Yes
Sign Up Procedure:	Contact: (604) 744-4553, or mark@dataflux.bc.ca

Mind Link!

105-20381 62nd Avenue
Langley, British Columbia
V3A 5E6
Tel: (604) 534-5663
Fax: (604) 534-7473
E-mail: info@mindlink.bc.ca
Internet Domain: mindlink.bc.ca

Service Area:	Lower Mainland from West Vancouver to Chilliwack
1-800 Service:	No
UUCP Service:	Yes Usenet News and Electronic Mail
Domain Registration:	No
Consulting Services:	Referral service
Commercial Traffic:	Yes
Sign Up Procedure:	Call (604) 576-1214 and login as "guest"

Mind Link! is the largest Internet access port in Western Canada, with over 3800 registered members. Mind Link offers a full range of access options: menu-driven interface for all Internet functions, multi-tasking Command Line access, UNIX shell access, and dial-up SLIP access.

Wimsey Information Services Inc.

8523 Commerce Court
Burnaby, British Columbia
V5A 4N3
Tel: (604) 421-4741
Fax: (604) 421-4742
E-mail: info@wimsey.com
Internet Domain: wimsey.com, wis.net

Service Area:	Vancouver and surrounding districts. Soon: BC Interior, Vancouver Island, and other provinces.
1-800 Service:	No
UUCP Service:	Yes Usenet News and Electronic Mail
Domain Registration:	Yes
Consulting Services:	Yes Internet consulting, UNIX, Novell, System Administration
Commercial Traffic:	Yes
Sign Up Procedure:	Phone, fax, dial-up (604) 937-7411; login as "help" password is <ENTER> key

Manitoba

GWR Human Resource Services

57 Home St.
Winnipeg, Manitoba
R3G 1W7
Tel: (204) 772-6475
Internet Domain: gwresource.mb.ca

Service Area:	Manitoba, Canada

1-800 Service:	No
UUCP Service:	Yes Usenet News and Electronic Mail
Domain Registration:	Yes
Consulting Services:	Yes Set up a variety of Internet network connections
Commercial Traffic:	Yes
Sign Up Procedure:	Phone (204) 772-6475 (voice), (204) 772-6487 (modem)

MBnet

Computer Services
University of Manitoba
15 Gillson Street
Winnipeg, Manitoba
R3T 5V6
Tel: (204) 474-9727
Fax: (204) 275-5420
E-mail: info@mbnet.mb.ca

Service Area:	Manitoba, Canada
1-800 Service:	No
UUCP Service:	Yes Usenet News and Electronic Mail
Domain Registration:	Yes
Consulting Services:	Yes
Commercial Traffic:	Yes
Sign Up Procedure:	For individuals, call (204) 474-9727 or e-mail info@mbnet.mb.ca By modem: (204) 275-6100, for 2400 bps or lower, login as mbnet, password is guest (204) 275-6132, for V.32bis/V.42bis, login as mbnet, password is guest

Newfoundland

Login Informatique

See this complete listing under the province of Quebec.

Ontario

Data Tech Canada

8-1 Routledge Street
Hyde Park, Ontario
N0M 1Z0
Tel: (519) 473-5694
Fax: (519) 645-6639
E-mail: info@dt-can.com

Service Area:	London
1-800 Service:	No
UUCP Service:	Yes Usenet News and Electronic Mail
Domain Registration:	Yes
Consulting Services:	Yes
Commercial Traffic:	Yes
Sign Up Procedure:	Call or send e-mail

HookUp Communications

1075 North Service Road
Suite 207
Oakville, Ontario
L6M 2G2
Tel: (905) 847-8000
Fax: (905) 847-8420
E-mail: info@hookup.net
Internet Domain: hookup.net

Service Area:	Toronto and vicinity, Kitchener-Waterloo, Cambridge, Guelph, Ottawa
1-800 Service:	Yes
UUCP Service:	Yes Usenet News and Electronic Mail
Domain Registration:	Yes For corporate accounts
Consulting Services:	No
Commercial Traffic:	Yes
Sign Up Procedure:	Phone (800) 363-0400 or e-mail info@hookup.net

Login Informatique

See this complete listing under the province of Quebec.

Mindemoya Computing and Design

794 Charlotte Street
Sudbury, Ontario   P3E 4C3
Tel: (705) 670-8129
Fax: (705) 522-6402
E-mail: info@mcd.on.ca
Internet Domain: mcd.on.ca

Service Area:	Sudbury
1-800 Service:	No
UUCP Service:	Yes Usenet News and Electronic Mail
Domain Registration:	Yes
Consulting Services:	No
Commercial Traffic:	Yes
Sign Up Procedure:	Call for information

NetAccess Systems Inc.

231 Main Street West, Suite E
Hamilton, Ontario   L8P 1J4
Tel: (905) 524-2544
Fax: (905) 524-3010
Internet Domain: netaccess.on.ca

Service Area:	Greater Hamilton Area
1-800 Service:	No
UUCP Service:	Yes Usenet News and Electronic Mail
Domain Registration:	Yes
Consulting Services:	Yes

Commercial Traffic:	Yes
Sign Up Procedure:	Call (905) 524-2544 or fax (905) 524-3010

NetAccess was incorporated in May of 1993 to provide Internet access on a subscription basis in the Greater Hamilton area. Our primary purpose is to provide high-quality access to computer-based communications and information services through the Internet for local area business and service organizations. As part of our wider mandate, NetAccess is committed to work with business, research, educational, service, and non-profit interests to encourage innovative use of computer technology for the benefit of the whole community.

Resudox Online Services

P/O Box 33067
Nepean, Ontario
K2C 3Y9
Tel: (613) 567-6925
Fax: (613) 567-8289
E-mail: info@Resudox.net
Internet Domain: resudox.net

Service Area:	613 / 819 area codes
1-800 Service:	No
UUCP Service:	Yes Usenet News and Electronic Mail
Domain Registration:	Yes
Consulting Services:	Yes
Commercial Traffic:	Yes
Sign Up Procedure:	Call (613) 567-1714 or telnet resudox.net

TDK Consulting

667 Pinerow Crescent
Unit 21
Waterloo, Ontario
N2T 2L5
Tel: (519) 888-0766
Internet Domain: waterloo-rdp.on.ca

Service Area:	Kitchener-Waterloo
1-800 Service:	No
UUCP Service:	Yes Usenet News and Electronic Mail
Domain Registration:	Yes
Consulting Services:	Yes
Commercial Traffic:	Yes
Sign Up Procedure:	Call (519) 888-0766 for information

UUISIS Electronic Mail Service

81 Tartan Drive
Nepean, Ontario
K2J 3V6
Tel: (613) 825-5324
postmaster@uuisis.isis.isis
Internet Domain: isis.org

Service Area:	National Capital Region. (Ontario: Ottawa, Nepean, Gloucester, Kanata, Vanier; Quebec: Hull, Gatineau, Aylmer)
1-800 Service:	No

21: Access Provider Directory

UUCP Service:	Yes Usenet News and Electronic Mail
Domain Registration:	No
Consulting Services:	No
Commercial Traffic:	Yes
Sign Up Procedure:	Modem (613) 823-6539, login as BBS, password is new, or Mail to above address - attention R. Beetham

UUnet Canada Inc.

1 Yonge Street
Suite 1400
Toronto, Ontario
M5E 1J9
Tel: (416) 368-6621
Fax: (416) 368-1350
E-mail: info@uunet.ca
Internet Domain: uunet.ca

Service Area:	National. Centered in greater Metro Toronto with POPs (points of presence) in Montreal, Ottawa, Calgary, Vancouver, Kitchener, London, and Hamilton
1-800 Service:	No
UUCP Service:	Yes Usenet News and Electronic Mail
Domain Registration:	Yes
Consulting Services:	Yes
Commercial Traffic:	Yes
Sign Up Procedure:	Contact us by phone (416) 368-6621, fax (416) 368-1350, or e-mail info@uunet.ca

UUNET Canada Inc. provides network infrastructure and services to access the resources of the worldwide Internet/UUCP community. These resources include Usenet news, electronic mail, telnet, ftp, and numerous other services and file archives.

VRx Network Services Inc.

87 Seymour Ave
Toronto, Ontario
M4J 3T6
Tel: (416) 778-5955
Fax: (416) 962-0079
Internet Domain: vrx.net

Service Area:	Canada
1-800 Service:	Yes
UUCP Service:	Yes Usenet News and Electronic Mail
Domain Registration:	Yes
Consulting Services:	Yes
Commercial Traffic:	Yes
Sign Up Procedure:	Call (416) 778-5955

Quebec

Login Informatique

4363 Jacques Bizard
Pierrefonds, Quebec (Montreal)
H9H 4W3
Tel: (514) 626-8086
E-mail: infos@login.qc.ca
Internet Domain: login.qc.ca

Service Area:	Metropolitan Montreal (we also have customers in Ontario and Newfoundland)
1-800 Service:	No
UUCP Service:	Yes Usenet News and Electronic Mail
Domain Registration:	Yes
Consulting Services:	Yes
Commercial Traffic:	Yes
Sign Up Procedure:	Contact us by phone, (we ask the customer about their exact needs)

Login is dedicated to providing access to the Internet for "highly motivated individuals" and small companies. Login Informatique is a gateway to the Internet; all customers are connected to the Internet via UUCP on their own system.

UUISIS Electronic Mail Service

See this complete listing under the province of Ontario.

Saskatchewan

SASK#net

Computing Services
Room 56, Physics Building
University of Saskatchewan
Saskatoon, Saskatchewan
S7N 0W0
Tel: (306) 966-4960
Fax (306) 966-4938
E-mail: dean.jones@usask.ca

Libraries and Information Services
Administration-Humanities Building
University of Regina
Regina, Saskatchewan
S4S 0A2
Tel: (306) 585-4132
Fax: (306) 585-4878
E-mail: wmaes@max.cc.uregina.ca
Internet Domain: sk.ca

Service Area:	Saskatchewan
1-800 Service:	No
UUCP Service:	Yes Usenet News and Electronic Mail
Domain Registration:	Yes
Consulting Services:	Yes
Commercial Traffic:	No
Sign Up Procedure:	Call Dean Jones at (306) 966-4860 or call William Maes at (306) 585-4132

SASK#net provides access in support of the research, educational, and technology transfer missions of its organizations. SASK#net is provided and managed jointly by the University of Regina and the University of Saskatchewan.

Europe

The Europe section of this directory includes the following:

>Service for All European Countries
>Austria
>Belgium
>Croatia
>Czech Republic
>Denmark
>France
>Germany
>Hungary
>Iceland
>Ireland
>Luxemburg
>The Netherlands
>Portugal
>Slovak Republic
>Slovenia
>Spain
>Sweden
>Switzerland
>United Kingdom

Service for All European Countries

ExNet Systems Ltd

37, Honley Road
Catford, SE6 2HY
London, United Kingdom
Tel: +44-81-244-0077

Fax: +44-81-244-0078
Internet Domain: exnet.com

Service Area:	Europe
1-800 Service:	Free calls to us from certain areas of England
UUCP Service:	Yes Usenet News and Electronic Mail
Domain Registration:	Yes
Consulting Services:	Yes
Commercial Traffic:	Yes Special prices and deals
Sign Up Procedure:	Ring us, fill in contract, one month free trial.

SpaceNet GmbH

Muenchener Technologiezentrum
Frankfurter Ring 193a
D-80807 Muenchen
Germany
Tel: +49-89-324683-0
Fax: +49-89-3234044
E-mail: vorstand@muc.de or info@spacenet.de
Internet domain: spacenet.de

Service Area:	All over Europe
1-800 Service:	No
UUCP Service:	Yes Usenet News and Electronic Mail
Domain Registration:	Yes
Consulting Services:	No
Commercial Traffic:	Yes
Sign Up Procedure:	Call for information

Sells Internet over satellite all over Europe. SpaceNet also works together with TLK, the European Telebit distributor.

Austria

EUnet EDV-Dienstleistungs-Gesellschaft

Thurngasse 8/16 A-1090
Wien, Austria
Tel: +43 1 3174969
Fax: +43 1 3106926
E-mail: info@austria.eu.net
Internet Domain: austria.eu.net , eunet.co.at

Service Area:	Austria, various points of presence in all major cities
1-800 Service:	No
UUCP Service:	Yes Usenet News and Electronic Mail
Domain Registration:	Yes
Consulting Services:	No
Commercial Traffic:	Yes
Sign Up Procedure:	E-mail, fax, or postal mail

Provider of quality Internet and UUCP services to commercial and governmental organizations and the general public in Austria.

Belgium

EUnet Belgium NV/SA

Stapelhuisstraat 13
3000 Leuven/Belgium
Tel: +32 16 236099
Fax: +32 16 232079
E-mail: info@Belgium.EU.net
Internet Domain: Belgium.EU.net or EUnet.BE

Service Area:	Belgium
1-800 Service:	No
UUCP Service:	Yes Usenet News and Electronic Mail
Domain RegistrationDomain Registration:	Yes
Consulting Services:	Yes
Commercial Traffic:	Yes
Sign Up Procedure:	Fax, letter, or e-mail

Internet Access Provider (VANS). EUnet Belgium NV/SA is the major full-service commercial Internet provider in Belgium.

Croatia

University Computing Centre

Ul. Josipa Marohnica bb
41000 Zagreb
Croatia
Tel: +385-41-510-099
Fax: +385-41-518-451
E-mail: cigaly@srce.hr
Internet Domain: srce.hr

Service Area:	Republic of Croatia
1-800 Service:	No
UUCP Service:	Yes Usenet News and Electronic Mail
Domain RegistrationDomain Registration:	Yes

Consulting Services:	Yes
Commercial Traffic:	Yes
Sign Up Procedure:	Call for information

Czech Republic

EUnet Czechia

COnet s.r.o.
Technicka 5
166 28
Czech Republic
Phone: +42 2 332 3242
Fax: +42 2 24310646
E-mail: info@EUnet.cz, pr@EUnet.cz
Internet Domain: EUnet.cz

Service Area:	Czech Republic
1-800 Service:	No
UUCP Service:	Yes Usenet News and Electronic Mail
Domain Registration:	Yes
Consulting Services:	No
Commercial Traffic:	Yes
Sign Up Procedure:	Call for information

Denmark

DKnet, EUnet Denmark

Copenhagen
Fruebjergvej 3
2100 Koebenhavn Oe
Denmark
Tel: +45 39 17 99 00
Fax: +45 39 17 98 97
E-mail: info@dknet.dk
Internet Domain: dknet.dk

Service Area:	Denmark
1-800 Service:	No
UUCP Service:	Yes Usenet News and Electronic Mail
Domain Registration:	Yes
Consulting Services:	Yes
Commercial Traffic:	Yes
Sign Up Procedure:	Contact us per e-mail/phone/fax and request order form

DKnet, Danish part of EUnet. Offering all Internet services from personal accounts to leased lines.

France

OLEANE

67 rue Monge
F-75005 Paris
Tel: +33 1 43.28.32.32
Fax: +33 1 43.28.46.21

E-mail: info@oleane.net
Internet Domain: oleane.net

Service Area:	France
1-800 Service:	No
UUCP Service:	Yes Usenet News and Electronic Mail
Domain Registration:	Yes
Consulting Services:	No
Commercial Traffic:	Yes
Sign Up Procedure:	Call for information

PIPEX

See this complete listing under the United Kingdom.

Germany

AllCon GmbH

D-24941 Flensburg, Germany
Lise Meitner Strasse 2
Tel: +49 461 9992 162
Fax: +49 461 9992 165
E-mail: svendi@allcon.net
Internet Domain: allcon.net

Service Area:	Northern Germany, Baltic countries
1-800 Service:	No

UUCP Service:	Yes Usenet News and Electronic Mail
Domain Registration:	Yes
Consulting Services:	Yes
Commercial Traffic:	Yes
Sign Up Procedure:	Call +49 461 9992 162 Fax +49 461 9992 165 E-mail svendi@allcon.net

EUnet Deutschland GmbH

Emil - Figge - Strasse 80
44227 Dortmund
Germany
Tel: +49 231 972 2222
Fax: +49 231 972 1111
E-mail: info@germany.eu.net
Internet Domain: EUnet.de, Germany.EU.net

Service Area:	All of Germany. Points of Presence in the following cities: Dortmund, Hamburg, Berlin, Kiel, Bremen/Oldenburg, Colone/Bonn, Munich, Aachen, Frankfurt, Halle/Leipzig, Hannover.
1-800 Service:	Service hotline (information and technical), 9am to 12am and 1pm to 5pm, Monday to Friday, +49 231 972 2222
UUCP Service:	Yes Usenet News and Electronic Mail
Domain Registration:	Yes EUnet Germany handles the registration of Internet Domains and IP Address clusters for its customers (registration via DE-NIC)
Consulting Services:	Yes EUnet Germany offers full managed network connections including installation and configuration of hardware and software
Commercial Traffic:	Yes
Sign Up Procedure:	Contact for detailed information: E-mail: info@germany.eu.net Phone: +49 231 972 2222 Fax: +49 231 972 1111

EUnet Germany offers EUnet Mail Electronic Mail service, EUnet News USENET News service, InterEUnet full Internet connection, EUnet Archive Archive services including ftp, fsp, gopher, WAIS, WWW and related server, Personal EUnet Internet connection for private persons and small companies, EUnet POP connection via local point of presence, EUnet VPN virtual private networks, EUnet database, interface to commercial databases.

FoeBuD e.V.

Markttstr. 18
D-33602 Bielefeld
Germany
Tel: +49-521-175254
Fax: +49-521-61172
BBS: +49-521-68000
E-Mail: zentrale@bionic.zer.de

Service Area:	Germany
1-800 Service:	No
UUCP Service:	Yes Usenet News and Electronic Mail
Domain Registration:	Yes
Consulting Services:	No
Commercial Traffic:	Yes
Sign Up Procedure:	Call for information

GFI DbR Oldenburg - NorthNet

Scheideweg 65
26121 Oldenburg
Germany
Tel: +49-0441-82724
Fax: +49-87004
E-mail: lord@olis.North.DE
Internet Domain: gfi.de

Service Area:	Northwestern Germany
1-800 Service:	No
UUCP Service:	Yes Usenet News and Electronic Mail
Domain Registration:	Yes
Consulting Services:	Yes Consulting and training
Commercial Traffic:	No Access for private persons only
Sign Up Procedure:	Call or send e-mail

NorthNet - Regionaldomain im Rahmen des Individual Network e.V.
Das NorthNet ist der regionale Zusammenschluss privater InterNet-Nutzer. Die Mitgliedschaft im NorthNet ermoeglicht Privatpersonen die Nutzung der Dienste E-Mail und News weltweit zum Pauschaltarif.
Die Kosten der Mitlgiedschaft betragen im Moment (Stand 2/94) DM 9 monatlich. Hinzu kommen die jeweiligen Servergebuehren des jew.
Serversystems. Im Raum Weser-Ems sind derartige Systeme in nahezu jeder Region zum Ortsoder Regionaltarif erreichbar. (Oldenburg, Bremen, Emden, Wilhelmshaven usw.)

Individual Network e.V.

Attn: Oliver Boehmer
Linkstr. 15
D-65933 Frankfurt
Germany
Tel: +49-69-39048413
Modem: +49-69-39048414 (+ others)

Service Area:	Germany
1-800 Service:	No
UUCP Service:	Yes Usenet News and Electronic Mail
Domain Registration:	Yes
Consulting Services:	No

Commercial Traffic:	No Non-commercial access only
Sign Up Procedure:	Call to sign up

I.S.A.R Netzwerke GbRmbH

Nymphenburgerstr. 209
80639 Muenchen (Munich)
Federal Republic of Germany
Phone: +49 89 1665238
Fax: +49 89 1675932
Internet Domain: info@isar.de

Service Area:	Munich and approximately 80 km around Munich
1-800 Service:	No
UUCP Service:	Yes Usenet News and Electronic Mail
Domain Registration:	Yes
Consulting Services:	Yes
Commercial Traffic:	Yes
Sign Up Procedure:	Call for information

A point of presence of the German Internet access provider NTG/Xlink. Additionally serve private people's Internet access via the Individual Network Association with less expensive conditions.

PIPEX

See this complete listing under the United Kingdom.

SpaceNet GmbH

Muenchener Technologiezentrum
Frankfurter Ring 193a
D-80807 Muenchen
Germany
Tel: +49-89-324683-0
Fax: +49-89-3234044
E-mail: vorstand@muc.de or info@spacenet.de
Internet domain: spacenet.de

Service Area:	All over Europe
1-800 Service:	No
UUCP Service:	Yes Usenet News and Electronic Mail
Domain Registration:	Yes
Consulting Services:	No
Commercial Traffic:	Yes
Sign Up Procedure:	Call for information

Sells Internet over satellite all over Europe. SpaceNet also works together with TLK, the European Telebit distributor.

SydLink

Alexander Finger
Im Winkel 8
24848 Kropp
Germany
Tel: +49-04621-29649
Internet Domain: syd.de

Service Area:	Landesteil Schleswig, Raum Rendsburg
1-800 Service:	No

UUCP Service:	Nutzer der Mailboxen und Mitglieder des Vereines koennen sich via UUCP an die Domain anschliessen.
Domain Registration:	Yes We are able to create subdomains under syd.de
Consulting Services:	Yes
Commercial Traffic:	Eine Kommerzielle Nutzung aus dem SydNet heraus ist nicht moeglich.
Sign Up Procedure:	Entweder per Antrag in einer Box oder per Brief an Alexander Finger, Im Winkel 8, 24848 Kropp.

SydLink ist ein Verein zur Foerderung der privaten Datenkommunikation.

Hungary

EUnet Hungary

1518 Budapest
PO Box 63
Hungary
Tel: +36 1 269 8281
Fax: +36 1 269 8288
E-mail: pr@hungary.eu.net
Internet Domain: sztaki.hu

Service Area:	Hungary
1-800 Service:	No
UUCP Service:	Yes Usenet News and Electronic Mail
Domain Registration:	Yes hostmaster@sztaki.hu
Consulting Services:	Yes
Commercial Traffic:	Yes
Sign Up Procedure:	E-mail pr@hungary.eu.net, phone, or fax

EUnet Hungary - as part of pan-european EUnet network - operates within the SZTAKI Computer and Automation Research Institute.

PIPEX

See this complete listing under the United Kingdom.

Iceland

ISnet

SURIS
Taeknigardi
Dunhaga 5
107 Reykjavik
Iceland
Tel: +354-1-694747
Fax: +354-1-28801
E-mail: isnet-info@isgate.is
Internet Domain: is

Service Area:	Iceland
1-800 Service:	No
UUCP Service:	Yes Usenet News and Electronic Mail
Domain Registration:	Yes
Consulting Services:	No
Commercial Traffic:	Yes
Sign Up Procedure:	Contact us directly

Ieunet's EmailLink service

Innovation Centre
Trinity College
Dublin 2, Ireland
Tel: +353 1 679 0832
Fax: +353 1 679 8039
E-mail: info@ieunet.ie
Internet Domain: All customers get assigned their own domain name in .ie

Service Area:	Whole of Ireland
1-800 Service:	No
UUCP Service:	Yes Usenet News and Electronic Mail
Domain Registration:	Yes
Consulting Services:	Yes
Commercial Traffic:	Yes
Sign Up Procedure:	Contact Ieunet for information pack and application form

PIPEX

See this complete listing under the United Kingdom.

Luxemburg

EUnet Luxemburg

162a, av. de la Faiencerie
L- 1511 Luxemburg
Tel: +352 47 02 61-361
Fax: +352 47 02 64
E-mail: info@luxemburg.eu.net

Service Area:	Luxemburg
1-800 Service:	No
UUCP Service:	Yes Usenet News and Electronic Mail
Domain Registration:	Yes
Consulting Services:	No
Commercial Traffic:	Yes
Sign Up Procedure:	Call for information

The Netherlands

NLnet

Amsterdam
Kruislaan 413
1098 SJ Amsterdam
The Netherlands
Phone: +31 20 592 4245
Fax: +31 20 665 5311
Email: info@NL.net
Internet Domain: NL.net

Service Area:	The Netherlands
1-800 Service:	No
UUCP Service:	Yes Usenet News and Electronic Mail
Domain Registration:	Yes
Consulting Services:	Yes
Commercial Traffic:	Yes
Sign Up Procedure:	Call for information

Internet connectivity in the Netherlands has been provided by the Dutch UNIX Users Group, the NLUUG, since 1982. The NLUUG is also the co-founder of the pan-European network, EUnet. In 1989, the Stichting NLnet was founded by the Dutch UNIX User Group to provide professional networking services to its members. A "stichting" is a common legal construct in The Netherlands for a non-profit organization. In 1993, the NLUUG membership constraint was dropped, making NLnet the only Dutch provider of IP connectivity for everyone. The only other provider of IP services in The Netherlands, SURFnet, is limited to governmental, academic, and research organizations. NLnet currently has more than 500 subscribers. Its subscribers are mainly organizations (ranging from small to large organizations), but NLnet also connects an increasing number of individuals.

Portugal

EUnet-PT - EUnet Portugal

Tel: +351 1 294 28 44
Fax: +351 1 295 77 86
Dialup: +351 1 315 09 85 / 6 / 7
E-mail: info@puug.pt or info@portugal.eu.net
Internet Domain: puug.pt, portugal.eu.net

Service Area:	Portugal
1-800 Service:	No
UUCP Service:	Yes Usenet News and Electronic Mail

Domain Registration:	Yes
Consulting Services:	No
Commercial Traffic:	Yes
Sign Up Procedure:	Call for information

EUnet Portugal is the Portuguese part of EUnet, the widest Pan-European network providing Internet access to over 8500 customer organizations in 26 countries.
EUnet - PT is operated by PUUG - The Portuguese UNIX Users Group. No special restrictions apply.

Slovak Republic

EUnet Slovakia

c/o Computing Centre of MFF UK
Mlynska dolina
842 15 Bratislava
Slovak Republic
Tel: +42 7 725 306, +42 7 377 434
Fax: +42 7 728 462, +42 7 377 433
E-mail: info@slovakia.eu.net

Service Area:	Slovak Republic
1-800 Service:	No
UUCP Service:	Yes Usenet News and Electronic Mail
Domain Registration:	Yes
Consulting Services:	No
Commercial Traffic:	Yes
Sign Up Procedure:	Call for details

21: Access Provider Directory

NIL Systems Integration & Consulting Ltd. (EUnet Slovenia)

Leskoskova 4
SLO-61000 Ljubljana
Slovenia
Phone : +386 61 1405 183, +386 61 1405 283
Telefax : +386 61 1405 381
E-mail : postmaster@slovenia.eu.net or info@slovenia.eu.net
    or register@slovenia.eu.net
Internet Domain: nil.si, slovernia.eu.net

Service Area:	Slovenia
1-800 Service:	No
UUCP Service:	Yes Usenet News and Electronic Mail
Domain Registration:	Yes
Consulting Services:	Yes
Commercial Traffic:	Yes
Sign Up Procedure:	Call for information

Internet Service Provider for non-academic organizations, companies and institutions including e-mail (EUMail), news (EUNews}, dial-up IP (DialEUnet), leased IP (InterEUnet), and Internet Consulting.

PIPEX

See this complete listing under the United Kingdom.

Spain

EUnet Spain

EUnet -- Goya
C/ Clara del Rey 8, 1-7
E-28046 Madrid
Spain
Tel: +34 1 413 48 56
Fax: +34 1 413 49 01
E-mail: info@eunet.es
Internet Domain: eunet.es

Service Area:	Spain
1-800 Service:	No
UUCP Service:	Yes Usenet News and Electronic Mail
Domain Registration:	Yes
Consulting Services:	No
Commercial Traffic:	Yes
Sign Up Procedure:	Call for information

Sweden

Tele2/SwipNet

P.O. Box 62
S-164 94 KISTA
Sweden
Tel: +46 8-6324058

Fax: +46 8-6324200
E-mail: wallner@swip.net
Internet Domain: swip.net

Service Area:	Sweden
1-800 Service:	No
UUCP Service:	Yes Usenet News and Electronic Mail
Domain Registration:	Yes
Consulting Services:	No
Commercial Traffic:	Yes
Sign Up Procedure:	Please contact us via phone or e-mail

PIPEX

See this complete listing under the United Kingdom.

Switzerland

EUnet Switzerland

Zweierstrasse 35
CH-8004 Zuerich
Tel: +41 1 291 45 80
Fax: +41 1 291 46 42
Internet Domain: info@eunet.ch

Service Area:	01 (Zuerich), 022 (Geneva), 031 (Bern), 091 (Lugano)
1-800 Service:	No
UUCP Service:	Yes Usenet News and Electronic Mail

Domain Registration:	Yes
Consulting Services:	No
Commercial Traffic:	Yes
Sign Up Procedure:	Call for information

United Kingdom

The Direct Connection

P O Box 931
London SE18 3PW
England
Internet Domain: dircon.co.uk

Service Area:	United Kingdom
1-800 Service:	No
UUCP Service:	Yes Usenet News and Electronic Mail
Domain Registration:	Yes
Consulting Services:	Yes
Commercial Traffic:	Yes
Sign Up Procedure:	We have a dial-up / demo service. Call 081 317 2222 using a modem and terminal software. Otherwise, contact us by phone or fax.

EUnet GB

Kent R&D Business Centre
Giles Lane
Canterbury CT2 7PB
United Kingdom

Service Area:	United Kingdom
1-800 Service:	No
UUCP Service:	Yes Usenet News and Electronic Mail
Domain Registration:	Yes
Consulting Services:	No
Commercial Traffic:	Yes
Sign Up Procedure:	Call for information

ExNet Systems Ltd

37 Honley Road
Catford, SE6 2HY
London, UK
Tel: +44-81-244-0077
Fax: +44-81-244-0078
Internet Domain: exnet.com

Service Area:	Europe
1-800 Service:	Free calls to us from certain areas of England.
UUCP Service:	Yes Usenet News and Electronic Mail
Domain Registration:	Yes
Consulting Services:	Yes

Commercial Traffic:	Yes Special prices and deals
Sign Up Procedure:	Ring us, fill in contract, one month free trial

PC User Group Ltd—CONNECT

P.O. Box 360
84-88 Pinner Road
Harrow HA1 4LQ
England
Tel: +44 (0)81-863 1191
Fax: +44 (0)81-863 6095
Internet Domain: ibmpcug.co.uk

Service Area:	U.K., London-based with access points around the U.K. for the second half of 1994.
1-800 Service:	No
UUCP Service:	Yes Usenet News and Electronic Mail
Domain Registration:	Yes
Consulting Services:	Yes
Commercial Traffic:	Yes
Sign Up Procedure:	Call Voice +44 (0)81-863 1191 or fax +44 (0)81-863 6095 if you have an email address email to request@ibmpcug.co.uk, Subject: MKS. UUCP Services under our domain can be set up automatically using script information that can be dowloaded from the above number or via the request address above or by phone/fax at the above numbers.

UK User Group, BBS Internet access plus individual and site UUCP access.

PIPEX

Public IP Exchange Limited - a subsidiary of Unipalm Group plc
216 Cambridge Science Park
Cambridge
CB4 4WA
Tel: 0500 64 65 66 / [outside UK] +44 223 250120
Fax: +44 223 250121
E-mail: pipex@pipex.net
Internet Domain: pipex.net

Service Area:	United Kingdom / Ireland, France, Benelux countries, Germany, Sweden, Hungary, Slovenia
1-800 Service:	No
UUCP Service:	Yes Usenet News and Electronic Mail
Domain Registration:	Yes
Consulting Services:	Yes
Commercial Traffic:	Yes
Sign Up Procedure:	Please call or email pipex@pipex.net, or ftp.pipex.net /pub/FAQ - or via WWW: http://www.pipex.net

One-stop shopping for Internet connectivity in the U.K. and several European countries, from low-cost dialup services for individuals (through subsidiary CityScape) and ISDN connnections, to high-speed digital leased line connections for corporate customers at 64 kbps/128 kbps/256 kbps and greater.

PIPEX offers commercial access to the Internet via a range of dialup and leased line services. These services are provided as a "one-stop-shop" where equipment/telecom installation and rental costs are included within our charges.

PIPEX is directly connected to the USA, EBone (European Backbone), JIPS, and SWIPnet networks. The network is designed to have no single point of failure, and significant international bandwidth allows us to offer excellent performance and 99.5% network availability.

PIPEX is a member of the CIX (Commercial Internet Exchange) and EBone'94 and as such can route commercial traffic worldwide. PIPEX does not restrict the type or volume of customer traffic in any way.

PIPEX has, at end of 94Q1, over 170 leased line customers in the UK and over 200 directly connected customers in all.

PIPEX-style services are now available in France, Germany, Benelux, Hungary, Slovenia, and Ireland exclusively through our partners: Oleane, MIS, INNet, Odin, Quantum, and Genesis; and a number of

U.K. resellers also sell low-cost dialup access across their PIPEX connections (details from sales@pipex.net).

Ukmail Network

White Bridge House
Old Bath Road
Charvil RG10 9QJ
United Kingdom
Tel: +44 734 344 000
Fax: +44 734 320 988
E-mail: pgoujard@infocom.co.uk

Service Area:	United Kingdom, London-based with access points around the U.K. for the second half of 1994.
1-800 Service:	No
UUCP Service:	Yes Usenet News and Electronic Mail
Domain Registration:	Yes
Consulting Services:	Yes
Commercial Traffic:	Yes
Sign Up Procedure:	Call 0734 344000. We send back an information pack.

Eurasia

The Eurasian section of this directory lists:

> Lithuania
> Russia
> Ukraine

Lithuania

ELNETA UAB

P.O. Box 2147
Vilnius 2017
Lithuania
Tel: (370-2) 263948
Internet Domain: elnet.lt

Service Area:	Lithuania
1-800 Service:	No
UUCP Service:	Yes Usenet News and Electronic Mail
Domain Registration:	Yes
Consulting Services:	Yes
Commercial Traffic:	Yes
Sign Up Procedure:	Call (370-2) 263948

InterCommunications Ltd.

107/25, Oborony st.
Rostov-on-Don
344007
Russia
Tel: +7 (863-2) 620562
Fax: +7 (863-2) 696951
E-mail: postmaster@icomm.md.su
Internet Domain: icomm.rnd.su

Service Area:	Rostov-on-Don
1-800 Service:	No
UUCP Service:	Yes Usenet News and Electronic Mail
Domain Registration:	Yes
Consulting Services:	Yes
Commercial Traffic:	Yes
Sign Up Procedure:	Please call for information

URAL-RELCOM Ltd.

Antona Valeka street, 13, 400
Russia, Ekatherinburg
Tel: +7 3432 571800
Internet Domain: it.e-burg.su (193.124.176.65) , mplik.e-burg.su, lik.e-burg.su,
faxnet38.e-burg.su

Service Area:	Urals region
1-800 Service:	No

UUCP Service:	Yes Usenet News and Electronic Mail
Domain Registration:	Yes
Consulting Services:	Yes
Commercial Traffic:	Yes
Sign Up Procedure:	By telephone/fax: +7 3432 571800 By e-mail: irina@mplik.e-burg.su

Regional host of Relcom net, regional host of Faxnet in Ekaterinburg (Russia). There are about 300 firms that use our services in the Urals region. We provide communication by Relcom, Faxnet, access to Internet, some information services.

Ukraine

Crimea Communication Centre

Simferopol, Crimea, Ukraine 33, Gorkogo
nternet Domain: snail.crimea.ua

Service Area:	Crimea peninsula
1-800 Service:	7 0652
UUCP Service:	Yes Usenet News and Electronic Mail
Domain Registration:	Yes
Consulting Services:	Yes
Commercial Traffic:	Yes
Sign Up Procedure:	Postal mail

CS/MONOLIT Network Centre

1/27 Likhacheva boul.
252195
Kiev, Ukraine
Tel: +7 044 2959080
Fax: 2953053
Internet Domain: ua.net

Service Area:	Ukraine
1-800 Service:	No
UUCP Service:	Yes Usenet News and Electronic Mail
Domain Registration:	Yes
Consulting Services:	Yes
Commercial Traffic:	Yes
Sign Up Procedure:	E-mail to info@ua.net Phone +7 044 2959080 Fax 2953053

We offer e-mail and news access to Internet; on-line accounts are also available.

PACO Links International Ltd.

App. 103, 4, Gazovy lane
Odessa, Ukraine, UA-270000
Tel: +7 0482 260704
Fax: +7 0482 200057
Internet Domain: vista.odessa.ua

Service Area:	Odessa region
1-800 Service:	No
UUCP Service:	Yes Usenet News and Electronic Mail
Domain Registration:	Yes

Consulting Services:	Yes
Commercial Traffic:	Yes
Sign Up Procedure:	Phone +7 0482 260704, +7 0482 200057

Africa

The Africa section of this directory includes:

> Egypt
> South Africa
> Tunisia

Egypt

Egyptian National STI Network (ENSTINET)

Academy of Scientific Research and Technology
101 Kasr El-Aini St, 12 floor
Cairo 11516
Egypt
Tel : +20-2-355-7253, +20-2-356-4421
Fax : +20-2-354-7807
E-mail: info@estinet.uucp, estinet!info@relay.eu.net

Service Area:	Egypt
1-800 Service:	No
UUCP Service:	Yes Usenet News and Electronic Mail
Domain Registration:	Yes
Consulting Services:	No

Commercial Traffic:	Yes
Sign Up Procedure:	Call for information

South Africa

The Internet Solution (Pty) Ltd

PO Box 273
Ferndale
2160
Tel: +27 11 7896071
Fax: +27 11 7891523
E-mail: ronnie@apollo.is.co.za
Internet Domain: is.co.za

Service Area:	Johannesburg and Pretoria
1-800 Service:	No
UUCP Service:	Yes Usenet News and Electronic Mail
Domain Registration:	Yes
Consulting Services:	Yes DNS, sendmail, routing,and WAN hardware. UNIX security and mail management customization.
Commercial Traffic:	Yes
Sign Up Procedure:	All our information is available with anonymous ftp from apollo.is.co.za in /pub

IRSIT

BP 212
2 Rue Ibn Nadim
1082 Cite Mahrajane
Tunis, Tunisia
Tel: +216 1 787 757 or 800 112 or 289 853
Fax: +216 1 787 827
E-mail: hostmaster@tunisia.eu.net
Internet Domain: rsinet.tn

Service Area:	Tunisia and North Africa
1-800 Service:	Yes Nota available in Tunisia
UUCP Service:	Yes Usenet News and Electronic Mail
Domain Registration:	Yes
Consulting Services:	Yes
Commercial Traffic:	Yes
Sign Up Procedure:	Send e-mail or fax

IRSIT is a national applied computer research Institute that deals with Informatics and Telecommunications. It manages the TN (TuNisia) national Internet Backbone.

Pacific Rim

The Pacific Rim section of this directory includes:

Australia
Hong Kong
Japan

Malaysia
Taiwan

Australia

AARNet

GPO Box 1142
CANBERRA, ACT
Tel: +61 6 2494968
Fax: +61 6 2491369
E-mail: admin@aarnet.edu.au
Internet Domain: .au

Service Area:	All (most) of Australia
1-800 Service:	No
UUCP Service:	Yes Usenet News and Electronic Mail
Domain Registration:	Yes
Consulting Services:	No
Commercial Traffic:	Yes
Sign Up Procedure:	E-mail to admin@aarnet.edu.au Commercial/non-private/non-personal use, ask for Connecting to AARNet Information Pack Private/hobby/personal use, ask for Network Access in Australia

AARNet, Australian Academic and Research Network. Provides access to the Australian backbone for all networks wishing to use AARNet, the Internet, and other peer networks.

connect.com.au pty ltd

29 Fitzgibbon Crescent
Caulfield Victoria
Australia 3161
Tel: +61 3 528 2239

Fax: +61 3 528 5887
E-mail: connect@connect.com.au
Internet Domain: connect.com.au

Service Area:	Adelaide, Brisbane, Canberra, Melbourne, Perth, Sydney
1-800 Service:	No
UUCP Service:	Yes Usenet News and Electronic Mail
Domain Registration:	Yes
Consulting Services:	Yes
Commercial Traffic:	Yes
Sign Up Procedure:	Send for brochure and application

Message Handling Systems Pty Ltd

1st Floor, 2 King Street
Newtown NSW 2042
Australia
Tel: 02 550-4448
Fax: 02 519-2551
E-mail: elaine@mhs.oz.au

Service Area:	Sydney, Melbourne and Brisbane (Australia)
1-800 Service:	No
UUCP Service:	Yes Usenet News and Electronic Mail
Domain Registration:	Yes
Consulting Services:	No
Commercial Traffic:	Yes
Sign Up Procedure:	Call for information

Pegasus Networks

PO Box 284
Broadway
Queensland, 4066
Australia
Tel: +61 7 257 1111 or 1-800-812-812
Fax: +61 7 257 1087
E-mail: pegasus@peg.apc.org or peg-info@peg.apc.org (automatic)
Internet domain: peg.apc.org, or pegasus.oz.au

Service Area:	Australia and Asia-Pacific neighbors
1-800 Service:	Yes
UUCP Service:	Yes Usenet News and Electronic Mail
Domain Registration:	Yes
Consulting Services:	Yes
Commercial Traffic:	Yes
Sign Up Procedure:	Call for information

Pegasus Networks provides an online communication and information service to subscribers across Australia. The network was established in 1989, offering services specifically to those with interests in the environment, development, education, media, health, and human rights. It has a rapidly growing user base of individuals and organizations (non-government, government, and private) involved in community, development, education, aid, research, media, management, and policy. Pegasus is a founding member of the international Association for Progressive Communications (APC).

Hong Kong

Hong Kong Internet Services Ltd.

1286 Telecom House
3 Gloucester Rd.
Wanchai, Hong Kong

Service Area:	Hong Kong
1-800 Service:	No
UUCP Service:	Yes Usenet News and Electronic Mail
Domain Registration:	Yes
Consulting Services:	No
Commercial Traffic:	Yes
Sign Up Procedure:	Send mail for information

Japan

Internet Initiative Japan, Inc.

Hoshigaoka Bldg.
2-11-2 Nagatacho, Chiyoda-ku
Tokyo 100 Japan
Tel: +81-3-3580-3781
Fax: +81-3-3580-3782
E-mail: info@iij.ad.jp
Internet Domain: iij.ad.jp

Service Area:	Japan
1-800 Service:	No
UUCP Service:	Yes Usenet News and Electronic Mail
Domain Registration:	Yes
Consulting Services:	Yes
Commercial Traffic:	Yes
Sign Up Procedure:	Contact info@iij.ad.jp and request application forms

TWICS

International Education Center Bldg.
1-21 Yotsuya, Shinjuku-ku
Tokyo 160 Japan
Tel: +81-3-3351-5977
Fax: +81-3-3353-6096
E-mail: info@twics.com
Internet Domain: twics.com, twics.co.jp

Service Area:	Japan (local access from 40 cities)
1-800 Service:	No
UUCP Service:	Yes Usenet News and Electronic Mail
Domain Registration:	Yes
Consulting Services:	Yes We can provide basic support in setting up UUCP for common systems. For more in-depth consulting, we prefer to work with professional systems integrators and will recommend one to potential customers.
Commercial Traffic:	Yes
Sign Up Procedure:	Contact us by: E-mail: info@twics.com Fax: +81-3-3353-6096 Tel: +81-3-3351-5977

TWICS is a public-access Internet system providing dial-up host and UUCP connections for individuals, schools, and businesses.

Malaysia

Malaysian Institute of Microelectronic Systems (MIMOS)

Jaring Network Operation Center,
7th Floor, Exchange Square,

Off Jalan Semantan, Damansara Heights
50490 Kuala Lumpur, Malaysia
Tel: +60-3-255-2700, 254-9601
Fax: +60-3-255-2755, 253-1898
E-mail: noc@jaring.my

Service Area:	Malaysia
1-800 Service:	No
UUCP Service:	Yes Usenet News and Electronic Mail
Domain Registration:	Yes
Consulting Services:	No
Commercial Traffic:	Yes
Sign Up Procedure:	Call to sign up

Taiwan

SEEDNET Service Center

Institute for Information Industry
10Fl. No.106   Sec. 2 Hoping E. Rd.
Taipei Taiwan R.O.C.
Tel: 886-2-733-8803
Fax: 886-2-737-0188
E-mail: liou@iiidns.iii.org.tw or liou@tpts1.seed.net.tw
Internet Domain: seed.net.tw or iii.org.tw

Service Area:	Taiwan
1-800 Service:	No
UUCP Service:	Yes Usenet News and Electronic Mail

Domain Registration:	Yes
Consulting Services:	Yes
Commercial Traffic:	Yes
Sign Up Procedure:	Call to get an application form

A

The Insides of the Internet

This appendix provides you with background information about the Internet, including a little history on how the Internet came to be.

What the Internet Isn't

The Internet is a global network of computer networks. Before we explain what that means, it's helpful to discuss what the Internet *isn't*:

- Internet is not a commercial enterprise, although many of the networks that make up Internet are commercial enterprises.

- Internet is not sponsored by any government, although important predecessors of Internet were sponsored by the U.S. Department of Defense.

- Internet is not administered or regulated by anyone, except for the individuals in charge of each separate system using the Internet.

Internet functions on consensus, tradition, peer pressure, natural selection, and the generosity of the sites and people who have decided "the net" is worth the effort needed to keep it going.

What the Internet Is

The Internet is commonly defined as a global network of computer networks. More importantly, however, the Internet is a *collaboration*: a collaboration of computer administrators, owners, and users, who all work together to support Internet services.

People have begun to call Internet an *electronic highway*: a way to ship data from one place to another. However, it's more like a highway *system*: a lot of individual roads and streets, each maintained locally. Highways are built and maintained by many jurisdictions—cities, counties, states—who coordinate their activities (most of the time, anyway) to make a usable set of roads. Similarly, the Internet consists of many different computers and computer networks, publicly or privately owned, who choose to work together to make certain services available to each other.

> **Definition:** For our purposes, a computer network is any group of computers that can exchange data with each other. The computers may send their data over phone lines or through direct hook-ups from one machine to another. They may be in constant communication with each other, or they may only make contact now and then (once a day, for example, or only when someone explicitly asks one system to call another).

Internet Services

To most people, the Internet is defined by the services it offers. Here's a quick list of the most important ones:

Electronic Mail (Also Called E-mail)

To send an electronic mail message, you type in a message on your computer and tell your computer to send it to another user, anywhere on the Internet. Typically, your computer transfers the message to a nearby computer, which in turn transfers it to another computer closer to the ultimate destination, and so on through a chain of computers until the message reaches the computer used by the intended recipient. That computer stores the message until the recipient asks to read his or her incoming mail.

This process may sound slow, but it can be extremely fast. Messages regularly travel from one side of the continent to the other in minutes, and it's not unusual for a message to go halfway around the globe in an hour or two.

Usenet News

The Usenet news service is comparable to an electronic bulletin board. In fact, it's like a collection of hundreds of electronic bulletin boards, each dedicated to a different topic and each shared by thousands of computers. These bulletin boards are called *newsgroups*, and they're organized into various classes: groups related to computers, business, science, recreational subjects, and so on.

People often use newsgroups to get answers to questions. For example, suppose you've just bought a new software package and are having trouble installing it. You might post an article to the newsgroup associated with your type of computer, describing your problems and asking for advice. Your computer transmits that article to other computers, which in turn relay it to still more computers, possibly reaching computers on every continent. (Yes, the Internet reaches Antarctica.)

On any of those systems, people can read the articles in that newsgroup. Your question may be read by hundreds or thousands of people around the world; those who have advice to offer may send an electronic mail message directly to you, or they may post their answers to the same newsgroup so that all readers of the group can benefit from the same information.

The administrators at each computer site choose which newsgroups that site will carry. For example, a particular company may choose to carry newsgroups related to computers and business concerns, but not newsgroups related to sports and entertainment.

Software packages called *news readers* make it easy for you to choose which newsgroups you want to follow and which messages you want to read within each newsgroup. Many sites offer several different news reader programs so you can pick the one most suited to your tastes.

Other Services

Dozens of other services are available through Internet, from databases on judicial precedents to the lyrics and guitar chords for popular songs. By following the right Usenet newsgroups (like *alt.internet services*), you'll be able to find out about existing services and about new services as they become available.

It's important to understand that many Internet services are offered out of sheer generosity. For example, someone in California faithfully types in the latest baseball scores every day so that people on Internet can find out who won. Perhaps this person would keep computer records of the scores anyway—baseball fans love statistics—but he chooses to make these records his contribution to the net as a whole.

> **Things You Shouldn't Do with Internet:** Usenet news
> should not be used for blatant commercial marketing. There
> are newsgroups where companies may make demure
> announcements of new products or services; but such
> announcements should be limited to a single message, with
> the emphasis on information, not hype. Internet is not the
> junk mail of the future.

Information Overload

The greatest challenge Internet users face is information overload. Through the net, people have access to files, programs, and people in almost every city of the world. Do you need a patch for your database software? It's out there. Do you fancy having all of Shakespeare on-line? It's out there. Do you want to correspond with folks who can explain black holes, white noise, or the Cincinnati Reds? They're out there, too.

Just reading Usenet news can become a full-time job. There are hundreds of newsgroups about computing alone. The newsgroup on baseball easily tops a hundred new messages a day during a pennant race. Many college students, exposed to Internet for the first time, jeopardize their grades by spending every evening reading and responding to news; and even if you devoted every waking hour to reading news, you couldn't cover more than a fraction of the information that flows through every day.

The trick is to locate information that could be useful or interesting to you, without getting bogged down in the intimidating "noise" of the net. Certain software packages (with names like Gopher and Archie) can help you track down information, but even they are only a start. Only experience will let you learn how to get the maximum benefit with the minimum amount of wasted time and aggravation.

A Brief History of the Internet

To be honest, Internet's success is partly accidental: it was in the right places at the right times. This section provides a little background to explain how Internet evolved from earlier computer networks.

Back in the Stone Age

It's easy to imagine how and why computer networks developed. Picture Fred working at a computer when he discovers that there is some useful information already stored on another computer nearby. Sure, he might be able to get a printout of the information, but nobody wants to retype long pages of facts and figures.

Wouldn't it be nice, he thinks, if I could connect these two machines some-how? If I wired together all the computers in the office so they could exchange information, I could save hours of work.

Then picture Fred's co-worker, Wilma, opening a branch office hundreds of miles away. She'd like to use the same computer system as everyone else in the company—it would keep the accounting procedures consistent and give her access to the most up-to-date information from the home office. So Wilma invests in a modem and writes some communications software to let her branch office keep in touch with headquarters. Most networks began as informal, local arrangements just like this.

Protocols

The people who created the earliest networks discovered that they needed rules to control the signals that computers send to each other when exchanging data. They called such rules *communications protocols*. A communications protocol is really just an agreement between computers on how information will be organized for exchange. A typical protocol covers how much information is passed at a time and how to check that it's been accurately transmitted.

You can compare a protocol to the rules of the road. In Great Britain, the rules of the road include an agreement that cars travel on the left side. In the United States, cars travel on the right. Drivers have to agree to a common set of rules before they can use the same highways; the same goes for computers using electronic highways.

A protocol is simply an agreement between two computers to use certain signals in a particular type of data transmission. The same computer can have different agreements with different computers; in other words, a single computer can use different protocols, depending on which computer is on the other end of the line. In fact, the same two computers can use different protocols in different situations.

ARPAnet

Large organizations such as government agencies and universities tend to own many computers, so they have the most to gain from linking those computers into networks. Thus, it's no surprise that the U.S. Department of Defense (DoD) was one of the first to experiment with a big network: something that went beyond wiring together neighboring machines or phoning home for data.

In 1969, the DoD introduced a modest network called ARPAnet, linking computer systems in universities and government labs. By 1983, as confidence in the network grew, it was divided into two sections: **MILnet** (for military computers) and **ARPAnet** (for research computers). The two networks were connected so that machines on one network could communicate with machines on the other.

The National Science Foundation (NSF), another agency of the U.S. government, soon recognized the usefulness of networking for scientific research. It built **NSFnet** to connect its supercomputer research centers to one another; in 1986, NSFnet connected to ARPAnet.

Eventually, NSFnet took over from ARPAnet as the mainstay of this group—NSFnet had newer, faster communication technology—so ARPAnet was phased out in the late 1980s. Most of the computer systems that were formerly connected through ARPAnet joined NSFnet instead. This is the basis of what we call Internet today.

UNIX and UUCPNET

ARPAnet originally ran on computers running an operating system called *Multics*. By the late 1970s, however, many of the computers on ARPAnet used the *UNIX* operating system.

The UNIX system originated at AT&T Bell Laboratories in the late 1960s. To begin with, UNIX was mostly a research tool, a system on which Bell Labs programmers could try out theories about how computers could be used more effectively. In the 1970s, federal regulations prevented AT&T from turning UNIX into a commercial software package; instead, AT&T made UNIX available to colleges and universities at rock-bottom prices.

The result was that professors and students at educational institutions could afford to "play around" with UNIX systems. In addition, the UNIX system was designed to let hot-shot programmers be as productive as possible. Thus, much of the most innovative software of the 1970s originated on UNIX.

> **TCP/IP:** The heart of ARPAnet and its sister networks was a family of communications protocols going under the name TCP/IP. Any computer that "spoke" the set of signals called TCP/IP could speak to ARPAnet machines. This is the reason that separate networks like ARPAnet, MILnet, and NSFnet could all communicate with each other: the machines all understood TCP/IP. TCP/IP is the protocol that underlies Internet.

It was natural that UNIX systems would become a major part of ARPAnet. Furthermore, the DoD was not the only organization interested in building networks on UNIX. While the DoD was developing the TCP/IP protocol for ARPAnet, other programmers produced a different protocol that could also be used to transmit data between UNIX systems. This protocol was called **UUCP**, short for "Unix-to-Unix CoPy."

The collection of computers that could communicate via UUCP constituted a network called **UUCPNET**. Just as you can define Internet as the set of all computers that "speak" TCP/IP, you can define UUCPNET as the set of all computers that "speak" UUCP.

Some UNIX systems were equipped to communicate using either TCP/IP or UUCP. You can picture such a system as a warehouse that has loading docks for trucks and for trains. This kind of "warehouse" system could send and receive data via the electronic highway (TCP/IP); but it could also send and receive data by railroad (UUCP). Even more important, such a system could transfer data from one mode of transportation to another; it could receive data by UUCP and ship it out by TCP/IP, or vice versa.

> **Gateway:** A system that can receive data by one protocol and ship it out by another is called a gateway machine. It operates as a "bridge" between networks.

Usenet News

The idea of users sharing news with each other dates back to at least the 1960s. For example, machines running the Multics operating system used a software package called *Forum* to share information and opinions with each other. A few other computer systems of the day had comparable facilities.

In the early 1980s, computers that could use the UUCP protocol began to share news postings, originally related only to computers, but soon on many other topics of interest to computer users. This sharing of news evolved into the Usenet news service.

Usenet news was *very* popular—so popular that news was soon being transported by many different data transfer protocols, not just UUCP. UUCP is still in wide use today, shipping news and other kinds of data too; however, news now travels by a variety of techniques, supported by a variety of software packages.

A Brief Comparison of DOS and UNIX

DOS is essentially a one-user system. It can really only do one thing at a time, even if software like Windows makes it look like several programs are working simultaneously. Furthermore, DOS lets any user work with any file on the system; there's no way to tell DOS that some files belong to user X while other files belong to user Y.

UNIX is a multiuser system. It's designed to let several people use the same computer simultaneously, each connected to the computer with a separate keyboard and monitor. Each user can set up his or her private files, inaccessible to other users; you can also set up files that are available to everyone. UNIX is also a *multitasking* system, which means that you can have many programs running and actively doing work at the same time.

Other Networks Join the Internet

In an earlier section, we discussed how gateway machines that could use both UUCP and TCP/IP could bridge the gap between UUCPNET and the Internet. Even if your machine only "spoke" UUCP, you could still obtain indirect access to a variety of Internet services by going through a gateway. In the late 1980s, many other networks used the same technique to link into Internet:

- **BITNET** (the "Because It's Time Network") is a collection of machines communicating through a protocol called NJE. Machines that can speak both NJE and TCP/IP now connect BITNET to the Internet.

- **FidoNet** is a cooperative worldwide network of personal computers communicating with each other through a special dial-up protocol. It is linked to Internet through machines that can use both this protocol and TCP/IP.

Over time, hundreds of other existing networks linked into the Internet in the same way. If any machine on a network can use TCP/IP, that machine can link the rest of the network to Internet and provide indirect access to selected Internet services.

Internet Growth

Although TCP/IP and UUCP began on UNIX systems, there are now many computers equipped to use these protocols. The reason is simple: success breeds success.

As more and more systems became accessible through the Internet and through UUCP, this kind of access became more attractive to other users. Companies that write software saw that their customers wanted the services that these protocols provided. Therefore, TCP/IP and UUCP became available on more and more machines—not just on UNIX systems, but on almost every type of computer available.

By the beginning of 1991, there were 313,000 computers accessible through the Internet. Since many of those computers had large numbers of users, a connection to the Internet gave you access to millions of people around the world. Companies knew how valuable that kind of connection could be, so they flocked to join Internet, too. By the end of 1992, just two years later, the number of computers with Internet access had ballooned to 1,136,000, an increase of 363%.

The Internet continues to grow at an exponential rate. By now, it's very difficult to count just how many computers have Internet access. After all, that would require taking an accurate census of hundreds of independent networks. You should also remember that the Internet population doesn't just grow by one machine at a time; it can grow in great leaps, as large multimachine networks suddenly gain access to the Internet by way of a gateway machine that has learned to speak TCP/IP.

As of August 1994, the number of computers connected to Internet is estimated at about 2.7 million systems…and the count is growing by 100,000 new systems every month.

Commercial Networks: CompuServe, GEnie, and Others

With all this talk of networks, you may be surprised that we haven't mentioned some of the prominent commercial networks: CompuServe, GEnie, Prodigy, and so on.

Most such networks have some degree of connection with Internet. Almost all of them can now exchange electronic mail with Internet sites—users have demanded this ability, and the commercial networks have complied.

Beyond this, however, the commercial networks don't have much incentive to enter the Internet world. For example, consider the news bulletin boards that the commercial networks run. If these networks started sending out their news to the Internet at large, millions of people would get the news free instead of paying the commercial networks for it.

If you're familiar with one or more of the commercial networks, you're in for a big surprise when you get a taste of Internet. First, Internet is vastly larger than any of the commercial nets: more news, more services, more users. Second, Internet is a brawling, sprawling anarchy, with no central authority to keep it genteel.

The commercial nets make an effort to keep their users civil, discouraging such things as vulgarity and verbal assaults on other users. Internet, on the other hand, isn't owned by anyone and isn't controlled by anyone. Some Internet newsgroups are blatantly pornographic, and almost every news-group occasionally suffers vicious bickering wars. This is the price you pay for the Internet's freedom—some people use their freedom to be rude and petty. On the other hand, Internet has so many other users that you can ignore the boors and enjoy the many gems in the Internet community.

Writer Tom Maddox has a neat analogy to put the networks into per-spective. The commercial networks are comparable to the suburbs, mostly tame and well-tended. The Internet is a full-fledged city, a metropolis like New York or Los Angeles, complete with high-class neighborhoods and places you might get mugged, interesting people with whom you can share thoughts and crazy people screaming in the night. At times, the Internet can make you furious; but it has a scope that none of the more controlled net-works can match.

Finding Your Way Around

The services available through Internet are offered by specific computers or sets of computers. For example, if you want to send an electronic mail message to someone, you have to tell the Internet where to deliver the message. This means that you need a unique way to refer to each of the different computers on the Internet.

Site Names

The first step is to give a name to every computer on the Internet. Companies might give their computer the same name as the company; individuals might come up with all kinds of special names for the computers, the way that people make up personalized license plates for their cars.

But naming your computer is only a beginning. Suppose, for example, you decide to call your computer `jojo`, and suppose that someone on another continent wants to send an electronic mail message to you. We've already mentioned that mail messages are transferred from computer to computer…but how does someone else's computer know which chain of computers will be able to transmit the message to you?

Site Addresses

In the early days of networks, you had to specify the chain explicitly. On UUCPNET, for example, if you wanted to send an electronic message to Dale in Detroit, it wasn't enough to say, "Send this to Dale at the Dimestore Inc. computer." You had to tell your computer the complete chain of machines through which the message had to travel to get to the Dimestore system. Dale's E-mail "address" might have looked something like this:

```
westworld!flatland!michdata!dimestore!dale
```

Obviously, such addresses were complicated to use, and people were eager to come up with a more practical way of writing an address.

Domain Addresses

In time, Internet users came up with the idea of *domains*. A domain is simply a group of computers with some common property—for example, the `ca` domain is made up of computers in Canada, while the `edu` domain is made up of computers at educational institutions. Often, a particular computer could belong to several domains; some educational institutions in Canada belong to the `ca` domain, while others belong to the `edu` domain. In this case, the people who run the computer may choose to belong to either or both domains.

Registries: Each domain has one or more sites that keep a registry of all the computers in the domain. To locate a particular computer, your computer's software just looks at the registry for that computer's domain. The registry provides all the information your computer needs to contact the other computer.

Think of it like this: domains are something like phone districts, and the registry is something like a phone book for every computer in that district. If you want to contact another computer, you have to know that computer's domain; then you can check the phone book for that domain to get the connection information.

> **Note:** You don't have to look up information in a domain registry by hand. It's all handled automatically by Internet software. You'll probably never know it's happening.

The Form of a Domain Address

The usual form of an Internet computer address is

```
machinename.domain
```

In other words, it's the name of the machine, followed by a dot (a period) followed by the domain name. For example, the White House has the address

```
whitehouse.gov
```

The name of the computer is `whitehouse` and the name of the domain is `gov`. As you might guess, the `gov` domain is for computers associated with the U.S. government.

To refer to a particular user on a computer, you use the address form

```
user@machinename.domain
```

For example, you might see

```
president@whitehouse.gov
vice-president@whitehouse.gov
```

for two different people who use the same machine. The `@` character is pronounced "at," so you'd read the first address above as "president at whitehouse dot gov."

> **Fully Qualified Domain Name:** Technically, an address of the form `user@machinename.domain` is called a fully qualified domain name (FQDN).

Subdomains

Many domains have *subdomains*. For example, the `ca` domain covers computers in Canada. Each province within Canada has its own separate subdomain. Thus, you might see machine addresses like

```
waterloo.on.ca
```

The `ca` domain stands for Canada and the `on` domain stands for Ontario, a province inside Canada.

As another example, the `edu` domain covers educational institutions. A school with a lot of computers on campus might create its own subdomain, and all the campus computers would belong to that subdomain. For example,

```
engrg.uwo.edu
```

is the main Engineering computer at `uwo` (University of Western Ontario), which is a subdomain of the `edu` domain.

When you send e-mail to a machine address like this, the mailing software checks the main registry first. The main domain registry contains a reference to a registry for the subdomain. The subdomain registry serves the same purpose as a domain registry, providing information on all the computers in the subdomain.

Internet Numbers: Domain names and domain addresses are mostly for the benefit of humans. Computers refer to other computers on the Internet using numbers. The registries for each domain give the Internet number that is associated with each domain name, and using this number, one machine on the Internet can find another. Internet numbers are written as four three-digit numbers, as in `137.186.128.113`.

Most users will never have to worry about Internet numbers...we hope. However, to the people who keep the Internet going, Internet numbers loom large in their minds at the moment. I won't go into the technical details, but the net was set up with a finite range of possible numbers, and with so many computers joining up in recent years, the net is running out of numbers. Sometime in the near future, Internet must expand the range of numbers somehow. We'll cross our fingers that the transition goes smoothly.

Some Popular Domains

Here are few domain names you're likely to see as you get to know the Internet:

`com`	Commercial businesses; for example, the company MKS that provided the software for this book is `mks.com`.
`edu`	Educational institutions.
`gov`	Government agencies.
`mil`	Military computers.
`net`	Sites that perform some administrative function for the net. For example, the backbone sites for NSFnet usually belong to the `net` domain.
`org`	Organizations such as advocacy groups and nonprofit agencies.

In addition to these, almost every country has a domain, often with additional domains for states, provinces, or even individual cities. Remember that a domain simply tells which "phone book" to use when your software is trying to locate a site. It doesn't really matter which phone book you're in, as long as you're registered somewhere.

Getting Onto the Internet

Now that you know what "the net" is, you'll want to know how to get there. First, you'll need some means of linking your computer to others. Your connection will be your telephone line. Your computer can use a *modem* to place phone calls to other computers on the Internet.

A Few Words on Modems

A *modem* is a machine used in making phone calls between computers. The modem translates everything your computer "says" into a series of high-pitched whistles. (If you eavesdrop on a modem "conversation" it sounds like duelling canaries.) This whistling is a code for transmitting information and for checking that it has been received correctly. There's a modem handling the other end of your call, too. It translates the whistles back into computer data and sends that data to the computer you're phoning.

Classic modems used to look like shoeboxes plugged into your computer, with a padded nest on top where you put the phone receiver. Today many modems are built right into the machine. All you see is a length of telephone cord with a plug that snaps directly into the phone jack in your wall.

If you make any significant use of Internet, you'll end up shipping a *lot* of data over phone lines. Most people find it's worth it to spend a little extra money to buy a fast modem—for example, one that can ship up to 19,200 bits per second. The faster your modem, the less you pay in phone bills and in connection charges (the cost of connecting your system to the computer that serves as an intermediary between you and the Internet).

> **Baud Rate vs. BPS:** The speed at which a modem works is measured either as a *baud rate* or in *bits per second* (*bps*). Technically speaking, the baud rate is the number of times per second that the modem changes the "condition" of its communication line. For simple types of communication, the condition of the line changes with every bit sent, so the baud rate comes out to be the same as the number of bits transferred in a second; this leads some people to believe that baud rate means "bits per second." However, more sophisticated types of communication can transfer several bits of data with each change in the communication line, so the *bps* speed is higher than the baud rate. In this book, we always use *bps* to measure modem speed, since that's a more meaningful way to measure how much information is actually being transmitted.

Finding an Access Provider

Once you have a modem for your DOS machine, you'll need to find another computer that is already linked to the Internet and that will let you connect to the computer using UUCP. This means you have to find an *access provider.* Chapters 20 and 21 provide more details about contacting access providers and discussing their services.

B
Registering a Site Name

Many access providers will register your chosen site name on your behalf. If so, you should certainly let them do the work for you. They'll set up a *domain address* which is then made known to the Internet. This makes it possible for other users on the Internet to send you electronic mail.

If you have to register your site name without your access provider's help, you should send an e-mail message to the UUCP Mapping Project. In return, they'll send back an e-mail message that is basically a form for you to fill out. The form provides further instructions about the registration process.

To get this process started, simply send an e-mail message to the address

```
uucpmap@rutgers.edu
```

In response, you'll receive the registration form that contains instructions on how to continue with the registration process.

C

Login Sequences

When your computer connects with your access provider or any other site, your computer usually has to go through a *login* process. Chapter 3 describes the simplest type of login process: your computer identifies itself by stating its *Login ID*, and then proves its identity by supplying a *Password*.

Unfortunately, some access providers have more complicated login procedures. They may require your computer to provide additional information before or after it states its *Login ID* and *Password*. This appendix explains how to set up MKS Internet Anywhere to cope with these more complicated logins.

Setting Up a Login Sequence

To begin setting up the necessary login information, start the Control Center by double-clicking on the *Control Center* icon in the MKS Internet Anywhere application group. This displays a window that looks something like this:

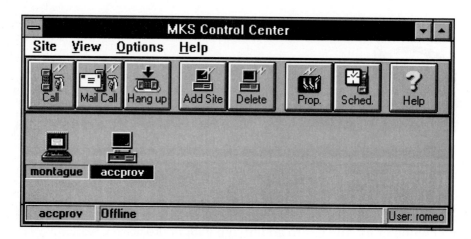

Once this window appears, follow these steps:

1. Click on the picture of the computer labeled with the site name of your access provider.

2. Click on the *Prop.* icon in the toolbar. (*Prop.* stands for *Properties*; this icon lets you set the properties of the connection to your access provider's site.) You'll see the following dialog box appear.

C: Login Sequences

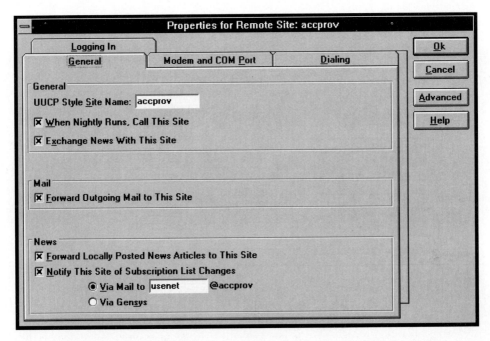

This window provides information about your connection to your access provider. For example, if you click on the *Modem and COM Port* tab, you'll see information about your modem.

The Login Sequence Box

Click on the *Logging In* tab of the dialog box on your screen. This displays the *Login Sequence Box*:

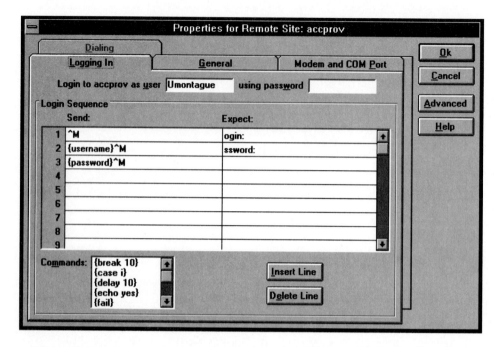

At the top of the box are blanks for a *username* and a *password* for identifying yourself to your access provider. Your access provider will tell you what name and password you should fill in here; if you use the prearranged connections with Rabbit or Portal, the first-time personalization program automatically sets up an appropriate name and password for you. (**Note:** this is a username for your *computer* not for you as a person. Your personal username is almost always different from your computer's username.)

Below the name and password are two lists: the *Send* list and the *Expect* list. In a normal login procedure, your computer sends the first line in the Send list, then waits to receive something that matches the first line in the Expect list. Then your computer sends the second line in the Send list, then waits to receive something that matches the second line in the Expect list. The process continues in the same way, back and forth, until your computer successfully establishes a connection with the other machine.

C: Login Sequences

To understand this process a little better, let's examine the lines of the above example:

`^M`
> The whole process starts with a line that says `^M`. This is a special code that stands for pressing the ENTER key. Thus, your computer starts everything by pressing ENTER.

`ogin:`
> The corresponding line in the Expect list is `ogin:`. Your computer quietly waits until the other computer sends these characters. The other computer may actually send a lot more than these characters; it might say any of

```
login:
Login:
Hello, hello, it's time to login:
```

> or anything else that ends in `ogin:`. The other computer may in fact send out several lines of text before getting around to the `ogin:` string of characters—that doesn't matter. Your computer won't do anything else until it sees `ogin:`.

`{username}^M`
> When your computer sees the expected string `ogin:`, it sends back your computer's *username*. You'll notice that this line ends in `^M` again, indicating that your computer presses ENTER after it has typed the username.

`ssword:`
> The corresponding line in the Expect list is `ssword:`. Normally, this will be a request for your computer to enter its password, as in

```
password:
Password:
Hey, buddy, gimme your password:
```

`{password}^M`
> Your computer replies with its password and presses ENTER again.

These steps make up the most common login sequence. If the actual process of connecting with your access provider is more complicated than this, you can add extra steps to cope with the complications.

For example, suppose that your access provider adds an extra step to the login process: after your computer has entered its Login ID and password, the access provider asks

```
Are you running MKS Internet Anywhere? (Yes or No)
```

Naturally, your computer should answer `Yes` to this question. Therefore, in the Expect list, you might add the entry

```
(Yes or No)
```

indicating that you expect to see a question that ends with those characters. Then in the Send list, you'd add the entry

```
Yes^M
```

to answer `Yes` to the question. Note that you put the notation `^M` after `Yes` to stand for pressing ENTER. You type this notation simply by typing the `^` character, then `M`; you don't actually press ENTER when you're filling in the entry.

> **Upper Case vs. Lower Case:** In the Expect list, you must specify characters exactly as your access provider's computer will send them, including the case of letters. For example, if the Expect list says `Login:` but the other computer sends `login:`, the two character strings don't match. This is why the standard Expect list only writes `ogin:`. That way it doesn't matter if the first letter in the string is `L` or `l`.

With the above additions to the Expect and Send lists, you'll get the following login sequence:

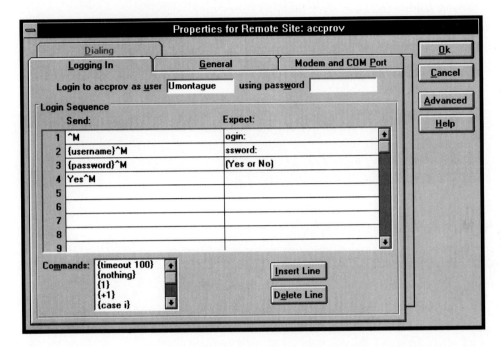

In a similar way, you can modify the Send and Expect lists to cope with any of your access provider's requirements. If you have to add a line before the ones that are already shown, click on the top line in the Send or Expect list and push the *Insert line* button. Similarly, click on the *Delete line* button to delete a line from both lists.

The *Commands* listed in the bottom left corner of the screen are used for special purposes. Consult the on-line help facilities for more information.

D Hints on Netiquette

This appendix offers a few suggestions on how to get along with your fellow Internet users. These tips particularly apply to posting Usenet news articles, since your articles may be read by thousands of strangers, some of whom are likely to take offense at the least provocation.

Mail messages are less of a problem, since you're only writing for a few readers, and often to people you know. However, it's still possible to make a bad impression if you don't pay attention to the niceties of computer communication.

Tone of Voice

News articles and mail messages are just lines of text on the screen. You can't use your tone of voice to indicate when you're completely serious or just joking…and neither can anyone else. Therefore, it's common for people to take harmless little jokes the wrong way.

> **Hint 1:** Be extremely careful when making a joke, or even a slightly sarcastic remark. Readers often can't tell when you're kidding, and they may get upset.

It's also easy to assume that your readers are much like yourself. This simply isn't true. Usenet reaches all around the world, to people in widely different circumstances. Many readers do not speak English as their first language; others hold cultural and political views different from your own, and may be actively hostile toward the things you hold precious.

> **Hint 2:** Be diplomatic, and remember that the Internet connects with people in every country, in all walks of life.

No matter how much you respect the diversity of the Internet, you may find yourself on the receiving end of a torrent of abuse; in any large enough group of people there's always someone who likes to pick fights, and the Internet community is a *huge* group of people.

Verbal assaults in Usenet news articles are called *flames*. A *flame war* is a back-and-forth series of angry news articles, usually accelerating in hostility. As in most wars, both sides usually lose; in this case, they lose the respect of other Usenet readers. No one remembers who started the war—they just remember how petty the participants were.

If someone attacks you in a newsgroup, keep your cool and try not to let it upset you. Ask yourself if you have to respond at all. If you decide that you must reply to a flame, do so as calmly and rationally as possible. The last thing you want is a worldwide reputation as a childish hothead.

> **Hint 3:** Be gracious under fire. Prove to other readers that you have more class than the person attacking you.

Smiley Symbols

Some people embellish their news articles with little marks to indicate when they're joking. They hope that these marks will prevent other readers from taking the jokes as serious comments. The classical "I'm joking" signal is

```
        :-)
```

This is called a *smiley* because it's a sideways version of a smiling face (eyes, nose, and smiling mouth). For example, you might see

```
   I think all cat owners should be shot.
        :-)
```

The smiley is supposed to indicate that the writer is not really serious about the preceding statement. Other versions of the smiley include:

;-)	A winking face
:-(	An unhappy face
:-o	A surprised or frightened face

You'll probably see many other variations on the same theme; some newsgroups hold contests to collect new smiley symbols.

The problem with smiley symbols is that they aren't very effective. First of all, they're easy to ignore—after you get used to them, your eye skips right over them. Secondly, some people mistakenly think that a smiley "makes everything better." For example, they may insult your mother, your car, and your taste in music, then put a smiley on the end, as if that lets them get away with all the preceding rudeness.

For all these reasons, you shouldn't depend on smileys to get you out of trouble. It's better to say what you mean clearly and rationally than to fix things with smileys after the fact.

> **Hint 4:** Smileys don't really hurt, but they usually don't help either.

Reducing Congestion

There are now more than two million computers connected to the Internet, and the number increases every day. Some of those computers do not receive Usenet news, but a good percentage of them do. This means that any article you post may be sent to, say, a million machines all over the world. If that's true, each and every character in your article takes up a megabyte of disk space worldwide, and an average article takes up hundreds or even thousands of megabytes on other people's disks.

Think about that every time you're tempted to post a news article. Don't let it intimidate you—you have as much right to use the Internet as anyone else—but avoid wasting other people's time and resources with trivialities.

For example, suppose you post an article asking a question and someone responds with another article giving an answer. **Don't** post an article saying thank you—that's not polite, that's a gigantic waste of other people's time and disk space. If you're really overflowing with gratitude, send an E-mail message saying thank you...but even that isn't usually necessary.

> **Hint 5:** Don't post an article unless it's genuinely important to you or to the newsgroup readership as a whole.

Other Tips

Here's a grab-bag of other tips you might find useful when posting.

- In newsgroups that discuss movies, books, or similar works, you may notice articles marked with the word `Spoiler`, either in the *Subject* line or at the beginning of the article. This means that the article gives away details of the plot that may spoil the surprise for people who haven't yet seen the movie or read the book. If you post this kind of article, you should do the same thing and display the word `Spoiler` or `Spoiler warning` before you start discussing such things; it's only polite.

- Usenet can be a wonderful place for teenagers to discuss issues of their own interest, but parents should keep an eye on what their children are reading. The concern is not just that young people may be exposed to "naughty" things (although there are plenty of newsgroups devoted to explicit sexual practices, anti-religious diatribes, drugs, and other topics that sections of the populace may find offensive). There are also newsgroups like *rec.pyrotechnics* which tell how to make explosives in the home...groups that distribute information that is downright dangerous, especially in the hands of adolescents. Be warned, and handle the situation with tact.

- Usenet has developed a number of short forms for common phrases. Here are a few:

IMHO	In my humble opinion
RSN	Real soon now (usually meant sarcastically)
BTW	By the way
RTFM	Read the @&#$ing manual (addressed to people who ask questions about a product when the questions are answered clearly in the product's documentation)
Lurker	A person who reads a newsgroup but never contributes to discussions in it

The Most Important Principle: Any news articles you post may be read by colleagues, friends, current or future employers, and other people whose opinions will affect your life. Conduct yourself accordingly.

E

Debugging the Configuration

This appendix suggests things you can do if you set up a connection to another computer but the connection doesn't work.

First Things First

Before you worry about more complicated things, check easy things first:

- Is your modem correctly plugged into an appropriate phone jack?

- If you connect an ordinary phone into the jack, do you get a dial tone?

- If you have other communications software that uses the same modem, does that software work? If it doesn't, there's a good chance your modem isn't properly connected to your computer.

Setup Information

If you don't find any problems after checking the easy things listed above, check the setup information for your access provider. To do this, you have to start the Control Center program by double-clicking on the Control Cen-

ter icon in the MKS Internet Anywhere application group. This displays
the Control Center window, which looks something like this:

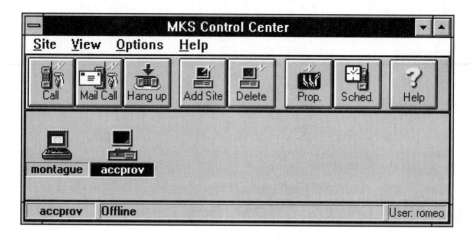

To check the setup information for your access provider, click on the computer picture that is labeled with the name of your access provider. Then
click on the *Prop.* (Properties) icon; this displays the Site Configuration
dialog box.

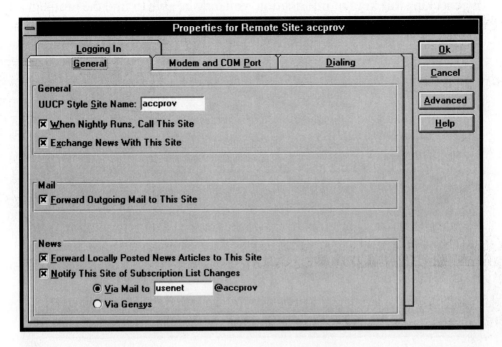

Check all the information entered in the dialog box against the information given to you by the other site. For example, if you can't connect to your chosen Internet access provider, check the information in the Site Configuration dialog box against the information provided by your provider.

- Do you have the right phone number? To check the phone number, click on the *Dialing* tab in the Site Configuration dialog box.

- Have you typed the login username and password *exactly* the way they were given to you? Remember that it matters whether letters are in upper or lower case. To check on the username and password, click on the *Logging In* tab in the Site Configuration dialog box.

- Have you set the modem type to your brand of modem? To check on the modem type, click on the *Modem and COM Port* tab in the Site Configuration dialog box.

By checking this kind of information, you may be able to find the problem. If not, contact your access provider to double-check that you got everything right. Also, consult the on-line help to obtain further suggestions for solving problems.

The Debug Window

If you've checked all the easy things and they look okay, it's time to dig deeper to see what's going on.

From the Site Configuration dialog box, click on *Ok* to return to the Control Center window. Then, pull down the *View* menu and choose the *Debug Messages* entry. This displays the *Debug window*.

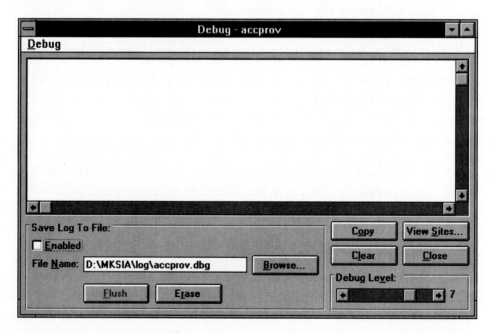

The Debug window displays all attempted interactions between your computer and your access provider. To see how this works, click on the *View*

Sites button (which returns to the Control Center window) and then click
on the *Call* icon in the Control Center window. This tells your computer to
try to call your access provider. As the software tries to make the connection, you'll see the interactions appear in the Debug window, as in:

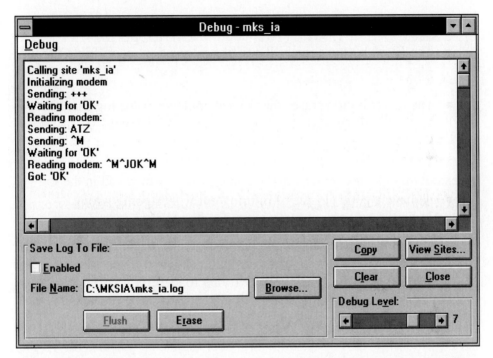

By examining the interactions, you may see what's going wrong. (You'll
probably have to consult your modem manual to understand the various
instructions that the software sends to the modem.)

Logging the Interaction

You'll notice that the Debug window contains an area labeled *Save Log To
File*. This lets you use a file to record the interactions that appear on the
Debug Screen. A file containing such records is called a *log file*.

The Debug window already contains a suggested name for this log file. If you prefer to save interactions in a different file, enter the name of the file in the space provided or click on *Browse* to locate an appropriate file. Once you have chosen the name of the log file, click on the *Enable* box to start recording interactions in the file.

You'll notice that there are two buttons beside the *Enable* box:

- The *Flush* button copies all existing interaction records into the log file.

- The *Erase* button erases the current contents of the log file. Obviously, you don't want to use this button if the log file contains information you want to keep.

By examining the interactions in the Debug window or saved in the log file, you'll have a good chance of figuring out what's going wrong.

> **Note:** Using the Debug window will make the software run considerably slower. Therefore, you should only use the Debug facilities when you are trying to identify the source of a problem; you shouldn't use the Debug window if everything is working correctly.

 *A List of Usenet Newsgroups*

This appendix lists of some of the currently active Usenet newsgroups as of April 1, 1994; the list was prepared by Gene Spafford and David C. Lawrence, and sent out in the *news.groups* newsgroup. It will certainly be out of date by the time you purchase this book, but it should give you an idea of what sort of Usenet newsgroups are available.

This list does not include any groups in the *alt* hierarchy. The *alt* hierarchy is almost as big as all the other hierarchies put together, and much more subject to change.

The comp Hierarchy

The *comp* hierarchy contains newsgroups devoted to computers and issues in the computing industry.

comp.admin.policy
  Discussions of site administration policies.

comp.ai
  Artificial intelligence discussions.

comp.ai.fuzzy
  Fuzzy set theory, aka fuzzy logic.

comp.ai.genetic
> Genetic algorithms in computing.

comp.ai.jair.announce
> Announcements and abstracts of the Journal of AI Research. (Moderated)

comp.ai.jair.papers
> Papers published by the Journal of AI Research. (Moderated)

comp.ai.nat-lang
> Natural-language processing by computers.

comp.ai.neural-nets
> All aspects of neural networks.

comp.ai.nlang-know-rep
> Natural Language and Knowledge Representation. (Moderated)

comp.ai.philosophy
> Philosophical aspects of artificial intelligence.

comp.ai.shells
> Artificial intelligence applied to shells.

comp.answers
> Repository for periodic Usenet articles. (Moderated)

comp.apps.spreadsheets
> Spreadsheets on various platforms.

comp.arch
> Computer architecture.

comp.arch.bus.vmebus
> Hardware and software for VMEbus systems.

comp.arch.storage
Storage system issues, both hardware and software.

comp.archives
Descriptions of public access archives. (Moderated)

comp.archives.admin
Issues relating to computer archive administration.

comp.archives.msdos.announce
Announcements about MSDOS archives. (Moderated)

comp.archives.msdos.d
Discussion of materials available in MSDOS archives.

comp.bbs.misc
All aspects of computer bulletin board systems.

comp.bbs.tbbs
The Bread Board System bulletin board software.

comp.bbs.waffle
The Waffle BBS and Usenet system on all platforms.

comp.benchmarks
Discussion of benchmarking techniques and results.

comp.binaries.acorn
Binary-only postings for Acorn machines. (Moderated)

comp.binaries.amiga
Encoded public domain programs in binary. (Moderated)

comp.binaries.apple2
Binary-only postings for the Apple II computer.

comp.binaries.atari.st
> Binary-only postings for the Atari ST. (Moderated)

comp.binaries.cbm
> For the transfer of 8-bit Commodore binaries. (Moderated)

comp.binaries.geos
> Binaries for the GEOS operating system. (Moderated)

comp.binaries.ibm.pc
> Binary-only postings for IBM PC/MS-DOS. (Moderated)

comp.binaries.ibm.pc.d
> Discussions about IBM/PC binary postings.

comp.binaries.ibm.pc.wanted
> Requests for IBM PC and compatible programs.

comp.binaries.mac
> Encoded Macintosh programs in binary. (Moderated)

comp.binaries.ms-windows
> Binary programs for Microsoft Windows. (Moderated)

comp.binaries.newton
> Apple Newton binaries, sources, books, and so on. (Moderated)

comp.binaries.os2
> Binaries for use under the OS/2 ABI. (Moderated)

comp.bugs.2bsd
> Reports of UNIX version 2BSD related bugs.

comp.bugs.4bsd
> Reports of UNIX version 4BSD related bugs.

comp.bugs.4bsd.ucb-fixes
    Bug reports/fixes for BSD UNIX. (Moderated)

comp.bugs.misc
    General UNIX bug reports and fixes (including V7 and uucp).

comp.bugs.sys5
    Reports of USG (System III, V, etc.) bugs.

comp.cad.cadence
    Users of Cadence Design Systems products.

comp.cad.compass
    Compass Design Automation EDA tools.

comp.cad.pro-engineer
    Parametric Technology's Pro/Engineer design package.

comp.cad.synthesis
    Research and production in the field of logic synthesis.

comp.client-server
    Topics relating to client/server technology.

comp.cog-eng
    Cognitive engineering.

comp.compilers
    Compiler construction, theory, and so on. (Moderated)

comp.compression
    Data compression algorithms and theory.

comp.compression.research
    Discussions about data compression research. (Moderated)

comp.constraints
>   Constraint processing and related topics.

comp.databases
>   Database and data management issues and theory.

comp.databases.informix
>   Informix database management software discussions.

comp.databases.ingres
>   Issues relating to INGRES products.

comp.databases.ms-access
>   MS Windows' relational database system, Access.

comp.databases.object
>   Object-oriented paradigms in database systems.

comp.databases.oracle
>   The SQL database products of the Oracle Corporation.

comp.databases.paradox
>   Borland's database for DOS and MS Windows.

comp.databases.pick
>   Pick-like, post-relational database systems.

comp.databases.rdb
>   The relational database engine RDB from DEC.

comp.databases.sybase
>   Implementations of the SQL Server.

comp.databases.theory
>   Discussing advances in database technology.

comp.databases.xbase.fox
    Fox Software's xBase system and compatibles.

comp.databases.xbase.misc
    Discussion of xBase (dBASE-like) products.

comp.dcom.cell-relay
    Forum for discussion of Cell Relay-based products.

comp.dcom.fax
    Fax hardware, software, and protocols.

comp.dcom.isdn
    The Integrated Services Digital Network (ISDN).

comp.dcom.lans.ethernet
    Discussions of the Ethernet/IEEE 802.3 protocols.

comp.dcom.lans.fddi
    Discussions of the FDDI protocol suite.

comp.dcom.lans.misc
    Local area network hardware and software.

comp.dcom.lans.token-ring
    Installing and using token ring networks.

comp.dcom.modems
    Data communications hardware and software.

comp.dcom.servers
    Selecting and operating data communications servers.

comp.dcom.sys.cisco
   Info on Cisco routers and bridges.

comp.dcom.sys.wellfleet
   Wellfleet bridge and router systems, hardware and software.

comp.dcom.telecom
   Telecommunications digest. (Moderated)

comp.dcom.telecom.tech
   Discussion of technical aspects of telephony.

comp.doc
   Archived public-domain documentation. (Moderated)

comp.doc.techreports
   Lists of technical reports. (Moderated)

comp.dsp
   Digital signal processing using computers.

comp.edu
   Computer science education.

comp.emacs
   EMACS editors of different flavors.

comp.fonts
   Typefonts—design, conversion, use, and so on.

comp.graphics
   Computer graphics, art, animation, and image processing.

comp.graphics.algorithms
  Algorithms used in producing computer graphics.

comp.graphics.animation
  Technical aspects of computer animation.

comp.graphics.avs
  The Application Visualization System.

comp.graphics.data-explorer
  IBM's Visualization Data Explorer, aka DX.

comp.graphics.explorer
  The Explorer Modular Visualisation Environment (MVE).

comp.graphics.gnuplot
  The GNUPLOT interactive function plotter.

comp.graphics.opengl
  The OpenGL 3D application programming interface.

comp.graphics.raytracing
  Ray-tracing software, tools, and methods.

comp.graphics.research
  Highly technical computer graphics discussion. (Moderated)

comp.graphics.visualization
  Info on scientific visualization.

comp.groupware
  Software and hardware for shared interactive environments.

comp.home.misc
> Media, technology, and information in domestic spaces. (Moderated)

comp.human-factors
> Issues related to human-computer interaction (HCI).

comp.infosystems
> Any discussion about information systems.

comp.infosystems.announce
> Announcements of internet information services. (Moderated)

comp.infosystems.gis
> All aspects of geographic information systems.

comp.infosystems.gopher
> Discussion of the Gopher information service.

comp.infosystems.interpedia
> The Internet Encyclopedia.

comp.infosystems.wais
> The Z39.50-based WAIS full-text search system.

comp.infosystems.www
> The World Wide Web information system.

comp.internet.library
> Discussing electronic libraries. (Moderated)

comp.ivideodisc
> Interactive videodiscs—uses, potential, and so on.

comp.lang.ada
>   Discussion about Ada.

comp.lang.apl
>   Discussion about APL.

comp.lang.basic.misc
>   Other dialects and aspects of BASIC.

comp.lang.basic.visual
>   Microsoft Visual Basic and App Basic; Windows and DOS.

comp.lang.c
>   Discussion about C.

comp.lang.c++
>   The object-oriented C++ language.

comp.lang.clos
>   Common Lisp Object System discussions.

comp.lang.dylan
>   For discussion of the Dylan language.

comp.lang.eiffel
>   The object-oriented Eiffel language.

comp.lang.forth
>   Discussion about Forth.

comp.lang.fortran
>   Discussion about FORTRAN.

comp.lang.functional
Discussion about functional languages.

comp.lang.hermes
The Hermes language for distributed applications.

comp.lang.idl-pvwave
IDL and PV-Wave language discussions.

comp.lang.lisp
Discussion about LISP.

comp.lang.lisp.mcl
Discussing Apple's Macintosh Common Lisp.

comp.lang.logo
The Logo teaching and learning language.

comp.lang.misc
Different computer languages not specifically listed.

comp.lang.ml
ML languages including Standard ML, CAML, Lazy ML, and so on. (Moderated)

comp.lang.modula2
Discussion about Modula-2.

comp.lang.modula3
Discussion about the Modula-3 language.

comp.lang.oberon
The Oberon language and system.

comp.lang.objective-c
  The Objective-C language and environment.

comp.lang.pascal
  Discussion about Pascal.

comp.lang.perl
  Discussion of Larry Wall's Perl system.

comp.lang.pop
  Pop11 and the Plug user group.

comp.lang.postscript
  The PostScript Page Description Language.

comp.lang.prograph
  Prograph, a visual object-oriented dataflow language.

comp.lang.prolog
  Discussion about PROLOG.

comp.lang.python
  The Python computer language.

comp.lang.sather
  The object-oriented computer language Sather.

comp.lang.scheme
  The Scheme Programming language.

comp.lang.sigplan
  Info and announcements from ACM SIGPLAN. (Moderated)

comp.lang.smalltalk
> Discussion about Smalltalk 80.

comp.lang.tcl
> The Tcl programming language and related tools.

comp.lang.verilog
> Discussing Verilog and PLI.

comp.lang.vhdl
> VHSIC Hardware Description Language, IEEE 1076/87.

comp.laser-printers
> Laser printers, hardware and software. (Moderated)

comp.lsi
> Large-scale integrated circuits.

comp.lsi.testing
> Testing of electronic circuits.

comp.mail.elm
> Discussion and fixes for the ELM mail system.

comp.mail.headers
> Gatewayed from the Internet header-people list.

comp.mail.maps
> Various maps, including UUCP maps. (Moderated)

comp.mail.mh
> The UCI version of the Rand Message Handling system.

comp.mail.mime
>Multipurpose Internet Mail Extensions of RFC 1341.

comp.mail.misc
>General discussions about computer mail.

comp.mail.mush
>The Mail User's Shell (MUSH).

comp.mail.sendmail
>Configuring and using the BSD sendmail agent.

comp.mail.uucp
>Mail in the uucp network environment.

comp.misc
>General topics about computers not covered elsewhere.

comp.multimedia
>Interactive multimedia technologies of all kinds.

comp.newprod
>Announcements of new products of interest. (Moderated)

comp.object
>Object-oriented programming and languages.

comp.object.logic
>Integrating object-oriented and logic programming.

comp.org.acm
>Topics about the Association for Computing Machinery.

comp.org.decus
>Digital Equipment Computer Users' Society newsgroup.

comp.org.eff.news
>News from the Electronic Frontier Foundation. (Moderated)

comp.org.eff.talk
>Discussion of EFF goals, strategies, and so on.

comp.org.fidonet
>FidoNews digest, official news of FidoNet Association. (Moderated)

comp.org.ieee
>Issues and announcements about the IEEE and its members.

comp.org.issnnet
>The International Student Society for Neural Networks.

comp.org.lisp-users
>Association of Lisp Users related discussions.

comp.org.sug
>Talk about/for the Sun User's Group.

comp.org.usenix
>USENIX Association events and announcements.

comp.org.usenix.roomshare
>Finding lodging during Usenix conferences.

comp.os.386bsd.announce
>Announcements relating to the 386bsd operating system. (Moderated)

comp.os.386bsd.apps
  Applications that run under 386bsd.

comp.os.386bsd.bugs
  Bugs and fixes for the 386bsd OS and its clients.

comp.os.386bsd.development
  Working on 386bsd internals.

comp.os.386bsd.misc
  General aspects of 386bsd not covered by other groups.

comp.os.386bsd.questions
  General questions about 386bsd.

comp.os.coherent
  Discussion and support of the Coherent operating system.

comp.os.cpm
  Discussion about the CP/M operating system.

comp.os.geos
  The GEOS operating system by GeoWorks for PC clones.

comp.os.linux.admin
  Installing and administering Linux systems.

comp.os.linux.announce
  Announcements important to the Linux community. (Moderated)

comp.os.linux.development
  Ongoing work on the Linux operating system.

comp.os.linux.help
Questions and advice about Linux.

comp.os.linux.misc
Linux-specific topics not covered by other groups.

comp.os.lynx
Discussion of LynxOS and Lynx Real-Time Systems.

comp.os.mach
The MACH OS from CMU and other places.

comp.os.minix
Discussion of Tanenbaum's MINIX system.

comp.os.misc
General OS-oriented discussion not carried elsewhere.

comp.os.ms-windows.advocacy
Speculation and debate about Microsoft Windows.

comp.os.ms-windows.announce
Announcements relating to Windows. (Moderated)

comp.os.ms-windows.apps
Applications in the Windows environment.

comp.os.ms-windows.misc
General discussions about Windows issues.

comp.os.ms-windows.nt.misc
General discussion about Windows NT.

comp.os.ms-windows.nt.setup
    Configuring Windows NT systems.

comp.os.ms-windows.programmer.misc
    Programming Microsoft Windows.

comp.os.ms-windows.programmer.tools
    Development tools in Windows.

comp.os.ms-windows.programmer.win32
    32-bit Windows programming interfaces.

comp.os.ms-windows.setup
    Installing and configuring Microsoft Windows.

comp.os.msdos.apps
    Discussion of applications that run under MS-DOS.

comp.os.msdos.desqview
    QuarterDeck's Desqview and related products.

comp.os.msdos.mail-news
    Administering mail and network news systems under MS-DOS.

comp.os.msdos.misc
    Miscellaneous topics about MS-DOS machines.

comp.os.msdos.pcgeos
    GeoWorks PC/GEOS and PC/GEOS-based packages.

comp.os.msdos.programmer
    Programming MS-DOS machines.

comp.os.msdos.programmer.turbovision
Borland's text application libraries.

comp.os.os2.advocacy
Supporting and flaming OS/2.

comp.os.os2.announce
Notable news and announcements related to OS/2. (Moderated)

comp.os.os2.apps
Discussions of applications under OS/2.

comp.os.os2.beta
All aspects of beta releases of OS/2 systems software.

comp.os.os2.bugs
OS/2 system bug reports, fixes and work-arounds.

comp.os.os2.games
Running games under OS/2.

comp.os.os2.misc
Miscellaneous topics about the OS/2 system.

comp.os.os2.multimedia
Multimedia on OS/2 systems.

comp.os.os2.networking
Networking in OS/2 environments.

comp.os.os2.networking.misc
Miscellaneous networking issues of OS/2.

comp.os.os2.networking.tcp-ip
    TCP/IP under OS/2.

comp.os.os2.programmer.misc
    Programming OS/2 machines.

comp.os.os2.programmer.oop
    Programming system objects (SOM, WPS, etc).

comp.os.os2.programmer.porting
    Porting software to OS/2 machines.

comp.os.os2.programmer.tools
    Compilers, assemblers, and interpreters under OS/2.

comp.os.os2.setup
    Installing and configuring OS/2 systems.

comp.os.os2.ver1x
    All aspects of OS/2 versions 1.0 through 1.3.

comp.os.os9
    Discussions about the os9 operating system.

comp.os.qnx
    Using and developing under the QNX operating system.

comp.os.research
    Operating systems and related areas. (Moderated)

comp.os.vms
    DEC's VAX line of computers and VMS.

comp.os.vxworks
  The VxWorks real-time operating system.

comp.os.xinu
  The XINU operating system from Purdue (D. Comer).

comp.parallel
  Massively parallel hardware/software. (Moderated)

comp.parallel.pvm
  The PVM system of multicomputer parallelization.

comp.patents
  Discussing patents of computer technology. (Moderated)

comp.periphs
  Peripheral devices.

comp.periphs.scsi
  Discussion of SCSI-based peripheral devices.

comp.programming
  Programming issues that transcend languages and OSs.

comp.programming.literate
  Literate programs and programming tools.

comp.protocols.appletalk
  Applebus hardware and software.

comp.protocols.dicom
  Digital Imaging and Communications in Medicine.

F: A List of Usenet Newsgroups

comp.protocols.ibm
   Networking with IBM mainframes.

comp.protocols.iso
   The ISO protocol stack.

comp.protocols.kerberos
   The Kerberos authentication server.

comp.protocols.kermit
   Info about the Kermit package. (Moderated)

comp.protocols.misc
   Various forms and types of protocol.

comp.protocols.nfs
   Discussion about the Network File System protocol.

comp.protocols.ppp
   Discussion of the Internet Point to Point Protocol.

comp.protocols.tcp-ip
   TCP and IP network protocols.

comp.protocols.tcp-ip.ibmpc
   TCP/IP for IBM(-like) personal computers.

comp.publish.cdrom.hardware
   Hardware used in publishing with CD-ROM.

comp.publish.cdrom.multimedia
   Software for multimedia authoring and publishing.

comp.publish.cdrom.software
> Software used in publishing with CD-ROM.

comp.realtime
> Issues related to real-time computing.

comp.research.japan
> The nature of research in Japan. (Moderated)

comp.risks
> Risks to the public from computers and users. (Moderated)

comp.robotics
> All aspects of robots and their applications.

comp.security.misc
> Security issues of computers and networks.

comp.security.unix
> Discussion of Unix security.

comp.simulation
> Simulation methods, problems, and uses. (Moderated)

comp.society
> The impact of technology on society. (Moderated)

comp.society.cu-digest
> The Computer Underground Digest. (Moderated)

comp.society.development
> Computer technology in developing countries.

comp.society.folklore
>Computer folklore and culture, past and present. (Moderated)

comp.society.futures
>Events in technology affecting future computing.

comp.society.privacy
>Effects of technology on privacy. (Moderated)

comp.soft-sys.khoros
>The Khoros X11 visualization system.

comp.soft-sys.matlab
>The MathWorks calculation and visualization package.

comp.soft-sys.powerbuilder
>Application development tools from PowerSoft.

comp.soft-sys.sas
>The SAS statistics package.

comp.soft-sys.shazam
>The SHAZAM econometrics computer program.

comp.soft-sys.spss
>The SPSS statistics package.

comp.soft-sys.wavefront
>Wavefront software products, problems, and so on.

comp.software-eng
>Software Engineering and related topics.

comp.software.config-mgmt
    Configuration management, tools, and procedures.

comp.software.licensing
    Software licensing technology.

comp.software.testing
    All aspects of testing computer systems.

comp.sources.3b1
    Source-code-only postings for the AT&T 3b1. (Moderated)

comp.sources.acorn
    Source-code-only postings for the Acorn. (Moderated)

comp.sources.amiga
    Source-code-only postings for the Amiga. (Moderated)

comp.sources.apple2
    Source code and discussion for the Apple2. (Moderated)

comp.sources.atari.st
    Source-code-only postings for the Atari ST. (Moderated)

comp.sources.bugs
    Bug reports, fixes, and discussion for posted sources.

comp.sources.d
    For any discussion of source postings.

comp.sources.games
    Postings of recreational software. (Moderated)

comp.sources.games.bugs
    Bug reports and fixes for posted game software.

comp.sources.hp48
    Programs for the HP48 and HP28 calculators. (Moderated)

comp.sources.mac
    Software for the Apple Macintosh. (Moderated)

comp.sources.misc
    Posting of software. (Moderated)

comp.sources.postscript
    Source code for programs written in PostScript. (Moderated)

comp.sources.reviewed
    Source code evaluated by peer review. (Moderated)

comp.sources.sun
    Software for Sun workstations. (Moderated)

comp.sources.testers
    Finding people to test software.

comp.sources.unix
    Postings of complete, UNIX-oriented sources. (Moderated)

comp.sources.wanted
    Requests for software and fixes.

comp.sources.x
    Software for the X windows system. (Moderated)

comp.specification
Languages and methodologies for formal specification.

comp.specification.z
Discussion about the formal specification notation Z.

comp.speech
Research and applications in speech science and technology.

comp.std.c
Discussion about C language standards.

comp.std.c++
Discussion about the C++ language and library standards.

comp.std.internat
Discussion about international standards.

comp.std.lisp
User group (ALU) supported standards. (Moderated)

comp.std.misc
Discussion about various standards.

comp.std.mumps
Discussion for the X11.1 committee on Mumps. (Moderated)

comp.std.unix
Discussion for the P1003 committee on UNIX. (Moderated)

comp.std.wireless
Examining standards for wireless network technology. (Moderated)

comp.sw.components
Software components and related technology.

comp.sys.3b1
Discussion and support of AT&T 7300/3B1/UnixPC.

comp.sys.acorn
Discussion on Acorn and ARM-based computers.

comp.sys.acorn.advocacy
Why Acorn computers and programs are better.

comp.sys.acorn.announce
Announcements for Acorn and ARM users. (Moderated)

comp.sys.acorn.tech
Software and hardware aspects of Acorn and ARM products.

comp.sys.alliant
Info and discussion about Alliant computers.

comp.sys.amiga.advocacy
Why an Amiga is better than XYZ.

comp.sys.amiga.announce
Announcements about the Amiga. (Moderated)

comp.sys.amiga.applications
Miscellaneous applications.

comp.sys.amiga.audio
Music, MIDI, speech synthesis, and other sounds.

comp.sys.amiga.datacomm
> Methods of getting bytes in and out.

comp.sys.amiga.emulations
> Various hardware and software emulators.

comp.sys.amiga.games
> Discussion of games for the Commodore Amiga.

comp.sys.amiga.graphics
> Charts, graphs, pictures, and so on.

comp.sys.amiga.hardware
> Amiga computer hardware, Q&A, reviews, and so on.

comp.sys.amiga.introduction
> Group for newcomers to Amigas.

comp.sys.amiga.marketplace
> Where to find it, prices, and so on.

comp.sys.amiga.misc
> Discussions not falling in another Amiga group.

comp.sys.amiga.multimedia
> Animations, video, and multimedia.

comp.sys.amiga.programmer
> Developers and hobbyists discuss code.

comp.sys.amiga.reviews
> Reviews of Amiga software and hardware. (Moderated)

comp.sys.apollo
> Apollo computer systems.

comp.sys.apple2
> Discussion about Apple II micros.

comp.sys.apple2.comm
> Apple II data communications.

comp.sys.apple2.gno
> The AppleIIgs GNO multitasking environment.

comp.sys.apple2.marketplace
> Buying, selling, and trading Apple II equipment.

comp.sys.apple2.programmer
> Programming on the Apple II.

comp.sys.apple2.usergroups
> All about Apple II user groups.

comp.sys.atari.8bit
> Discussion about 8-bit Atari micros.

comp.sys.atari.advocacy
> Attacking and defending Atari computers.

comp.sys.atari.st
> Discussion about 16-bit Atari micros.

comp.sys.atari.st.tech
> Technical discussions of Atari ST hard/software.

comp.sys.att
> Discussions about AT&T microcomputers.

comp.sys.cbm
> Discussion about Commodore micros.

comp.sys.concurrent
> The Concurrent/Masscomp line of computers. (Moderated)

comp.sys.convex
> Convex computer systems, hardware and software.

comp.sys.dec
> Discussions about DEC computer systems.

comp.sys.dec.micro
> DEC Micros (Rainbow, Professional 350/380)

comp.sys.encore
> Encore's MultiMax computers.

comp.sys.harris
> Harris computer systems, especially real-time systems.

comp.sys.hp.apps
> Discussion of software and apps on all HP platforms.

comp.sys.hp.hardware
> Discussion of Hewlett Packard system hardware.

comp.sys.hp.hpux
> Issues pertaining to HP-UX and 9000 series computers.

comp.sys.hp.misc
    Issues not covered in any other comp.sys.hp group.

comp.sys.hp.mpe
    Issues pertaining to MPE and 3000 series computers.

comp.sys.hp48
    Hewlett-Packard's HP48 and HP28 calculators.

comp.sys.ibm.pc.demos
    Demonstration programs that showcase programmer skill.

comp.sys.ibm.pc.digest
    The IBM PC, PC-XT, and PC-AT. (Moderated)

comp.sys.ibm.pc.games.action
    Arcade-style games on PCs.

comp.sys.ibm.pc.games.adventure
    Adventure (non-rpg) games on PCs.

comp.sys.ibm.pc.games.announce
    Announcements for all PC gamers. (Moderated)

comp.sys.ibm.pc.games.flight-sim
    Flight simulators on PCs.

comp.sys.ibm.pc.games.misc
    Games not covered by other PC groups.

comp.sys.ibm.pc.games.rpg
    Role-playing games on the PC.

comp.sys.ibm.pc.games.strategic
>   Strategy/planning games on PCs.

comp.sys.ibm.pc.hardware.cd-rom
>   CD-ROM drives and interfaces for the PC.

comp.sys.ibm.pc.hardware.chips
>   Processor, cache, memory chips, and so on.

comp.sys.ibm.pc.hardware.comm
>   Modems and communication cards for the PC.

comp.sys.ibm.pc.hardware.misc
>   Miscellaneous PC hardware topics.

comp.sys.ibm.pc.hardware.networking
>   Network hardware and equipment for the PC.

comp.sys.ibm.pc.hardware.storage
>   Hard drives and other PC storage devices.

comp.sys.ibm.pc.hardware.systems
>   Whole IBM PC computer and clone systems.

comp.sys.ibm.pc.hardware.video
>   Video cards and monitors for the PC.

comp.sys.ibm.pc.misc
>   Discussion about IBM personal computers.

comp.sys.ibm.pc.rt
>   Topics related to IBM's RT computer.

comp.sys.ibm.pc.soundcard
    Hardware and software aspects of PC sound cards.

comp.sys.ibm.ps2.hardware
    Microchannel hardware, any vendor.

comp.sys.intel
    Discussions about Intel systems and parts.

comp.sys.isis
    The ISIS distributed system from Cornell.

comp.sys.laptops
    Laptop (portable) computers.

comp.sys.m6809
    Discussion about 6809s.

comp.sys.m68k
    Discussion about 6800s.

comp.sys.m68k.pc
    Discussion about 6800-based PCs. (Moderated)

comp.sys.m88k
    Discussion about 8800-based computers.

comp.sys.mac.advocacy
    The Macintosh computer family compared to others.

comp.sys.mac.announce
    Important notices for Macintosh users. (Moderated)

comp.sys.mac.apps
 Discussions of Macintosh applications.

comp.sys.mac.comm
 Discussion of Macintosh communications.

comp.sys.mac.databases
 Database systems for the Apple Macintosh.

comp.sys.mac.digest
 Apple Macintosh: info and uses, but no programs. (Moderated)

comp.sys.mac.games
 Discussions of games on the Macintosh.

comp.sys.mac.graphics
 Macintosh graphics: paint, draw, 3D, CAD, and animation.

comp.sys.mac.hardware
 Macintosh hardware issues and discussions.

comp.sys.mac.hypercard
 The Macintosh Hypercard: info and uses.

comp.sys.mac.misc
 General discussions about the Apple Macintosh.

comp.sys.mac.oop.macapp3
 Version 3 of the MacApp object-oriented system.

comp.sys.mac.oop.misc
 Object-oriented programming issues on the Mac.

comp.sys.mac.oop.tcl
  Symantec's THINK Class Library for object programming.

comp.sys.mac.portables
  Discussion particular to laptop Macintoshes.

comp.sys.mac.programmer
  Discussion by people programming the Apple Macintosh.

comp.sys.mac.scitech
  Using the Macintosh in scientific and technological work.

comp.sys.mac.system
  Discussions of Macintosh system software.

comp.sys.mac.wanted
  Postings of "I want XYZ for my Mac."

comp.sys.mentor
  Mentor Graphics products and the Silicon Compiler System.

comp.sys.mips
  Systems based on MIPS chips.

comp.sys.misc
  Discussion about computers of all kinds.

comp.sys.ncr
  Discussion about NCR computers.

comp.sys.newton.announce
  Newton information posts. (Moderated)

comp.sys.newton.misc
    Miscellaneous discussion about Newton systems.

comp.sys.newton.programmer
    Discussion of Newton software development.

comp.sys.next.advocacy
    The NeXT religion.

comp.sys.next.announce
    Announcements related to the NeXT computer system. (Moderated)

comp.sys.next.bugs
    Discussion and solutions for known NeXT bugs.

comp.sys.next.hardware
    Discussing the physical aspects of NeXT computers.

comp.sys.next.marketplace
    NeXT hardware, software, and jobs.

comp.sys.next.misc
    General discussion about the NeXT computer system.

comp.sys.next.programmer
    NeXT-related programming issues.

comp.sys.next.software
    Function, use, and availability of NeXT programs.

comp.sys.next.sysadmin
    Discussions related to NeXT system administration.

comp.sys.novell
    Discussion of Novell Netware products.

comp.sys.nsc.32k
    National Semiconductor 32000 series chips.

comp.sys.palmtops
    Super-powered calculators in the palm of your hand.

comp.sys.pen
    Interacting with computers through pen gestures.

comp.sys.powerpc
    General PowerPC Discussion.

comp.sys.prime
    Prime Computer products.

comp.sys.proteon
    Proteon gateway products.

comp.sys.psion
    Discussion about PSION Personal Computers and Organizers.

comp.sys.pyramid
    Pyramid 90x computers.

comp.sys.ridge
    Ridge 32 computers and ROS.

comp.sys.sequent
    Sequent systems (Balance and Symmetry).

comp.sys.sgi.admin
System administration on Silicon Graphics's Irises.

comp.sys.sgi.announce
Announcements for the SGI community. (Moderated)

comp.sys.sgi.apps
Applications that run on the Iris.

comp.sys.sgi.bugs
Bugs found in the IRIX operating system.

comp.sys.sgi.graphics
Graphics packages and issues on SGI machines.

comp.sys.sgi.hardware
Base systems and peripherals for Iris computers.

comp.sys.sgi.misc
General discussion about Silicon Graphics's machines.

comp.sys.sinclair
Sinclair computers, such as the ZX81, Spectrum and QL.

comp.sys.stratus
Stratus products, including System/88, CPS-32, VOS and FTX.

comp.sys.sun.admin
Sun system administration issues and questions.

comp.sys.sun.announce
Sun announcements and Sunergy mailings. (Moderated)

F: A List of Usenet Newsgroups

comp.sys.sun.apps
   Software applications for Sun computer systems.

comp.sys.sun.hardware
   Sun Microsystems hardware.

comp.sys.sun.misc
   Miscellaneous discussions about Sun products.

comp.sys.sun.wanted
   People looking for Sun products and support.

comp.sys.tahoe
   CCI 6/32, Harris HCX/7, and Sperry 7000 computers.

comp.sys.tandy
   Discussion about Tandy computers: new and old.

comp.sys.ti
   Discussion about Texas Instruments.

comp.sys.transputer
   The Transputer computer and OCCAM language.

comp.sys.unisys
   Sperry, Burroughs, Convergent, and Unisys systems.

comp.sys.xerox
   Xerox 1100 workstations and protocols.

comp.sys.zenith.z100
   The Zenith Z-100 (Heath H-100) family of computers.

comp.terminals
   All sorts of terminals.

comp.text
   Text processing issues and methods.

comp.text.desktop
   Technology and techniques of desktop publishing.

comp.text.frame
   Desktop publishing with FrameMaker.

comp.text.interleaf
   Applications and use of Interleaf software.

comp.text.sgml
   ISO 8879 SGML, structured documents, and markup languages.

comp.text.tex
   Discussion about the TeX and LaTeX systems and macros.

comp.theory.info-retrieval
   Information retrieval topics. (Moderated)

comp.unix.admin
   Administering a UNIX-based system.

comp.unix.advocacy
   Arguments for and against UNIX and UNIX versions.

comp.unix.aix
   IBM's version of UNIX.

comp.unix.amiga
    Minix, SYSV4, and related systems on an Amiga.

comp.unix.aux
    The version of UNIX for Apple Macintosh II computers.

comp.unix.bsd
    Discussion of Berkeley Software Distribution UNIX.

comp.unix.dos-under-unix
    MS-DOS running under UNIX by whatever means.

comp.unix.internals
    Discussions on hacking UNIX internals.

comp.unix.large
    UNIX on mainframes and in large networks.

comp.unix.misc
    Various topics that don't fit other groups.

comp.unix.osf.misc
    Various aspects of Open Software Foundation products.

comp.unix.osf.osf1
    The Open Software Foundation's OSF/1.

comp.unix.pc-clone.16bit
    UNIX on 286 architectures.

comp.unix.pc-clone.32bit
    UNIX on 386 and 486 architectures.

comp.unix.programmer
Q&A for people programming under Unix.

comp.unix.questions
UNIX neophytes group.

comp.unix.shell
Using and programming the Unix shell.

comp.unix.sys3
System III UNIX discussions.

comp.unix.sys5.misc
Versions of System V that predate Release 3.

comp.unix.sys5.r3
Discussing System V Release 3.

comp.unix.sys5.r4
Discussing System V Release 4.

comp.unix.ultrix
Discussions about DEC's Ultrix.

comp.unix.unixware
Discussion about Novell's UnixWare products.

comp.unix.user-friendly
Discussion of UNIX user-friendliness.

comp.unix.wizards
For only true UNIX wizards. (Moderated)

comp.unix.xenix.misc
  General discussions regarding XENIX (except SCO).

comp.unix.xenix.sco
  XENIX versions from the Santa Cruz Operation.

comp.virus
  Computer viruses and security. (Moderated)

comp.windows.garnet
  The Garnet user interface development environment.

comp.windows.interviews
  The InterViews object-oriented windowing system.

comp.windows.misc
  Various issues about windowing systems.

comp.windows.news
  Sun Microsystems' NeWS window system.

comp.windows.open-look
  Discussion about the Open Look GUI.

comp.windows.suit
  The SUIT user-interface toolkit.

comp.windows.x
  Discussion about the X Window System.

comp.windows.x.apps
  Getting and using, not programming, applications for X.

comp.windows.x.i386unix
The XFree86 window system and others.

comp.windows.x.intrinsics
Discussion of the X toolkit.

comp.windows.x.pex
The PHIGS extension of the X Window System.

The misc Hierarchy

The misc hierarchy includes newsgroups on many different topics.

misc.activism.progressive
Information for Progressive activists. (Moderated)

misc.answers
Repository for periodic Usenet articles. (Moderated)

misc.books.technical
Discussion of books about technical topics.

misc.consumers
Consumer interests, product reviews, and so on.

misc.consumers.house
Discussion about owning and maintaining a house.

misc.education
Discussion of the educational system.

misc.education.adult
Adult education and adult literacy practice/research.

misc.education.language.english
    Teaching English to speakers of other languages.

misc.education.multimedia
    Multimedia for education. (Moderated)

misc.emerg-services
    Forum for paramedics and other first responders.

misc.entrepreneurs
    Discussion on operating a business.

misc.fitness
    Physical fitness, exercise, bodybuilding, and so on.

misc.forsale
    Short, tasteful postings about items for sale.

misc.forsale.computers.d
    Discussion of misc.forsale.computers.

misc.forsale.computers.mac
    Apple-Macintosh-related computer items.

misc.forsale.computers.other
    Selling miscellaneous computer stuff.

misc.forsale.computers.pc-clone
    IBM-PC-related computer items.

misc.forsale.computers.workstation
    Workstation-related computer items.

misc.handicap
  Items of interest for/about the handicapped. (Moderated)

misc.headlines
  Current interest: drug testing, terrorism, and so on.

misc.health.alternative
  Alternative, complementary, and holistic health care.

misc.health.diabetes
  Discussion of diabetes management in day-to-day life.

misc.int-property
  Discussion of intellectual property rights.

misc.invest
  Investments and the handling of money.

misc.invest.canada
  Investing in Canadian financial markets.

misc.invest.funds
  Sharing info about bond, stock, and real estate funds.

misc.invest.real-estate
  Property investments.

misc.invest.stocks
  Forum for sharing info about stocks and options.

misc.invest.technical
  Analyzing market trends with technical methods.

misc.jobs.contract
    Discussions about contract labor.

misc.jobs.misc
    Discussion about employment, workplaces, careers.

misc.jobs.offered
    Announcements of positions available.

misc.jobs.offered.entry
    Job listings only for entry-level positions.

misc.jobs.resumes
    Postings of resumes and "situation wanted" articles.

misc.kids
    Children, their behavior, and activities.

misc.kids.computer
    The use of computers by children.

misc.kids.vacation
    Discussion on all forms of family-oriented vacationing.

misc.legal
    Legalities and the ethics of law.

misc.legal.computing
    Discussing the legal climate of the computing world.

misc.legal.moderated
    All aspects of law. (Moderated)

misc.misc
> Various discussions not fitting in any other group.

misc.news.east-europe.rferl
> Radio Free Europe/Radio Liberty Daily Report. (Moderated)

misc.news.southasia
> News from Bangladesh, India, Nepal, and so on. (Moderated)

misc.rural
> Devoted to issues concerning rural living.

misc.taxes
> Tax laws and advice.

misc.test
> For testing of network software. Very boring.

misc.test.moderated
> Testing of posting to moderated groups. (Moderated)

misc.wanted
> Requests for things that are needed (NOT software).

misc.writing
> Discussion of writing in all of its forms.

The news Hierarchy

The news hierarchy contains newsgroups related to Usenet news itself.

news.admin.misc
> General topics of network news administration.

news.admin.policy
   Policy issues of Usenet.

news.admin.technical
   Technical aspects of maintaining network news. (Moderated)

news.announce.conferences
   Calls for papers and conference announcements. (Moderated)

news.announce.important
   General announcements of interest to all. (Moderated)

news.announce.newgroups
   Calls for new groups and announcements of same. (Moderated)

news.announce.newusers
   Explanatory postings for new users. (Moderated)

news.answers
   Repository for periodic Usenet articles. (Moderated)

news.config
   Postings of system down times and interruptions.

news.future
   The future technology of network news systems.

news.groups
   Discussions and lists of newsgroups.

news.groups.questions
   Where can I find talk about topic X?

news.groups.reviews
    What is going on in group or mailing list named X? (Moderated)

news.lists
    News-related statistics and lists. (Moderated)

news.lists.ps-maps
    Maps relating to Usenet traffic flows. (Moderated)

news.misc
    Discussions of Usenet itself.

news.newsites
    Postings of new site announcements.

news.newusers.questions
    Q&A for users new to Usenet.

news.software.anu-news
    VMS B-news software from Australian National University.

news.software.b
    Discussion about B-news-compatible software.

news.software.nn
    Discussion about the "nn" news reader package.

news.software.notes
    Notesfile software from the University of Illinois.

news.software.readers
    Discussion of software used to read network news.

The rec Hierarchy

The rec hierarchy contains newsgroups devoted to recreational activities.

rec.answers
> Repository for periodic Usenet articles. (Moderated)

rec.antiques
> Discussing antiques and vintage items.

rec.aquaria
> Keeping fish and aquaria as a hobby.

rec.arts.animation
> Discussion of various kinds of animation.

rec.arts.anime
> Japanese animation fen discussion.

rec.arts.anime.info
> Announcements about Japanese animation. (Moderated)

rec.arts.anime.marketplace
> Things for sale in the Japanese animation world.

rec.arts.anime.stories
> All about Japanese comic fanzines. (Moderated)

rec.arts.bodyart
> Tattoos and body decoration discussions.

rec.arts.bonsai
> Dwarfish trees and shrubbery.

rec.arts.books
> Books of all genres and the publishing industry.

rec.arts.books.tolkien
> The works of J. R. R. Tolkien.

rec.arts.cinema
> Discussion of the art of cinema. (Moderated)

rec.arts.comics.info
> Reviews, convention information, and other comics news. (Moderated)

rec.arts.comics.marketplace
> The exchange of comics and comic-related items.

rec.arts.comics.misc
> Comic books, graphic novels, and sequential art.

rec.arts.comics.strips
> Discussion of short-form comics.

rec.arts.comics.xbooks
> The Mutant Universe of Marvel Comics.

rec.arts.dance
> Any aspects of dance not covered in another newsgroup.

rec.arts.disney
> Discussion of any Disney-related subjects.

rec.arts.drwho
> Discussion about Dr. Who.

rec.arts.erotica
> Erotic fiction and verse. (Moderated)

rec.arts.fine
> Fine arts and artists.

rec.arts.int-fiction
> Discussions about interactive fiction.

rec.arts.manga
> All aspects of the Japanese storytelling art form.

rec.arts.marching.drumcorps
> Drum and bugle corps.

rec.arts.marching.misc
> Marching-related performance activities.

rec.arts.misc
> Discussions about the arts not in other groups.

rec.arts.movies
> Discussions of movies and movie-making.

rec.arts.movies.reviews
> Reviews of movies. (Moderated)

rec.arts.poems
> For the posting of poems.

rec.arts.prose
> Short works of prose fiction and followup discussion.

rec.arts.sf.announce
Major announcements of the SF world. (Moderated)

rec.arts.sf.fandom
Discussions of SF fan activities.

rec.arts.sf.marketplace
Personal for-sale notices of SF materials.

rec.arts.sf.misc
Science fiction lovers' newsgroup.

rec.arts.sf.movies
Discussing SF motion pictures.

rec.arts.sf.reviews
Reviews of science fiction/fantasy/horror works. (Moderated)

rec.arts.sf.science
Real and speculative aspects of SF science.

rec.arts.sf.starwars
Discussion of the Star Wars universe.

rec.arts.sf.tv
Discussing general television SF.

rec.arts.sf.tv.babylon5
Babylon 5 creators meet Babylon 5 fans.

rec.arts.sf.written
Discussion of written science fiction and fantasy.

rec.arts.startrek.current
New Star Trek shows, movies, and books.

rec.arts.startrek.fandom
Star Trek conventions and memorabilia.

rec.arts.startrek.info
Information about the universe of Star Trek. (Moderated)

rec.arts.startrek.misc
General discussions of Star Trek.

rec.arts.startrek.reviews
Reviews of Star Trek books, episodes, films, and so on. (Moderated)

rec.arts.startrek.tech
Star Trek's depiction of future technologies.

rec.arts.theatre
Discussion of all aspects of stage work and theatre.

rec.arts.tv
The boob tube, its history, and past and current shows.

rec.arts.tv.soaps
Postings about soap operas.

rec.arts.tv.uk
Discussions of telly shows from the U.K.

rec.arts.wobegon
"A Prairie Home Companion" radio show discussion.

rec.audio
   High-fidelity audio.

rec.audio.car
   Discussions of automobile audio systems.

rec.audio.high-end
   High-end audio systems. (Moderated)

rec.audio.pro
   Professional audio recording and studio engineering.

rec.autos
   Automobiles, automotive products, and laws.

rec.autos.antique
   Discussing all aspects of automobiles over 25 years old.

rec.autos.driving
   Driving automobiles.

rec.autos.marketplace
   Buy/Sell/Trade automobiles, parts, tools, and accessories.

rec.autos.misc
   Miscellaneous discussion about automobiles.

rec.autos.rod-n-custom
   High-performance automobiles.

rec.autos.simulators
   Discussion of automotive simulators.

rec.autos.sport
Discussion of organized, legal auto competitions.

rec.autos.tech
Technical aspects of automobiles *et al.*

rec.autos.vw
Issues pertaining to Volkswagen products.

rec.aviation.announce
Events of interest to the aviation community. (Moderated)

rec.aviation.answers
Frequently asked questions about aviation. (Moderated)

rec.aviation.homebuilt
Selecting, designing, building, and restoring aircraft.

rec.aviation.ifr
Flying under Instrument Flight Rules.

rec.aviation.military
Military aircraft of the past, present, and future.

rec.aviation.misc
Miscellaneous topics in aviation.

rec.aviation.owning
Information on owning airplanes.

rec.aviation.piloting
General discussion for aviators.

rec.aviation.products
Reviews and discussion of products useful to pilots.

rec.aviation.simulators
Flight simulation on all levels.

rec.aviation.soaring
All aspects of sailplanes and hang-gliders.

rec.aviation.stories
Anecdotes of flight experiences. (Moderated)

rec.aviation.student
Learning to fly.

rec.backcountry
Activities in the Great Outdoors.

rec.bicycles.marketplace
Buying, selling, and reviewing items for cycling.

rec.bicycles.misc
General discussion of bicycling.

rec.bicycles.racing
Bicycle racing techniques, rules, and results.

rec.bicycles.rides
Discussions of tours and training or commuting routes.

rec.bicycles.soc
Societal issues of bicycling.

rec.bicycles.tech
Cycling product design, construction, maintenance, and so forth.

rec.birds
Hobbyists interested in bird watching.

rec.boats
Hobbyists interested in boating.

rec.boats.paddle
Talk about any boats with oars, paddles, and so on.

rec.climbing
Climbing techniques, competition announcements, and so forth.

rec.collecting
Discussion among collectors of many things.

rec.collecting.cards
Collecting all sorts of sport and nonsport cards.

rec.collecting.stamps
Discussion of all things related to philately.

rec.crafts.brewing
The art of making beers and meads.

rec.crafts.jewelry
All aspects of jewelry making and lapidary work.

rec.crafts.metalworking
All aspects of working with metal.

rec.crafts.misc
   Handiwork arts not covered elsewhere.

rec.crafts.quilting
   All about quilts and other quilted items.

rec.crafts.textiles
   Sewing, weaving, knitting, and other fiber arts.

rec.crafts.winemaking
   The tasteful art of making wine.

rec.equestrian
   Discussion of things equestrian.

rec.folk-dancing
   Folk dances, dancers, and dancing.

rec.food.cooking
   Food, cooking, cookbooks, and recipes.

rec.food.drink
   Wines and spirits.

rec.food.drink.beer
   All things beer.

rec.food.historic
   The history of food-making arts.

rec.food.recipes
   Recipes for interesting food and drink. (Moderated)

rec.food.restaurants
   Discussion of dining out.

rec.food.sourdough
   Making and baking with sourdough.

rec.food.veg
   Vegetarians.

rec.food.veg.cooking
   Vegetarian recipes, cooking, and nutrition. (Moderated)

rec.gambling
   Articles on games of chance and betting.

rec.games.abstract
   Perfect information, pure strategy games.

rec.games.backgammon
   Discussion of the game of backgammon.

rec.games.board
   Discussion and hints on board games.

rec.games.board.ce
   The Cosmic Encounter board game.

rec.games.board.marketplace
   Trading and selling of board games.

rec.games.bolo
   The networked strategy war game Bolo.

rec.games.bridge
    Hobbyists interested in bridge.

rec.games.chess
    Chess and computer chess.

rec.games.chinese-chess
    Discussion of the game of Chinese chess, Xiangqi.

rec.games.corewar
    The Core War computer challenge.

rec.games.deckmaster
    The Deckmaster line of games.

rec.games.design
    Discussion of game-design-related issues.

rec.games.diplomacy
    The conquest game Diplomacy.

rec.games.empire
    Discussion and hints about Empire.

rec.games.frp.advocacy
    Flames and rebuttals about various role-playing systems.

rec.games.frp.announce
    Announcements of happenings in the role-playing world. (Moderated)

rec.games.frp.archives
    Archivable fantasy stories and other projects. (Moderated)

rec.games.frp.cyber
> Discussions of cyberpunk-related role-playing games.

rec.games.frp.dnd
> Fantasy role-playing with TSR's Dungeons and Dragons.

rec.games.frp.live-action
> Live-action role-playing games.

rec.games.frp.marketplace
> Role-playing game materials wanted and for sale.

rec.games.frp.misc
> General discussions of role-playing games.

rec.games.go
> Discussion about Go.

rec.games.hack
> Discussion, hints, and so forth about the Hack game.

rec.games.int-fiction
> All aspects of interactive fiction games.

rec.games.mecha
> Giant robot games.

rec.games.miniatures
> Tabletop wargaming.

rec.games.misc
> Games and computer games.

rec.games.moria
    Comments, hints, and info about the Moria game.

rec.games.mud.admin
    Administrative issues of multi-user dungeons.

rec.games.mud.announce
    Informational articles about multi-user dungeons. (Moderated)

rec.games.mud.diku
    All about DikuMuds.

rec.games.mud.lp
    Discussions of the LPMUD computer role-playing game.

rec.games.mud.misc
    Various aspects of multi-user computer games.

rec.games.mud.tiny
    Discussion about Tiny muds, like MUSH, MUSE, and MOO.

rec.games.netrek
    Discussion of the X window system game Netrek (XtrekII).

rec.games.pbm
    Discussion about Play by Mail games.

rec.games.pinball
    Discussing pinball-related issues.

rec.games.programmer
    Discussion of adventure game programming.

rec.games.rogue
> Discussion and hints about Rogue.

rec.games.roguelike.angband
> The computer game Angband.

rec.games.roguelike.announce
> Major info about rogue-styled games. (Moderated)

rec.games.roguelike.misc
> Rogue-style dungeon games without other groups.

rec.games.trivia
> Discussion about trivia.

rec.games.video.3do
> Discussion of 3DO video game systems.

rec.games.video.advocacy
> Debate on merits of various video game systems.

rec.games.video.arcade
> Discussions about coin-operated video games.

rec.games.video.arcade.collecting
> Collecting, converting, repairing, and so on.

rec.games.video.atari
> Discussion of Atari's video game systems.

rec.games.video.classic
> Older home video entertainment systems.

rec.games.video.marketplace
    Home video game stuff for sale or trade.

rec.games.video.misc
    General discussion about home video games.

rec.games.video.nintendo
    All Nintendo video game systems and software.

rec.games.video.sega
    All Sega video game systems and software.

rec.games.xtank.play
    Strategy and tactics for the distributed game Xtank.

rec.games.xtank.programmer
    Coding the Xtank game and its robots.

rec.gardens
    Gardening, methods and results.

rec.guns
    Discussions about firearms. (Moderated)

rec.heraldry
    Discussion of coats of arms.

rec.humor
    Jokes and the like. May be somewhat offensive.

rec.humor.d
    Discussions on the content of rec.humor articles.

rec.humor.funny
Jokes that are funny (in the moderator's opinion). (Moderated)

rec.humor.oracle
Sagacious advice from the Usenet Oracle. (Moderated)

rec.humor.oracle.d
Comments about the Usenet Oracle's comments.

rec.hunting
Discussions about hunting. (Moderated)

rec.juggling
Juggling techniques, equipment, and events.

rec.kites
Talk about kites and kiting.

rec.mag
Magazine summaries, tables of contents, and so on.

rec.martial-arts
Discussion of the various martial art forms.

rec.misc
General topics about recreational/participant sports.

rec.models.railroad
Model railroads of all scales.

rec.models.rc
Radio-controlled models for hobbyists.

rec.models.rockets
Model rockets for hobbyists.

rec.models.scale
Construction of models.

rec.motorcycles
Motorcycles and related products and laws.

rec.motorcycles.dirt
Riding motorcycles and ATVs off-road.

rec.motorcycles.harley
All aspects of Harley-Davidson motorcycles.

rec.motorcycles.racing
Discussion of all aspects of racing motorcycles.

rec.music.a-cappella
Vocal music without instrumental accompaniment.

rec.music.afro-latin
Music with Afro-Latin, African, and Latin influences.

rec.music.beatles
Postings about the Fab Four and their music.

rec.music.bluenote
Discussion of jazz, blues, and related types of music.

rec.music.cd
CDs—availability and other discussions.

rec.music.celtic
> Traditional and modern music with a Celtic flavor.

rec.music.christian
> Christian music, both contemporary and traditional.

rec.music.classical
> Discussion about classical music.

rec.music.classical.guitar
> Classical music performed on guitar.

rec.music.classical.performing
> Performing classical (including early) music.

rec.music.compose
> Creating musical and lyrical works.

rec.music.country.western
> C&W music, performers, performances, and so forth.

rec.music.dementia
> Discussion of comedy and novelty music.

rec.music.dylan
> Discussion of Bob's works and music.

rec.music.early
> Discussion of pre-classical European music.

rec.music.folk
> Folks discussing folk music of various sorts.

rec.music.funky
> Funk, rap, hip-hop, house, soul, r&b, and related.

rec.music.gaffa
> Discussion of Kate Bush and other alternative music. (Moderated)

rec.music.gdead
> A group for (Grateful) Dead-heads.

rec.music.indian.classical
> Hindustani and Carnatic Indian classical music.

rec.music.indian.misc
> Discussing Indian music in general.

rec.music.industrial
> Discussion of all industrial-related music styles.

rec.music.info
> News and announcements on musical topics. (Moderated)

rec.music.makers
> For performers and their discussions.

rec.music.makers.bass
> Upright bass and bass guitar techniques and equipment.

rec.music.makers.builders
> Design, building, and repair of musical instruments.

rec.music.makers.guitar
> Electric and acoustic guitar techniques and equipment.

rec.music.makers.guitar.acoustic
Discussion of acoustic guitar playing.

rec.music.makers.guitar.tablature
Guitar tablature/chords.

rec.music.makers.marketplace
Buying & selling used music-making equipment.

rec.music.makers.percussion
Drum & other percussion techniques and equipment.

rec.music.makers.piano
Piano music, performing, composing, learning, and styles.

rec.music.makers.synth
Synthesizers and computer music.

rec.music.marketplace
Records, tapes, and CDs: wanted, for sale, and so on.

rec.music.misc
Music lovers' group.

rec.music.newage
"New Age" music discussions.

rec.music.phish
Discussing the musical group Phish.

rec.music.reggae
Roots, rockers, and dancehall reggae.

rec.music.rem
> The musical group R.E.M.

rec.music.reviews
> Reviews of music of all genres and mediums. (Moderated)

rec.music.video
> Discussion of music videos and music video software.

rec.nude
> Hobbyists interested in naturist/nudist activities.

rec.org.mensa
> Talking with members of the high-IQ society Mensa.

rec.org.sca
> Society for Creative Anachronism.

rec.outdoors.fishing
> All aspects of sport and commercial fishing.

rec.parks.theme
> Entertainment theme parks.

rec.pets
> Pets, pet care, and household animals in general.

rec.pets.birds
> The culture and care of indoor birds.

rec.pets.cats
> Discussion about domestic cats.

rec.pets.dogs
> Any and all subjects relating to dogs as pets.

rec.pets.herp
> Reptiles, amphibians, and other exotic vivarium pets.

rec.photo
> Hobbyists interested in photography.

rec.puzzles
> Puzzles, problems, and quizzes.

rec.puzzles.crosswords
> Making and playing gridded word puzzles.

rec.pyrotechnics
> Fireworks, rocketry, safety, and other topics.

rec.radio.amateur.antenna
> Antennas: theory, techniques, and construction.

rec.radio.amateur.digital.misc
> Packet radio and other digital radio modes.

rec.radio.amateur.equipment
> All about production amateur radio hardware.

rec.radio.amateur.homebrew
> Amateur radio construction and experimentation.

rec.radio.amateur.misc
> Amateur radio practices, contests, events, rules, and so on.

rec.radio.amateur.policy
    Radio use and regulation policy.

rec.radio.amateur.space
    Amateur radio transmissions through space.

rec.radio.broadcasting
    Discussion of global domestic broadcast radio. (Moderated)

rec.radio.cb
    Citizen-band radio.

rec.radio.info
    Informational postings related to radio. (Moderated)

rec.radio.noncomm
    Topics relating to noncommercial radio.

rec.radio.scanner
    "Utility" broadcasting traffic above 30 MHz.

rec.radio.shortwave
    Shortwave radio enthusiasts.

rec.radio.swap
    Offers to trade and swap radio equipment.

rec.railroad
    For fans of real trains, ferroequinologists.

rec.roller-coaster
    Roller coasters and other amusement park rides.

rec.running
    Running for enjoyment, sport, exercise, and so on.

rec.scouting
    Scouting youth organizations worldwide.

rec.scuba
    Hobbyists interested in scuba diving.

rec.skate
    Ice skating and roller skating.

rec.skiing
    Hobbyists interested in snow skiing.

rec.skiing.alpine
    Downhill skiing technique, equipment, and so forth.

rec.skiing.announce
    FAQ, competition results, and automated snow reports. (Moderated)

rec.skiing.nordic
    Cross-country skiing technique, equipment, and so forth.

rec.skiing.snowboard
    Snowboarding technique, equipment, and so on.

rec.skydiving
    Hobbyists interested in skydiving.

rec.sport.baseball
    Discussion about baseball.

rec.sport.baseball.college
> Baseball on the collegiate level.

rec.sport.baseball.fantasy
> Rotisserie (fantasy) baseball play.

rec.sport.basketball.college
> Hoops on the collegiate level.

rec.sport.basketball.misc
> Discussion about basketball.

rec.sport.basketball.pro
> Talk of professional basketball.

rec.sport.basketball.women
> Women's basketball at all levels.

rec.sport.cricket
> Discussion about the sport of cricket.

rec.sport.cricket.scores
> Scores from cricket matches around the globe. (Moderated)

rec.sport.disc
> Discussion of flying-disc-based sports.

rec.sport.fencing
> All aspects of swordplay.

rec.sport.football.australian
> Discussion of Australian (rules) football.

F: A List of Usenet Newsgroups

rec.sport.football.canadian
> All about Canadian rules football.

rec.sport.football.college
> U.S.-style college football.

rec.sport.football.fantasy
> Rotisserie (fantasy) football play.

rec.sport.football.misc
> Discussion about American-style football.

rec.sport.football.pro
> U.S.-style professional football.

rec.sport.golf
> Discussion about all aspects of golfing.

rec.sport.hockey
> Discussion about ice hockey.

rec.sport.hockey.field
> Discussion of the sport of field hockey.

rec.sport.misc
> Spectator sports.

rec.sport.olympics
> All aspects of the Olympic Games.

rec.sport.paintball
> Discussing all aspects of the survival game paintball.

rec.sport.pro-wrestling
> Discussion about professional wrestling.

rec.sport.rowing
> Crew for competition or fitness.

rec.sport.rugby
> Discussion about the game of rugby.

rec.sport.soccer
> Discussion about soccer (Association Football).

rec.sport.swimming
> Training for and competing in swimming events.

rec.sport.table-tennis
> Things related to table tennis (aka ping pong).

rec.sport.tennis
> Things related to the sport of tennis.

rec.sport.triathlon
> Discussing all aspects of multi-event sports.

rec.sport.volleyball
> Discussion about volleyball.

rec.sport.water-polo
> Discussion of water polo.

rec.sport.waterski
> Waterskiing and other boat-towed activities.

rec.toys.lego
   Discussion of Lego and Duplo (and compatible) toys.

rec.toys.misc
   Discussion of toys that lack a specific newsgroup.

rec.travel
   Traveling all over the world.

rec.travel.air
   Airline travel around the world.

rec.travel.marketplace
   Tickets and accommodations wanted and for sale.

rec.video
   Video and video components.

rec.video.cable-tv
   Technical and regulatory issues of cable television.

rec.video.production
   Making professional-quality video productions.

rec.video.releases
   Pre-recorded video releases on laserdisc and videotape.

rec.video.satellite
   Getting shows via satellite.

rec.windsurfing
   Riding the waves as a hobby.

rec.woodworking
>   Hobbyists interested in woodworking.

The sci Hierarchy

The sci hierarchy includes groups devoted to science, engineering, and mathematics.

sci.aeronautics
>   The science of aeronautics and related technology. (Moderated)

sci.aeronautics.airliners
>   Airliner technology. (Moderated)

sci.agriculture
>   Farming, agriculture, and related topics.

sci.answers
>   Repository for periodic Usenet articles. (Moderated)

sci.anthropology
>   All aspects of studying humankind.

sci.anthropology.paleo
>   Evolution of man and other primates.

sci.aquaria
>   Only scientifically-oriented postings about aquaria.

sci.archaeology
>   Studying antiquities of the world.

sci.astro
> Astronomy discussions and information.

sci.astro.fits
> Issues related to the Flexible Image Transport System.

sci.astro.hubble
> Processing Hubble Space Telescope data. (Moderated)

sci.astro.planetarium
> Discussion of planetariums.

sci.bio
> Biology and related sciences.

sci.bio.ecology
> Ecological research.

sci.bio.ethology
> Animal behavior and behavioral ecology.

sci.bio.evolution
> Discussions of evolutionary biology. (Moderated)

sci.bio.herp
> Biology of amphibians and reptiles.

sci.chem
> Chemistry and related sciences.

sci.chem.organomet
> Organometallic chemistry.

sci.classics
> Studying classical history, languages, art, and more.

sci.cognitive
> Perception, memory, judgment, and reasoning.

sci.comp-aided
> The use of computers as tools in scientific research.

sci.cryonics
> Theory and practice of biostasis, suspended animation.

sci.crypt
> Different methods of data en/decryption.

sci.data.formats
> Modeling, storage, and retrieval of scientific data.

sci.econ
> The science of economics.

sci.econ.research
> Research in all fields of economics. (Moderated)

sci.edu
> The science of education.

sci.electronics
> Circuits, theory, electrons, and discussions.

sci.energy
> Discussions about energy, science, and technology.

sci.energy.hydrogen
All about hydrogen as an alternative fuel.

sci.engr
Technical discussions about engineering tasks.

sci.engr.advanced-tv
HDTV/DATV standards, formats, equipment, and practices.

sci.engr.biomed
Discussing the field of biomedical engineering.

sci.engr.chem
All aspects of chemical engineering.

sci.engr.civil
Topics related to civil engineering.

sci.engr.control
The engineering of control systems.

sci.engr.lighting
Light, vision, and color in architecture, media, and so on.

sci.engr.manufacturing
Manufacturing technology.

sci.engr.mech
The field of mechanical engineering.

sci.engr.semiconductors
Semiconductor devices, processes, materials, and physics.

sci.environment
   Discussions about the environment and ecology.

sci.fractals
   Objects of non-integral dimension and other chaos.

sci.geo.fluids
   Discussion of geophysical fluid dynamics.

sci.geo.geology
   Discussion of solid earth sciences.

sci.geo.meteorology
   Discussion of meteorology and related topics.

sci.geo.satellite-nav
   Satellite navigation systems, especially GPS.

sci.image.processing
   Scientific image processing and analysis.

sci.lang
   Natural languages, communication, and so forth.

sci.lang.japan
   The Japanese language, both spoken and written.

sci.life-extension
   Slowing, stopping, or reversing the ageing process.

sci.logic
   Logic—math, philosophy, and computational aspects.

sci.materials
> All aspects of materials engineering.

sci.math
> Mathematical discussions and pursuits.

sci.math.research
> Discussion of current mathematical research. (Moderated)

sci.math.symbolic
> Symbolic algebra discussion.

sci.med
> Medicine and its related products and regulations.

sci.med.aids
> AIDS: treatment, pathology/biology of HIV, and prevention. (Moderated)

sci.med.dentistry
> Dental-related topics; all about teeth.

sci.med.nursing
> Nursing questions and discussion.

sci.med.nutrition
> Physiological impacts of diet.

sci.med.occupational
> Preventing, detecting, and treating occupational injuries.

sci.med.pharmacy
> The teaching and practice of pharmacy.

sci.med.physics
>Issues of physics in medical testing/care.

sci.med.psychobiology
>Dialogue and news in psychiatry and psychobiology.

sci.med.radiology
>All aspects of radiology.

sci.med.telemedicine
>Clinical consulting through computer networks.

sci.military
>Discussion about science and the military. (Moderated)

sci.misc
>Short-lived discussions on subjects in the sciences.

sci.nanotech
>Self-reproducing molecular-scale machines. (Moderated)

sci.nonlinear
>Chaotic systems and other nonlinear scientific study.

sci.op-research
>Research, teaching, and application of operations research.

sci.optics
>Discussion relating to the science of optics.

sci.philosophy.tech
>Technical philosophy: math, science, logic, and so on.

sci.physics
  Physical laws, properties, and so forth.

sci.physics.accelerators
  Particle accelerators and the physics of beams.

sci.physics.electromag
  Electromagnetic theory and applications.

sci.physics.fusion
  Info on fusion, especially "cold" fusion.

sci.physics.particle
  Particle physics discussions.

sci.physics.research
  Current physics research. (Moderated)

sci.polymers
  All aspects of polymer science.

sci.psychology
  Topics related to psychology.

sci.psychology.digest
  PSYCOLOQUY: Refereed Psychology Journal and Newsletter.
  (Moderated)

sci.research
  Research methods, funding, ethics, and whatever.

sci.research.careers
  Issues relevant to careers in scientific research.

sci.research.postdoc
>Anything about postdoctoral studies, including offers.

sci.skeptic
>Skeptics discussing pseudo-science.

sci.space.news
>Announcements of space-related news items. (Moderated)

sci.space.policy
>Discussions about space policy.

sci.space.science
>Space and planetary science and related technical work. (Moderated)

sci.space.shuttle
>The space shuttle and the STS program.

sci.space.tech
>Technical and general issues related to space flight. (Moderated)

sci.stat.consult
>Statistical consulting.

sci.stat.edu
>Statistics education.

sci.stat.math
>Statistics from a strictly mathematical viewpoint.

sci.systems
>The theory and application of systems science.

sci.techniques.microscopy
    The field of microscopy.

sci.techniques.spectroscopy
    Spectrum analysis.

sci.techniques.xtallography
    The field of crystallography.

sci.virtual-worlds
    Virtual Reality—technology and culture. (Moderated)

sci.virtual-worlds.apps
    Current and future uses of virtual-worlds technology. (Moderated)

The soc Hierarchy

The soc hierarchy includes newsgroups on social issues.

soc.answers
    Repository for periodic Usenet articles. (Moderated)

soc.bi
    Discussions of bisexuality.

soc.college
    College, college activities, campus life, and so on.

soc.college.grad
    General issues related to graduate schools.

soc.college.gradinfo
    Information about graduate schools.

soc.college.org.aiesec
    The International Association of Business and Commerce Students.

soc.college.teaching-asst
    Issues affecting collegiate teaching assistants.

soc.couples
    Discussions for couples (cf. soc.singles).

soc.couples.intercultural
    Intercultural and interracial relationships.

soc.culture.afghanistan
    Discussion of the Afghan society.

soc.culture.african
    Discussions about Africa and things African.

soc.culture.african.american
    Discussions about Afro-American issues.

soc.culture.arabic
    Technological and cultural issues, not politics.

soc.culture.argentina
    All about life in Argentina.

soc.culture.asean
    Countries of the Association of SE Asian Nations.

soc.culture.asian.american
    Issues of and discussion about Asian-Americans.

soc.culture.australian
Australian culture and society.

soc.culture.austria
Austria and its people.

soc.culture.baltics
People of the Baltic states.

soc.culture.bangladesh
Issues of and discussion about Bangladesh.

soc.culture.bosna-herzgvna
The independent state of Bosnia and Herzegovina.

soc.culture.brazil
Talking about the people and country of Brazil.

soc.culture.british
Issues about Britain and those of British descent.

soc.culture.bulgaria
Discussing Bulgarian society.

soc.culture.burma
Politics, culture, news, and discussion about Burma.

soc.culture.canada
Discussions of Canada and its people.

soc.culture.caribbean
Life in the Caribbean.

soc.culture.celtic
> Irish, Scottish, Breton, Cornish, Manx, and Welsh.

soc.culture.chile
> All about Chile and its people.

soc.culture.china
> About China and Chinese culture.

soc.culture.croatia
> The lives of people of Croatia.

soc.culture.czecho-slovak
> Bohemian, Slovak, Moravian, and Silesian life.

soc.culture.europe
> Discussing all aspects of European society.

soc.culture.filipino
> Group about the Filipino culture.

soc.culture.french
> French culture, history, and related discussions.

soc.culture.german
> Discussions about German culture and history.

soc.culture.greek
> Group about Greeks.

soc.culture.hongkong
> Discussions pertaining to Hong Kong.

soc.culture.hongkong.entertainment
Entertainment in Hong Kong.

soc.culture.indian
Group for discussion about India and things Indian.

soc.culture.indian.info
Info group for soc.culture.indian groups. (Moderated)

soc.culture.indian.telugu
The culture of the Telugu people of India.

soc.culture.indonesia
All about the Indonesian nation.

soc.culture.iranian
Discussions about Iran and things Iranian/Persian.

soc.culture.israel
Israel and Israelis.

soc.culture.italian
The Italian people and their culture.

soc.culture.japan
Everything Japanese, except the Japanese language.

soc.culture.jewish
Jewish culture and religion. (cf. talk.politics.mideast)

soc.culture.korean
Discussions about Korea and things Korean.

soc.culture.laos
> Cultural and social aspects of Laos.

soc.culture.latin-america
> Topics about Latin America.

soc.culture.lebanon
> Discussion about things Lebanese.

soc.culture.maghreb
> North African society and culture.

soc.culture.magyar
> The Hungarian people and their culture.

soc.culture.malaysia
> All about Malaysian society.

soc.culture.mexican
> Discussion of Mexico's society.

soc.culture.misc
> Group for discussion about other cultures.

soc.culture.native
> Aboriginal people around the world.

soc.culture.nepal
> Discussion of people and things in and from Nepal.

soc.culture.netherlands
> People from the Netherlands and Belgium.

soc.culture.new-zealand
   Discussion of topics related to New Zealand.

soc.culture.nordic
   Discussion about culture up north.

soc.culture.pakistan
   Topics of discussion about Pakistan.

soc.culture.palestine
   Palestinian people, culture, and politics.

soc.culture.peru
   All about the people of Peru.

soc.culture.polish
   Polish culture, Polish past, and Polish politics.

soc.culture.portuguese
   Discussion of the people of Portugal.

soc.culture.romanian
   Discussion of Romanian and Moldavian people.

soc.culture.scientists
   Cultural issues about scientists and scientific projects.

soc.culture.singapore
   The past, present, and future of Singapore.

soc.culture.soviet
   Topics relating to Russian or Soviet culture.

soc.culture.spain
Spain and the Spanish.

soc.culture.sri-lanka
Things and people from Sri Lanka.

soc.culture.swiss
Swiss culture.

soc.culture.taiwan
Discussion about things Taiwanese.

soc.culture.tamil
Tamil language, history, and culture.

soc.culture.thai
Thai people and their culture.

soc.culture.turkish
Discussion about things Turkish.

soc.culture.ukrainian
The lives and times of the Ukrainian people.

soc.culture.uruguay
Discussions of Uruguay for those at home and abroad.

soc.culture.usa
The culture of the United States of America.

soc.culture.venezuela
Discussion of topics related to Venezuela.

soc.culture.vietnamese
> Issues and discussions of Vietnamese culture.

soc.culture.yugoslavia
> Discussions of Yugoslavia and its people.

soc.feminism
> Discussion of feminism and feminist issues. (Moderated)

soc.history
> Discussions of things historical.

soc.history.moderated
> All aspects of history. (Moderated)

soc.libraries.talk
> Discussing all aspects of libraries.

soc.men
> Issues related to men, their problems, and relationships.

soc.misc
> Socially oriented topics not in other groups.

soc.motss
> Issues pertaining to homosexuality.

soc.net-people
> Announcements, requests, and so on about people on the net.

soc.penpals
> In search of net.friendships.

soc.politics
    Political problems, systems, and solutions. (Moderated)

soc.politics.arms-d
    Arms discussion digest. (Moderated)

soc.religion.bahai
    Discussion of the Baha'i Faith. (Moderated)

soc.religion.christian
    Christianity and related topics. (Moderated)

soc.religion.christian.bible-study
    Examining the Holy Bible. (Moderated)

soc.religion.eastern
    Discussions of Eastern religions. (Moderated)

soc.religion.islam
    Discussions of the Islamic faith. (Moderated)

soc.religion.quaker
    The Religious Society of Friends.

soc.religion.shamanism
    Discussion of the full range of shamanic experience. (Moderated)

soc.rights.human
    Human rights and activism (e.g., Amnesty International).

soc.roots
    Discussing genealogy and genealogical matters.

soc.singles
> Newsgroup for single people, their activities, and so on.

soc.veterans
> Social issues relating to military veterans.

soc.women
> Issues related to women, their problems and relationships.

The talk Hierarchy

The talk hierarchy includes newsgroups for chatting about almost anything.

talk.abortion
> All sorts of discussions and arguments on abortion.

talk.answers
> Repository for periodic Usenet articles. (Moderated)

talk.bizarre
> The unusual, bizarre, curious, and often stupid.

talk.environment
> Discussing the state of the environment and what to do.

talk.origins
> Evolution versus creationism (sometimes hot!).

talk.philosophy.misc
> Philosophical musings on all topics.

talk.politics.animals
    The use and/or abuse of animals.

talk.politics.china
    Discussion of political issues related to China.

talk.politics.crypto
    The relation between cryptography and government.

talk.politics.drugs
    The politics of drug issues.

talk.politics.guns
    The politics of firearm ownership and (mis)use.

talk.politics.medicine
    The politics and ethics involved with health care.

talk.politics.mideast
    Discussion and debate over Middle Eastern events.

talk.politics.misc
    Political discussions and ravings of all kinds.

talk.politics.soviet
    Discussion of Soviet politics, domestic and foreign.

talk.politics.theory
    Theory of politics and political systems.

talk.politics.tibet
    The politics of Tibet and the Tibetan people.

talk.rape
    Discussions on stopping rape; not to be cross-posted.

talk.religion.misc
    Religious, ethical, and moral implications.

talk.religion.newage
    Esoteric and minority religions and philosophies.

talk.rumors
    For the posting of rumors.

Glossary

This glossary defines terms used in the main body of the book. When a term inside a definition is shown in *italics*, it means that the term has its own definition in the glossary.

Access provider:
> A company that provides you with a connection to the *Internet*. Chapter 21 offers a directory of some willing to supply you with a connection.

Active Newsgroups Table:
> A list of the *newsgroups* you receive from your *access provider*. You can modify the active newsgroups table to create, delete, and update newsgroups on your system.

Address:
> A string of characters used in sending a *mail message*. An Internet-style address has three parts: the name of a person (the *username*); the name of the computer that the person uses (the *site name*); and additional *domain* information which tells more about the computer (such as its location or purpose). These are written as

```
username@sitename.domain
```

Address Book:
> A helpful feature of the *Mail Composer*. The Address Book lets you keep a list of people with whom you regularly exchange *electronic mail* and their Internet mailing *addresses*.

Article:

Lines of text sent to one or more *Usenet newsgroups* to share information or opinions with other users. News articles have *header lines* providing information about the article, and a *body* containing the text of the article itself.

Attachment:

A file whose contents are sent out along with a normal *mail message*. People who receive such a message can save the file contents on their own systems. In this way, attachments let people ship files from one computer to another.

Baud rate:

A measure of how fast data can be transmitted over a connection between two computers. The higher the baud rate, the faster data can be shipped. Technically, the baud rate is the number of times the communications line changes its state every second. Note that baud rate is not the same as "bps" (bits per second), even though the two are often confused with each other.

Bcc:

Short for Blind Carbon Copies. If you send out an *electronic mail* message to someone, you can add a Bcc: line so that copies of the message are sent to other people. People receiving the message do not see the Bcc: line, so they don't know that you've sent out copies to the specified recipients. Contrast with Cc:.

Binary file:

A file containing data not intended for direct human reading. This includes word processor files, spreadsheet data files, and executable programs.

Body:
> Part of a *mail message* or *Usenet news* article. The body contains the actual text of the message or article. Information about the message or article is contained in *header lines*.

Cc:
> Short for Carbon Copies. If you send out an *electronic mail* message to someone, you can add a Cc: line so that copies of the message are sent to other people. People receiving the message can see the Cc: line, so they know that you've sent out copies of the message to the specified *addresses*. Contrast with Bcc:.

Clipboard:
> A temporary storage location used to transfer data between documents and between programs. When you cut or copy text from a document, it is stored in the clipboard; when you paste anything into your document, the material comes from the clipboard. Refer to your Microsoft Windows documentation for more information on the Windows Clipboard facility.

COM port:
> A connection on a DOS computer where you can plug in a printer, a modem, or some other device.

Compacting the database:
> Shrinking the *news database* file so that it doesn't take up as much disk space.

Compression:
> A way to reduce the amount of disk space that a particular file takes up. By compressing *attachments*, you can reduce the amount of time needed to transfer the data from one computer to another.

Configuration:

The process of setting up the MKS Internet Anywhere package after you have installed it. For example, you must provide the software with information about how to connect with your *access provider*; otherwise, the software has no way to connect you with the *Internet*.

Control Center:

The MKS Internet Anywhere program that lets you control how your computer connects with other computers.

Cross-posting:

Sending the same *news article* to more than one *newsgroup*.

Database:

See *news database*.

Dialog box:

A window that appears temporarily to request information. Every dialog box in MKS Internet Anywhere is explained in the "Commands" section of the on-line help.

Distribution code:

A short code that determines which geographical areas receive a particular *Usenet news* article. Distribution codes include `world` (for the entire Internet) and `na` (for North America). Ask your *access provider* for information about valid distribution codes.

Domain:

Part of an Internet mailing *address*. A domain is attached to the end of the *site name* part of the address to help the *electronic mail* software find the destination machine. It serves much the same purpose as an area code does in a normal telephone number. Some domains have additional *subdomains* to provide more information; for example, the domain associated with a country may have separate subdomains for states or provinces within that country.

Electronic mail:
A way that people on the same computer system or on different systems can exchange messages with each other. The sender composes a message; the sender's computer then transfers the message to another computer, which transfers it to another, and so on, until the message finally reaches the computer used by the intended recipient. The message waits on the recipient's machine until the recipient reads it. The name "electronic mail" is frequently shortened to e-mail.

Encryption:
Transforming the contents of a file into an unreadable format, for security reasons. An encryption operation requires you to supply an encryption key, which is used in decrypting the file back to its original form.

Expiration List:
A list that controls when *Usenet news* articles *expire*.

Expire:
The process of getting rid of *Usenet news* articles from the news *database* so that you have disk space to receive new articles.

Feed:
See *news feed*.

Flame:
A *Usenet news* article, written as a personal attack on another Internet user. A flame war is a sequence of flames sent back and forth between two or more people.

Folder:

A *text file* containing electronic *mail messages.*

Followup:

A *Usenet news* article posted in response to another article. Contrast with a "reply"—a *mail message* sent in response to another article.

Header lines:

Part of an *electronic mail* message or *Usenet news* article. The header lines provide information about the message or article: who sent it, when it was sent, what it's about, and so on. Some headers are created automatically by the software; others are created by the person who writes the message or article.

Index:

The area of the *Mail Reader* window that lists available *mail messages*, and the area of the *News Reader* window that lists available *Usenet news* articles.

Information highway:

A term often used to describe the *Internet*, because the Internet transports information in the same way that highways transport goods.

Internet:

A *network* of computer networks. Basically, the Internet consists of a huge number of computers whose owners have agreed to collaborate in providing services like *electronic mail* and *Usenet news*. The Internet as a whole is not controlled by any single agency. Instead, various parts of the Internet are publicly or privately owned, and each may make its own rules about the way their computers may be used.

Local site:
> A term denoting your computer when you communicate on the Internet. When your computer connects with another computer, your computer is called the local site, and the other computer is called the *remote site*.

Log file:
> A file containing records of interactions between your computer and another computer. See Appendix E for more details.

Login:
> A process for identifying yourself to a computer. In a typical login, you type in a special *username* (who you are) and a *password* (to prove you are who you say you are). Often, when one computer connects to another, the computer itself will log in to the other computer, to verify its identity.

Login program:
> The MKS Internet Anywhere program that lets you customize how other computers log in to your computer. It is not included in your application group, but you can invoke it from the Windows File Manager by double-clicking on its filename from the `mksia` directory.

Mail Composer:
> The MKS Internet Anywhere program that lets you write and send *mail messages* to be sent to other people.

Mail message:
> Lines of text send by one user to another via *electronic mail*. Mail messages have *header lines* providing information about the sender, and a *body* containing the text of the message itself.

Mail Reader:
> The MKS Internet Anywhere program that lets you read incoming electronic *mail messages.*

Mailbox:
> Sometimes used to refer to a file where *electronic mail* is stored. MKS Internet Anywhere uses the term *folder* for the same thing.

Mailing list:
> A group of *Internet* users who exchange electronic *mail messages* about a particular topic. Mailing list members send messages to a central site, which then redirects incoming messages to all the people on the list.

Menu bar:
> The part of a computer window that contains the names of pull-down menus.

Modem:
> A machine that translates the output of a computer from ones and zeroes into electronic "chirps" that can be transmitted over telephone lines. A modem on the other end of the phone translates the chirps back into digits and sends them as input into another computer.

Moderated:
> A word used to describe certain *newsgroups* and *mailing lists.* These groups and lists are controlled by a person who examines all submissions and decides which submissions are actually distributed to readers. Contrast with *unmoderated.*

Moderator backbone site:
> A *site* that provides up-to-date information on *moderated news-groups* and automatically directs your postings to the appropriate moderator.

Netiquette:
> Courteous behavior on the Internet, especially in *Usenet news* articles.

Netnews:
> Same as *Usenet news*.

Network:
> Any group of computers that can exchange information with each other. Often, a network is defined by the method used by the computers to exchange information.

New message or article:
> A *mail message* or *Usenet news* article that has arrived on your computer since the last time you read mail or news. This is not the same as an *unread* message or article, which may have been around for a long time and just hasn't been read yet.

News Control:
> The MKS Internet Anywhere program that lets you control the way *Usenet news* is handled by your computer.

News database:
> The file that contains all the *Usenet news* articles on your system, as well as information to control how Usenet news works on your computer.

News feed:
> A service provided by an *access provider*, supplying you with *Usenet news*. Before you can read Usenet news, you must acquire a news feed from an access provider.

News hierarchy:
> A collection of *newsgroups* that are all related to a particular field of interest. For example, the *comp* news hierarchy deals with topics related to computing, while the *rec* news hierarchy deals with recreational topics.

News Poster:
> The MKS Internet Anywhere program for posting a *Usenet news* article to one or more *newsgroups*.

News Reader:
> The MKS Internet Anywhere program that lets you read incoming *Usenet news* articles.

News thread:
> See *thread*.

Newsgroup:
> Comparable to a bulletin board where people can post articles related to a particular topic. Newsgroups have names made up of several components, with dot (.) characters between components, as in *comp.sys.ibm.pc.hardware*.

Notify box:
> A box in the *Mail Reader* window which notifies you that you have received a new *mail message*.

Permissions:
   A list of instructions telling what you'll let outsiders do on your
   computer. For example, if you want to receive *Usenet news* and
   electronic mail, you have to give another computer permission to
   copy news and mail to your machine.

Personal system folder:
   The *folder* that holds all of your incoming *mail messages*.

Public UUCP Directory:
   A computer directory that outside users can access with *UUCP*.
   Depending on how you set your *permissions*, outsiders may be able
   to write files to the public directory (and its subdirectories), but not
   to other directories on your machine.

Remote site:
   Any computer with which you communicate on the *Internet*. When
   your computer connects with another computer, your computer is
   called the *local site*, and the other computer is called the remote
   site.

Remote user:
   Any person using the computer known as the *remote site*.

Retry:
   An attempt to connect with a *site* after an initial attempt has failed.

Scheduler:
   The MKS Internet Anywhere program that lets you schedule the
   execution of any program, including the times you connect with
   other computers.

Service provider:
   Same as *access provider*.

Signature:

Lines of text that appear at the end of all *mail messages* and *Usenet news* articles that you write with MKS Internet Anywhere. Signatures usually contain such information as your name, title, organization, and e-mail address; often, they also include a clever quote or slogan.

Site:

Any computer with which you can communicate over the *Internet*. For example, your computer can be called your site. When your computer connects with another computer, your computer is called the *local site* and the other computer is called the *remote site*. Every Internet site is uniquely identified by a combination of a *site name* and a *domain name*.

Site name:

A name for a computer on the *Internet*. Also called the computer's *system name*.

Smiley:

The symbol : -) or some variation, looking like a smiling face shown sideways. Smileys are often used to indicate jokes inside news articles or mail messages, although they frequently don't meet with much success.

Spoiler:

The word Spoiler in the *Subject* line of a *Usenet news* article or near the beginning of the article. This indicates that the article gives away plot points about a book, movie, or some similar work. A spoiler warning helps avoid ruining the surprise for people who haven't yet read the book or seen the movie.

Spooling directory:

A directory where other computers can deposit incoming *electronic mail* messages and *Usenet news* articles, and where they can pick up any outgoing messages or articles waiting to be sent. For the purposes of MKS Internet Anywhere, you can think of a spooling directory as a holding area that is accessible to other computers.

Store-and-Forward Networking:

A term describing file transfer software like *UUCP*. When you ask UUCP to transfer a file from one computer to another, it may not start the transfer right away. Instead, it may store your request and honor that request at a more appropriate time.

Subdomain:

Part of an *Internet* mailing *address*. It attaches to the *domain* to provide more detail about the location of a computer.

Subject:

Part of the *header* information in a *mail message* or *Usenet news* article. The sender can use the *Subject* line to create a capsule summary of what the message or article is about.

Subscribing:

Deciding to read a chosen *newsgroup* or *mailing list*.

Supplier:

Same as *access provider*.

System distribution table:

A list of the *newsgroups* your computer sends to other computers.

System name:

See *site name*.

Text file:
> A file that contains only printable characters (letters, digits, and punctuation). Files like spreadsheets, databases, and word processor documents contain other characters (called "control characters") that cannot be part of *mail messages* or *Usenet news* articles.

Thread:
> A set of *Usenet news* articles that all deal with the same subject.

Toolbar:
> The part of a window that contains icons (pictures) for performing various actions quickly.

Unmoderated:
> A word used to describe *newsgroups* and *mailing lists* where all submissions are sent out to readers without being reviewed by a moderator. Contrast with *moderated.*

Unread message or article:
> A *mail message* or *Usenet news* article that you have not read. This includes *new* messages and articles as well as older ones that you haven't looked at yet.

Updating:
> Changing the contents of a mail *folder* to reflect actions you've performed on that folder. For example, while you're reading *electronic mail* messages, you can mark a message to say you want that message deleted. However, the message is not actually deleted from the folder until you update the folder.

Usenet news:
> A way that computer users can share information and opinions with each other. Usenet news resembles a collection of hundreds of

separate bulletin boards, called *newsgroups*. Users may read articles from newsgroups and may (usually) post articles of their own.

Username:
A special name given to a person using a computer, to distinguish that person from other people using the same computer.

Users program:
The MKS Internet Anywhere program that lets you manage multiple users. It lets you identify yourself to the software so that the software lets you read your mail instead of someone else's, set options to your preference, and so on.

UUCP:
Short for Unix-to-Unix CoPy. UUCP refers to a class of signals and procedures that computers can use to exchange data. UUCP software originated on the UNIX operating system, but is now available on many different types of computer systems.

UUCP connection:
The type of connection that MKS Internet Anywhere uses to interact with other computers. *UUCP* refers to a class of signals and procedures that computers can use to exchange data.

Uudecode:
See *uuencode*.

Uuencode:
A process for translating non-text files into a special text format so that they can be transmitted by *electronic mail*. The reverse (translating the special text format back into non-text files) is called the "uudecode" process.

Working folder:
    The *folder* that you are currently reading with the *Mail Reader*.

Index

The Rabbit Network
Brings You the Internet

The Rabbit Network Inc. is dedicated to providing access to the Internet for users in the United States and Canada, concentrating on helping those who are new to the Internet learn how to use its vast array of resources.

Founded in 1991, Rabbit provides access to the Internet through dedicated (leased) lines and dial-up modem either by connection directly to a terminal server or via a continent-wide toll free (800) number. Services offered include UUCP USENET and E-Mail feeds, Domain Name Service, Mail Forwarding, a nation-wide TELNET server, SLIP or PPP dial-up connections, and dedicated (leased) line access to the Internet.

FREE OFFER

If you select Internet Anywhere's automatic installation option, you will be connected to The Rabbit Network. Rabbit has worked with the development team at MKS to ensure that this connection is reliable and automatic. In addition, Rabbit is offering you 30 days of FREE Internet access via a toll free (800) number.

After the free 30 days, you can elect to continue using Rabbit's services. Please phone or email for information on our rates.

The Rabbit Network Inc.
31511 Harper Ave.
St. Clair Shores, MI   48082
800-456-0094 (voice)
810-790-0156 (fax)

info@rabbit.net (email)

Portal Is Your Gateway to the Internet

Portal wants to be your gateway to the Internet. We were the first company in the United States to offer a commercial email gateway and provide Usenet access. We grew up in the Silicon Valley with the cutting edge companies of the computer industry and our easy access and reliability are well known across the Internet.

To ensure you get a simple, reliable, high quality solution Portal has conducted extensive testing of Internet Anywhere with our UUCP service. We also have local access numbers in over 700 cities across the United States so you won't have to incur expensive long distance calls.

Free Offer!

If you select Internet Anywhere's automatic installation option and The Rabbit Network is unavailable, you will be connected to Portal. Alternatively, you can choose to override the automatic option and select Portal as your access provider. Portal is offering a free 30 day trial of Standard UUCP Service, including 5 free hours of connect time.*

After the free 30 days, you can elect to continue using Portal's services. Please phone or email for information on our rates.

The Portal Information Network
20863 Stevens Creek Boulevard
Suite 200
Cupertino, CA 95014 USA
408-973-9111 (voice)
408-725-1580 (fax)

cs@portal.com (email)
info@portal.com (auto-response)

*Offer applies to new members only. A valid credit card is required for immediate access. Your credit card will not be charged until the 5 free hours are completed or after the first 30 days, whichever comes first. After the 5 free hours, your card will be charged at the rate of $2.95 per hour.

"We're at Your Commands"

We are the MKS Toolkit team. As developers, our job is to create high quality tools for developers. We understand your need for development tools that make your job easier, increase your productivity and allow you more time for creativity. We answer this need with the powerful MKS Toolkit.

The power and flexibility of MKS Toolkit comes not only from the sheer number of commands (190+), but from the ability to combine these commands to perform complex programming tasks.

Developers just like you use MKS Toolkit for:

- Advanced PC-to-PC and PC-to-UNIX communication
- Cross platform development and porting
- Editing and security tools
- File backup and transfer utilities
- Concise, clearly written documentation
- Quick prototyping of complex applications
- 100% UNIX compatibility
- Development on a broad choice of operating systems: Windows, DOS, OS/2, Windows NT
- PC access to the Internet (via Usenet news and electronic mail)
- Our make utility; for precise, uniform, repeatable builds
- Interoperability with UNIX, POSIX, OpenVMS, MVS OpenEdition, MPE/ix, CTOS, and AS/400

Imagine if you had to buy all of these tools separately—for each of the operating systems you develop on. It would cost thousands of dollars.

We know how tight budgets are, and we save you money by bundling all these tools into one single product. After all, we're developers too.

ORDER TODAY: See the coupon on page 437 to receive more than 25% off the retail price of MKS Toolkit.

A SAVINGS OF $80 (U.S.)

SOFTWARE **Development** *PRODUCT EXCELLENCE AWARD 1993*

MKS TOOLKIT

MORTICE KERN SYSTEMS INC.

30 day money back guarantee.

The MKS Toolkit Development team: Back row (l-r) Jeff Moll, Mark Haygarth, Dale Gass, Hilary Jamnik. Front row (l-r) Seán Goggin, Alex White, Fred Walter

MKS Toolkit is a registered trademark of Mortice Kern Systems Inc. All other Trademarks are acknowledged.

MICROSOFT® WINDOWS™ COMPATIBLE

KEEP YOUR SOURCE INTEGRITY™

M K S

RCS

**REVISION
CONTROL
SYSTEM**

Keep your Source Integrity with the absolute best configuration management system available for Client/Server development.

Project Management

MKS RCS thinks and works the way you do – in terms of projects. You can automatically track all files included within any project. You can also track who is currently modifying a file and which version of an archive should be used for the next build.

This tracking is essential for you and your team to easily find the information necessary to perform your job.

Sandboxes

Sandboxes guarantee you have the most up-to-date project data and allow you to fully test any changes you make to the project before committing your version to the master.

Production Control

You can promote a project, or source file, from one level of the software development life cycle to another. MKS RCS tracks exactly what stage each project or file is in at all times.

"MKS gave us the solution we needed across platforms" - Lotus Development Corporation

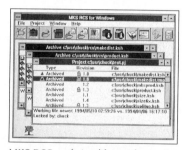

MKS RCS *works just like you do – project oriented, team based and cross platform.*

Visual Basic Integration

MKS RCS has integrated hooks to give you configuration management functionality right from your familiar Visual Basic environment. Think of the time you and your team will save.

"MKS RCS has easily paid for itself with the time it has saved our engineers"
- Glenn Lewis, Intel

Enhanced NetWare Security

Take full advantage of Novell NetWare's security with our new NetWare NLM. Your source code deserves the top notch security provided only by MKS RCS.

And More...

Designed by developers for developers, MKS RCS gives you:

- Make/Configuration Builder for no additional cost – update your builds with the click of a mouse

- Unlimited branching and merging, locking, binary file support, access lists

- Multi-platform support
  - DOS ● Windows ● UNIX
  - OS/2 ● Windows NT ● & More

- Fully documented API available

- Network pricing available

Upgrade from competing CM products - call now for special price reductions!

"We give the project management edge to MKS RCS."
- PC Week, January 1994

MORTICE KERN SYSTEMS INC.

SPECIAL OFFERS

FROM

MKS

MORTICE KERN SYSTEMS INC.

☐ **YES** I want to purchase **MKS TOOLKIT** for more than 25% off the regular price.

☐ **YES** I want to purchase **MKS RCS** for more than 25% off the regular price.

ORDER FORM

To take advantage of these exclusive offers from MKS, just complete and fax this order form to **(519) 884-8861**. To order MKS Toolkit or MKS RCS by phone, or for more information on MKS products and services, multi-user pricing, or Preferred Customer Support, call toll free at **1-800-265-2797**.

This offer is not valid in conjunction with any other special offer from MKS.

30-DAY MONEY BACK GUARANTEE

■ **Please complete:**

_____ MKS Toolkit @ $219.00	$ _____	
_____ MKS RCS @ $289.00	$ _____	
Shipping add $10.00 per unit	$ _____	
COD add $4.50 per unit	$ _____	
Total amount of order	$ _____	

Prices in US dollars and subject to change without notice.

■ **Select your method of payment:**

☐ **VISA**   ☐ **MasterCard**   ☐ **AMERICAN EXPRESS**

Card #: _____

Exp. Date: _____

Phone #: _____

Signature: _____

☐ Check Enclosed   ☐ COD   ☐ Money Order

NAME: _____

COMPANY NAME: _____ POSITION: _____

ADDRESS: _____

CITY: _____ STATE: _____ ZIP: _____

PHONE: _____ FAX: _____ E-MAIL: _____

Mortice Kern Systems Inc.
Licensing Agreement

This is a legal agreement between you, the end user, and Mortice Kern Systems Inc. (MKS). Carefully read the following terms and conditions before opening the sealed disk package. By opening this package, you are agreeing to be bound by the terms and conditions of this agreement. If you do not agree with them, do not open this package or install software, and promptly return the unopened disk package, accompanying written materials, and proof of purchase for a full refund.

Grant of License: MKS grants you the right to use one copy of the enclosed MKS software program (SOFTWARE) on a single computer. If you install the SOFTWARE on a network or any computer configuration which permits more than one user to have access to the SOFTWARE, then you must purchase a separate copy of the SOFTWARE or a license for each additional user, so that you have licenses for the maximum number of users who will be accessing the SOFTWARE at the same time. If you are acquiring the SOFTWARE for network use, MKS grants to you the right to use the SOFTWARE on a LICENSED COMPUTER NETWORK. A LICENSED COMPUTER NETWORK is a computer network for which you have acquired and dedicated at least one license per user. If more than one user wishes to use the SOFTWARE on a computer network at the same time, then you may add authorized users by acquiring additional licenses. In no event may the total number of users on a network exceed the number of licenses acquired for the network.

If you make additional copies of the SOFTWARE or the documentation contrary to this agreement or if you use the SOFTWARE on a number of computers greater than that for which you have paid a license fee, then, in addition to any other remedies MKS may have, MKS may require that you immediately make payment to MKS for such copies and/or such use at the then current list price.

Copyright: This SOFTWARE is owned by MKS and is protected by copyright laws and international treaty provisions. MKS authorizes you to make up to two archival copies of the SOFTWARE for the sole purpose of protecting your investment from loss. You may not copy the written materials accompanying the SOFTWARE.

Other Restrictions: You may not rent, lease, or permit others to use the SOFTWARE, but you may transfer your rights to use the SOFTWARE on a permanent basis provided you transfer all copies of the SOFTWARE and all accompanying written materials, and the recipient agrees to the terms of this Agreement. You may not modify, reverse engineer, decompile or disassemble the SOFTWARE. Any transfer must include the most recent update and all prior versions.

Warranty: With respect to the physical diskette and physical documentation enclosed herein, MKS warrants the same to be free from defects in materials and workmanship under normal use for a period of 60 days from date of receipt. MKS's entire liability and your exclusive remedy shall be, provided that you have given MKS written notification within the warranty period of the defects, replacement of the defective diskette or documentation. Except for the express warranty above, the SOFTWARE, diskette and documentation are provided on an "as is" basis, without any other warranties, or conditions, express or implied, including but not limited to warranties of merchantability and fitness for a particular purpose, or those arising by law, statute, usage of trade or course of dealing. The entire risk as to the results and performance of the SOFTWARE is assumed by you. In particular, MKS shall not have any responsibility whatsoever for any portions of the SOFTWARE which have been modified by you or on your behalf.

IN NO EVENT SHALL MKS OR ITS DISTRIBUTORS BE LIABLE FOR ANY OTHER DAMAGES WHATSOEVER (INCLUDING BUT NOT LIMITED TO DAMAGES FOR LOSS OF BUSINESS PROFITS, BUSINESS INTERRUPTION, LOSS OF BUSINESS INFORMATION OR OTHER PECUNIARY LOSS) ARISING OUT OF THE USE OR INABILITY TO USE THE SOFTWARE, THE DISKETTE OR THE DOCUMENTATION (WHETHER SUCH CLAIM IS BASED ON BREACH OF CONTRACT, INDEMNITY, WARRANTY, TORT (INCLUDING NEGLIGENCE), STRICT LIABILITY OR OTHERWISE), EVEN IF MKS HAS BEEN ADVISED OF THE POSSIBILITY OF SUCH DAMAGES. IN ANY CASE, MKS'S ENTIRE LIABILITY UNDER THIS AGREEMENT OR OTHERWISE WITH RESPECT TO THE SOFTWARE, DISKETTE OR DOCUMENTATION SHALL BE LIMITED TO THE AMOUNT ACTUALLY PAID BY YOU FOR THE SOFTWARE, DISKETTE AND DOCUMENTATION.

General: This Agreement is the entire agreement between MKS and you, supersedes any other agreements or discussions, oral or written, and may not be changed except by written amendment signed by MKS. This Agreement shall be governed by and construed in accordance with the laws of the Province of Ontario, Canada, excluding the United Nations Convention on Contracts for the International Sale of Goods. If any provision of this Agreement is declared by a court of competent jurisdiction to be invalid, illegal or unenforceable, such provision shall be severed from this Agreement and the other provisions shall remain in full force and effect. The parties have requested that this Agreement and all documents contemplated hereby be drawn up in English. Les parties aux présentes ont exigé que cette entente et tous autres documents envisagés par les présentes soient redigé en anglais.

This software may contain material licensed under U.S. Patent No. 4,558,302 or material copyright © 1987 by the Software Development Group, University of Waterloo, Ontario.